*Patriotism
for Profit*

The Fred W. Morrison
Series in Southern Studies

Patriotism for Profit

Georgia's Urban Entrepreneurs and the Confederate War Effort

by Mary A. DeCredico

The University of North Carolina Press

Chapel Hill and London

© 1990 The University of North Carolina Press
All rights reserved
Manufactured in the United States of America

The paper in this book meets the guidelines for permanence and
durability of the Committee on Production Guidelines for Book
Longevity of the Council on Library Resources.

94 93 92 91 90   5 4 3 2 1

Library of Congress Cataloging-in-Publication Data

DeCredico, Mary A.
   Patriotism for profit : Georgia's urban entrepreneurs and the
Confederate war effort / by Mary A. DeCredico.
      p.   cm.—(The Fred W. Morrison series in Southern studies)
   Includes bibliographical references.
   ISBN 0-8078-1891-7 (alk. paper)
   1. Georgia—Economic policy. 2. Georgia—Industries—
History—19th century. 3. Businessmen—Georgia—History—
19th century. 4. Entrepreneurship—Georgia—History—19th
century. 5. Industrial mobilization—Georgia—History—19th
century. 6. Georgia—History—Civil War, 1861–1865. I. Title.
II. Series.
HC107.G4D43   1990
338.09758'09'034—dc20   89-39132
                                                               CIP

Publication of this work was aided by a grant included in the
Mrs. Simon Baruch University Award of the United Daughters of
the Confederacy.

Portions of this work appeared earlier in somewhat different
form in Mary A. DeCredico, "War Is Good Business: Georgia's
Urban Entrepreneurs and the Confederate War Effort," *Georgia
Historical Quarterly* 73 (Summer 1989): 231–49, and are repro-
duced here by permission of the *Georgia Historical Quarterly*.

Design by April Leidig-Higgins

*For my parents
and to the memory
of my grandfather*

Contents

Tables and Maps

Illustrations

Preface

The composition and character of Southern society during the antebellum and immediate postbellum years have been the subject of numerous studies of the roots and nature of Southern distinctiveness. Despite a vast literature on the subject, however, historians are no closer to a resolution of the debate. Many of the monographs produced in the last twenty years have portrayed the South as an essentially static, tradition-bound society, complete with the "moonlight and magnolias" of legend, and epitomized by gentlemen planters of the Ashley Wilkes variety. Those historians have argued persuasively that the region's minority population of white planters exercised a socioeconomic and political hegemony out of proportion to their actual numbers. That elite, they argue, kept the South stagnant by erecting social barriers that acted as constraints to the growth and activity of an urban industrial middle class that would have threatened the planters' hegemony. Thus the South remained a "prebourgeois" society: planters operated fully in the liberal capitalist order, and benefited from it, but did not share in the bourgeois value system of thrift, hard work, and profit-seeking for its own sake. Some scholars have carried the analysis a step further and have conceded that a middle class did, in fact, exist in the antebellum South. Still, this class remained frightfully small and totally dependent upon and subservient to the planter elite.[1]

Drawing upon the pathbreaking work of Eugene Genovese and Barrington Moore, Marxist historians applied similar theories to the postbellum South. Scholars such as Jonathan Wiener and Dwight Billings argue that even the twin debacles of Civil War defeat and Reconstruction did not diminish the planters' control of Southern society. Rather, they claim that the elite adapted to the new order created by emancipation and developed new institutions (such as tenancy) to reassert their dominant position in Southern society. These historians point to the continued reliance upon agriculture and the lack of industrialization until the end of the nineteenth century—and later—as proof of their assertions.[2]

These interpretations have been challenged only recently. Local studies of Virginia and Alabama, for example, provide evidence that an urban industrial middle class not only existed but actively pursued the twin goals of industrial growth and diversification. Although these studies conclude on the eve of the Civil War, they suggest that this urban middle class remained a vigorous force during the war years and after. Further, they imply that this middle class was imbued with bourgeois values and remained independent of planter domination.[3]

In attempting to explain Southern backwardness or progress, scholars have manifested a singular unwillingness to come to terms with the Civil War period. Several historians have recognized the catalytic impact the war had on Southern society, but they have explained that impact in general terms, falling back on Marxist interpretations that deny any elements of qualitative modernity in the antebellum South.[4] Such treatment of the war years is curious, for scholars of virtually every historiographical school acknowledge that the Civil War had a tremendous impact on every sector of Southern society.

This study addresses this gap in the literature by examining the experience of mobilizing for the Civil War in the South and the way that mobilization affected the dynamics of Southern society. More specifically, it explores Georgia's response to the demands of Confederate mobilization to show how the war years influenced entrepreneurs in four of the state's urban centers: Atlanta, Augusta, Columbus, and Savannah. By identifying and reconstructing the pattern of mobilization in a specific locale, it is possible to gauge the impact of the war years on Southern society.

Georgia is a particularly appropriate state to illuminate this question for in many ways Georgia's history and growth present a microcosm of the Southern experience. Its colonization and the development of a plantation-based economy in the southern and eastern portions of the state paralleled the experience of the upper South. Differences in terrain and the later organization (vis-à-vis the Georgia coast) of the northern and western quadrants of Georgia produced patterns of development found on the frontier and in the lower South in the early nineteenth century.

Like other Southern states, Georgia grew and prospered throughout the antebellum era. Ironically, the catalyst for Georgia's initial growth was the depression that followed the Panic of 1837. That economic crisis prompted many far-seeing Georgians to press for diversification—seeking opportunities for investment in railroads, manufacturing, and mining. The state government proved to be a staunch ally of the boosters' quest for economic development and diversification. In the 1840s, successive administrations extended tax incentives and passed liberal incorporation statutes to provide ambitious entrepreneurs with the security needed to embark on nonagricultural ventures. By Southern standards, the results were impressive. In 1860, Georgia ranked first in the South in textile manufacturing; it boasted the region's second most extensive railroad system; and it had laid the foundations of heavy industry with the creation of iron furnaces and rolling mills. Georgia had become a Southern leader and something of a novelty. Still, similar advances in Virginia, Tennessee, and South Carolina make Georgia's achievements illustrative of the Southern experience. Only a short but decidedly virulent outburst of popular anticorporate sentiment in the late 1850s halted an otherwise uninterrupted trend of economic growth and diversification.

Georgia's achievements were not lost on Southern fire-eaters who agitated for Southern independence. They recognized that Georgia's economic might and political clout were essential for the consummation of Southern secession and the establishment of a Southern nation. Hence those political leaders eagerly welcomed Georgia into the nascent Confederacy in 1861, for it brought a generation of wealth, prestige, and entrepreneurial achievement to the Southern cause.

The Confederacy embarked upon its quest for independence lacking virtually everything—save, perhaps, arrogance. While patriots danced in the streets and engaged in grandiloquent boasting, more sober souls realized that King Cotton notwithstanding, the South needed arms, equipment, and ammunition. Given Georgia's reputation as the "Empire State of the South," it was almost axiomatic that Confederate War Department officials would look to Georgia as a key to successful mobilization.

Those officials were not disappointed with Georgia's response. Businessmen in Atlanta, Augusta, Columbus, and Savannah eagerly embraced the challenge of mobilization. These businessmen converted existing factories to war-related production or created entirely new concerns, seemingly overnight. The exigencies of war created new opportunities for those antebellum boosters of diversification to resume their drive for a balanced local and state economy. Established businesses formed the vanguard of the effort, but their successes and the adulation they received as "patriots" prompted less experienced but equally ambitious entrepreneurs to emulate their example. By the summer of 1863, Georgia's urban entrepreneurs had built upon and expanded the antebellum economic base to create what Emory M. Thomas has termed a "military-industrial complex."[5] Persistent short-ages of raw materials and skilled labor stymied and eventually crip-pled Georgia's mobilizers, but their successes enabled the Southern legions to continue in the field for four years. For a region considered precapitalist and agrarian, that was no small feat.

Virtually all Georgians who embraced the challenge of economic diversification during the mobilization benefited personally. Estab-lished manufacturers expanded production and branched out into new lines of goods. Merchants, grocers, clerks—individuals from vir-tually every occupational category—seized the opportunity to embark upon new careers in a society made fluid by war. All seemed to embrace, and indeed personify, the bourgeois ethic. Yet success in war-related activities did not guarantee continued achievement in an era of peace. Those who had led Georgia's antebellum industrial revo-lution reestablished themselves as soon as it was physically and finan-cially possible. Others who had switched to manufacturing solely to gain government contracts were, with few exceptions, less successful. The opportunities of war appear to have had no consistent effect on postwar accomplishment.

These various wartime experiences and postwar decisions created different responses and results in urban Georgia. That reality under-scores the influence, both positive and negative, of the entrepreneur-ial class on the state's subsequent development. Scholars of entrepre-neurship have demonstrated the connection between entrepreneurial activity and economic change: those individuals who form new com-binations and who react creatively to perceived opportunities will prompt changes in the socioeconomic organization of society. More-over, those innovators will enjoy society's respect and approval, thus encouraging them to continue as innovators.[6]

The experience of urban Georgia before, during, and after the Civil War demonstrates the validity of such conclusions. Georgia's urban mobilizers were consistently recognized for their exploits on behalf of Confederate independence—economic as well as political. After the war, the desire to "out-Yankee the Yankee" became a potent rallying cry, exhorting Georgians to rebuild the state. Such appeals, however, went only so far in cities such as Columbus and Augusta. There, physical obstacles (the destruction of Columbus) and perhaps psycho-logical ones (the burden of defeat) prevented the continued quest for local and state development. Ironically, those same obstacles would create a totally different response in Savannah and Atlanta—a response more in tune with the entrepreneurial creed. In these cities, urban businessmen overcame unfavorable conditions to pursue their quest for a balanced urban economy. These were the men who would lay the foundation for the urban-industrial New South of the 1880s.

Urban Georgia's contradictory response to the postbellum era highlights the impact of the war mobilization. War experiences created a reference point for many. Those who used the past—the prewar and wartime experiences in organization and management—could apply those lessons to the pursuit of a New South in Georgia. For them, the entrepreneurial ethos was not stunted by a hegemonic planter elite, nor was it consumed in the holocaust of 1865. Instead, it was a viable creed that held the key to Georgia's future.

Acknowledgments

Anyone who writes a book incurs tremendous debts, scholarly and otherwise. I am no exception. This project began at Vanderbilt University, where it evolved under the steady guidance of Professor Don H. Doyle. Knowing of my love of the Civil War and Southern history, Professor Doyle encouraged me to pursue a topic that would hold my interest for an extended period. He performed service worthy of Georgia's entrepreneurs, helping me to iron out hazy conceptualizations and dubious ideas. His assistance, kindness, and knowledge enhanced whatever merit the original manuscript had.

The research conducted in Georgia, North Carolina, Ohio, and Massachusetts could not have been accomplished had it not been for the generous fellowship aid I received from Vanderbilt and the Naval Academy Research Council. Grants from Vanderbilt and NARC allowed me to use the vast collections of the Georgia Historical Society, the University of Georgia, the Georgia Department of Archives and History, the Georgia State Library, the Atlanta Historical Society, the Baker Library at the Harvard University Graduate School of Business Administration, the Southern Historical Collection at the University of North Carolina at Chapel Hill, and the Western Reserve Historical Society. The staffs of those archives were of inestimable assistance in helping me locate manuscripts, official reports, photographs, and the like. They humored my more outrageous requests and allowed me to stay past closing time "just to finish one more document." Research at Vanderbilt and the Naval Academy was also made easier by the staffs of the interlibrary loan offices, who worked diligently in helping me locate vital microfilm reproductions of official reports. Supplemental NARC funding also facilitated the reproduction of the photographs and maps in the text. Special thanks are due to Bill Christ of B C Graphics, the Library of Congress and National Archives Photographic Reproduction Services, and Joseph DeCredico for their contributions to the illustrations contained herein.

My colleagues at the Naval Academy have been a continual source of support and assistance. I presented portions of the book to the Department's Works-in-Progress seminar. There, it was subjected to perceptive questioning and penetrating critiques. The participants in those meetings were a tremendous help, for they forced me to reassess and clarify numerous propositions. One colleague, however, deserves special mention. Craig L. Symonds proved to be my most helpful sounding board, and his careful reading tightened considerably the final manuscript.

Others in the academic community were also important to the completion of this book. Eugene Genovese read the manuscript carefully, and although he did not always agree with my arguments, he still encouraged me to rethink and reformulate. Michael Chesson and Emory Thomas were instrumental in helping me sort out some weak arguments. Their attention to detail and their general encouragement of the project were much appreciated.

I also benefited from the financial support I received from the United Daughters of the Confederacy. The manuscript was awarded the Mrs. Simon Baruch University Award, which included a substantial publication grant. The encouragement and generosity of the United Daughters of the Confederacy were truly gratifying.

Lewis Bateman of the University of North Carolina Press followed the project and encouraged it from the very beginning. Ron Maner, Trudie Calvert, and others in the editorial department rendered invaluable assistance in helping to make the final version cogent and consistent. Any errors that remain are mine alone.

Other members of the academic and nonacademic communities played roles in this project. During my graduate student days, Doug Flamming, Susan Benton, and Michael Carrafiello provided much needed moral support. They plied me with coffee and good cheer and never let me take Georgia too seriously. My family, too, has tolerated my fits of depression and encouraged, consoled, and commiserated with my travails. To my parents, Joseph and Alexandra Jack DeCredico, I owe an emotional debt I can never begin to repay. They, more than all others, sustained me during my protracted sojourn in Civil War Georgia. I dedicate this book to them with love and thanks, and also to the memory of the first and best scholar in our family, my grandfather, Robert Alexander Jack.

Patriotism
for Profit

1 *The Antebellum Legacy*

The Foundations of Entrepreneurialism

When the members of the Georgia delegation to the Provisional Congress of the Confederate States of America journeyed to Montgomery, Alabama, in February 1861, few of them comprehended the magnitude of the struggle that was about to unfold. Nor could they foresee the fate of their beloved Empire State of the South in the following years. Yet the Georgians were conscious that they represented a prosperous and diversified state, whose strength and stature guaranteed that secession was not a threat but an established fact. That Georgia was a crucial political keystone was recognized by all; that it would become the nascent Confederacy's economic backbone was perceived by only the prescient few.

Georgia's contributions to the Confederate war effort were in part the result of the state's antebellum economic development. Geography and climate dictated Georgia's colonial economy. The development of the rice and cotton culture determined that Georgia would follow its fellow Southern states in the creation of a plantation slave-based economy. But Georgia did not remain wedded to a traditional agricultural economy; industrialization and urbanization took root and flourished. And Georgia was not an atypical case. Trends toward economic diversification in late antebellum Georgia were occurring elsewhere in the South—changes that belie the notion of a static, retrogressive society.

Political policies implemented in the mid-1830s produced profound consequences for the national economy. President Andrew Jackson's attack on the national banking system, coupled with a decline in world cotton prices, set off a chain reaction that culminated in the Panic of 1837. Jackson's hand-picked successor, Martin Van Buren, gained the dubious distinction of presiding over the economic tailspin that reached rock bottom by 1840. Investment capital dried up, bankruptcies were distressingly common, and credit was sharply curtailed. Conditions did not improve until 1843.[1]

This depression was the most severe economic crisis in the nation's history. Yet contemporaries, and even latter-day historians, underestimated the impact of this economic downturn on the South. The full force of the depression did not hit the region until 1839, but from that year until well into the 1840s, the South felt the full weight of the financial contraction. Internal improvement projects were abandoned; bank and credit facilities dried up; and numerous merchants, planters, and farmers were bankrupted. Full recovery was not achieved until 1846, when cotton prices finally rebounded.[2]

Georgia's experience during the depression mirrored that of the South as a whole. Yet the experience prompted many farsighted individuals to analyze the state's economic problems. Planters, merchants, editors, and others began to advocate agricultural diversification and the development of Georgia's natural resources as a defense against future panics. They urged the construction of more railroads and bank and credit facilities to help the state recover its prosperity and guard against future economic dislocations.[3] Financial recovery did not stifle these demands. Rather, with the return of high crop prices, the easing of money markets, and the revival of commerce, the calls for agricultural diversification and industrial development became even more strident. The future greatness of Georgia, state boosters argued, lay in the establishment and cultivation of manufacturing enterprises and in the exploitation of the state's vast natural resources.[4]

The new economic spirit was most pronounced in Georgia's towns and cities. The city of Augusta appeared in the vanguard of Georgia's attempts to reap the rewards of economic diversification. Augusta had long been a vital trade center on the fall line of the Savannah River and shared in the economic vicissitudes that wracked the state and nation in the 1840s. Economic contractions were exacerbated by natural disasters: a drought in 1839 and a flood and devastating yellow fever epidemic in 1840.[5] Augustans proved hardy; they weathered nature's afflictions, recouped their fortunes, and embarked upon a drive to restore their city's economy. Some local business leaders perceived that the Savannah River represented an untapped boon to Augusta's economy. Those men believed that by harnessing the water power of the river, manufacturing enterprises could be established in the city and a "new spirit" infused in the region. In 1845, a consortium of five prominent community leaders raised the requisite funding to incorporate the Augusta Canal Company. Shortly thereafter, they petitioned the City Council for a charter of incorporation to build the canal.[6]

As the final touches were added to the Augusta Canal, a second group of local entrepreneurs established the Augusta Manufacturing Company in 1847. Each of the eleven directors used part of his personal fortune to capitalize the new company at $200,000.[7] Other local merchants quickly imitated the Augusta Manufacturing Company and created additional manufacturing concerns. In due course, these men and others organized the Augusta Machine Works (originally capitalized at $70,000), the Augusta Paper Manufacturing Company, the Belleville Factory (capitalized at $50,000 to $75,000), and other, smaller concerns.[8] Within just a few years, the Augusta Manufacturing Company possessed 15,000 spindles and 462 looms; the Belleville's spindles and looms produced 400,000 yards of cotton osnaburgs a year; and the Augusta Machine Works became the major supplier for the Georgia Railroad Company. Profits and production grew to such an extent that the officers of the various companies had little trouble obtaining stock subscriptions for their enterprises, and plans for new and larger mills moved from Augusta boardrooms to local contractors' drawing tables. Capitalists and stockholders reaped handsome gains, and local planters and farmers benefited from providing for the needs of the urban population, which slowly rebounded from the effects of disease and flood. Optimism and prosperity pervaded Augusta, and most were won over to the idea of building factories in the fields.[9]

Rising concurrently with Augusta during this period was the town of Columbus, located in the southwestern corner of the state. Like Augusta, Columbus was blessed with an excellent location. Situated on the falls of the Chattahoochee River, it was able to tap that resource to power local mills and other manufacturing enterprises. Moreover, the town possessed an active and enterprising group of capitalists who were willing to exploit its advantages. J. Shivers & Company launched the first manufacturing establishment in Columbus in 1834. Situated on the Chattahoochee, the Columbus Factory produced the town's first textile products.[10] Not until the 1840s, however, were other enterprises established. Here, too, local capitalists had to endure the depression, which halted plans to build dams to harness the river. Once the dams were built, the town and its manufacturing concerns grew rapidly.

Textile mills formed the backbone of Columbus's manufacturing economy. The Columbus Factory was soon joined by the Coweta Manufacturing Company and the Howard Factory. Colonel John H. Howard was the driving force behind these two concerns. Local credit agents considered Howard and fellow stockholders John E. Dawson,

William L. Jeter, and John L. Bacon "gentlemen of high char[acter] & g[oo]d [property]." The Coweta Manufacturing Company represented a capital investment of $80,000; it operated 145 looms and 3,700 spindles. Capitalized at $85,000, the Howard Factory housed 75 looms and 5,000 spindles.[11]

Another of Columbus's pioneer industrialists was Colonel John H. Winter. Winter opened the Rock Island Paper Manufacturing Company in 1849 and presided over a concern worth an estimated half-million dollars. The enterprising colonel also built two smaller textile mills: the Variety Works, which manufactured woolen cloth, and Winter's Merchant Mill, whose 3,000 spindles produced cotton yarn.[12]

Columbus also boasted two large grain mills. Colonel T. Jones, worth an estimated $1 million, took over the City Mills in the mid-1850s and expanded their productive facilities. Jones's chief competition came from Randolph L. Mott, who built the Palace Mills in 1848. Local credit agents considered Mott and his partners, Thomas Tallman, George W. Winter, and John Mustian, good businessmen with ample personal capital. By 1860, the Palace Mills had outdistanced its competitors and virtually cornered the area's flour market.[13]

Columbus's capitalists were local men of means, often plantation owners and farmers. The planters of the area were commonly in the vanguard of development efforts. As one historian has noted, those interior planters "were said to be in a ferment seeking new enterprises in which they could earn more on their capital."[14] By the late 1840s, these planters and their merchant colleagues had combined to establish a board of trade, which resolved "to encourage manufacturing and commerce" in the city.[15]

Evidently, the Columbus Board of Trade served its function well, for by 1850 articles in the irrepressible *DeBow's Review* were exalting Columbus manufacturing establishments and the strides they had made. One such piece noted that the Carter Factory contained 200 looms and 10,000 spindles; the Coweta Manufacturing Company had 2,500 spindles that produced between 1,400 and 1,800 pounds of thread daily and 1,800 yards of heavy osnaburgs; and pioneer John H. Howard's Howard Manufacturing Company possessed 5,000 spindles and over 100 looms. The article also called attention to Columbus's two iron foundries, concluding that the city's entrepreneurs did not live by textiles alone.[16] Between manufacturing, an active wagon trade, and the start of railroad connections to the Gulf of Mexico, the city's prosperity was firmly based. Best of all for Columbus, these diverse endeavors were the product of local brains and capital, drawn from a population that increased 62 percent in a decade.[17]

Columbus and Augusta represented most graphically the changes that swept the state between the mid-1840s and 1860. In 1840, Georgia's textile establishments were of insignificant product value compared with those elsewhere in the South and the nation. Yet by 1850, Georgia ranked eighth nationally and first regionally in value added by cotton manufacture.[18] Such strides produced popular optimism and faith in the state's future development in manufacturing and economic diversification. The *Columbus Times* boasted that the city "will be a Georgia Lowell before long and some of these days will beat her."[19] A Tennessee paper proclaimed that Georgia seemed to be the "New England of the South," and DeBow argued that the state had just claim to its sobriquet, Empire State of the South.[20] DeBow went on to state grandiloquently: "Georgia . . . makes more cotton and corn—has more railroads—more manufactures—more shipping (save perhaps for New Orleans)— . . . has more diversified mineral wealth—[and] is nearly ready to furnish her own citizens and those of her sister states with flour to eat, clothes to wear, [and] iron to work."[21] The praises that were sung were not hollow: by 1860, Georgia possessed almost 21 percent of all Southern cotton manufacturing establishments, 29.3 percent of the South's cotton spindlage, and slightly over 29 percent of value added to products in the region.[22]

The dispersed nature of Georgia's manufacturing and commercial centers added impetus to the desire to develop an effective transportation network. Rail promoters believed that connecting Georgia's nascent manufacturing centers to market areas would promote further growth and diversification. Hence Georgia's textile boom complemented the drive to create a comprehensive rail network within the state.

Actually, the Georgia railroad craze began in the late 1820s. Previous concentration on plank roads and canals was undercut by neighboring South Carolina's charter of the Charleston & Hamburg Railroad. This line threatened to divert much of Augusta's cotton and wagon trade to Charleston and thus elicited consternation, not only in that city but in Charleston's rival, Savannah, as well.[23] Augusta and Savannah's previous indifference toward the railroads ended abruptly in 1831, when numerous delegates representing thirty-three counties met in Eatonton, Georgia, to discuss railroad proposals. Although the assembled county representatives drew up resolutions calling for the building of rail lines and state support for internal improvement projects, interest lagged after the meeting adjourned. Once the rival South Carolina line was completed, however, interest was piqued anew, and in 1833 the Georgia General Assembly endorsed the Eatonton resolutions and gave them legislative sanction. It granted charters of incorporation to the Georgia Railroad Company (which proposed to link Athens to Augusta), the Central of Georgia Railroad (Savannah to Macon), and the Monroe Railroad Company (Macon to Forsyth).[24]

The motive behind the renewed desire to build a state transportation system was not hard to find. The delegates to Georgia's railroad meetings were fully aware that the Atlantic seaboard had become a battleground of sorts. With the completion of the Erie Canal, eastern states, not the least of which was Georgia, felt compelled to challenge New York's monopoly of the western trade. Georgia railroad promoters envisioned an extensive state system that would tap the markets of the Tennessee and Mississippi valleys and hence bolster the export and import sectors of the economy.[25] In short, Georgia's railroad entrepreneurs believed that railroads held the key to the development and prosperity of the state's economy.

Athens promoters struck first and began building the Georgia Railroad in 1834. Led by James Camak, the directors of the Georgia Railroad were prominent businessmen who sought to improve trade connections between Athens and other parts of the state. More specifically, the Georgia Railroad's founders envisioned the proposed road as the key to Athens's economic development: the road would ultimately tap the interior of the state and make the "Classic City" central Georgia's industrial and commercial center.[26] Unfortunately for Camak and his supporters, the depression intervened. Work on the road slowed considerably and came to a halt in 1841, after Athens and Madison had been linked. Tight money, little credit, and the death of its guiding light, James Camak, seemed to spell doom for the Georgia road. Late in 1841, however, the line's fortunes changed dramatically, when prominent Augusta businessman John P. King took over as president of the financially troubled company. Using his personal fortune and substantial personal credit, King pushed the construction of the road forward. By 1845, the Georgia Railroad had reached its terminus near Marthasville.[27]

The Georgia Railroad's chief rival during this period was the Savannah-based Central of Georgia Railroad, also chartered in 1833. The

Central's directors believed that a connection to the state's interior cotton belt would counter the threats to Savannah's cotton trade that the Charleston & Hamburg Railroad and the Savannah, Ogeechee and Altamaha Canal portended. Under the aegis of William W. Gordon, work on the 195-mile road began in 1836, but like the Georgia Railroad, the Central fell victim to the depression. The city of Savannah tendered the company liberal financial aid, and local business interests also invested in the Central, but mounting costs and tight credit dimmed the company's prospects. State aid, in the form of a bank charter, and careful management saw the Central through its lean years. In 1843, the road from Savannah to Macon was complete.[28]

Intrastate connections, the development of the urban hinterlands, and, ultimately, trade with the West were clearly on the minds of those boosters who backed the Central of Georgia and Georgia railroads.[29] The staunchest proponent of this quest, however, was Governor Wilson Lumpkin. An early and outspoken advocate of internal improvements, Lumpkin presided over the legislature that granted the first railroad charters. More important, Lumpkin personally surveyed the state's interior to assess the feasibility of a rail line to the Tennessee River. Lumpkin perceived great developmental advantages redounding to Georgia if rail connections to the West could be built. Not only would railroads open new areas of trade, they would also foster economic diversification and prosperity that would benefit all Georgians. Lumpkin's dream of a state system of railways was translated into reality when the Georgia General Assembly chartered and funded a state-owned and operated railroad: the Western & Atlantic.[30]

Grading on the Western & Atlantic began in 1837, but the onset of the depression considerably delayed its completion. Despite annual legislative appropriations, high costs forced the suspension of the work for two years. Construction renewed in earnest in 1843, and by 1847, the Western & Atlantic stretched from Atlanta to Dalton. The final spike was driven in 1850 at Chattanooga, Tennessee.

Critics of the Western & Atlantic (often called the state road) argued from the beginning that the road was an unnecessary and unneeded drain on the state's treasury—especially during the depression years. The road's annual reports tended to corroborate that assertion, but state funds continued to pour into Lumpkin's project. Beginning in 1854, the gamble began to pay off, and thereafter the state road began to pay, on the average, $200,000 a year into state coffers.[31]

Construction of the Western & Atlantic prompted the Georgia Railroad and the Central of Georgia to seek connections with the state line at Atlanta. With the completion of the state road, Georgia's two major private companies finally had a link to Georgia's interior cotton belt and to the long-sought western markets in the Tennessee Valley. As might be expected, the managers of these two railroads moved aggressively to tap these newly available markets, for they offered the prospect of new goods, more commerce, and additional capital for the state and local economies.

John P. King's Georgia Railroad moved to consolidate its route to the West by investing in other railroads that were also being built during the period. King and his board of directors bought stock in the Atlanta & LaGrange (later the Atlanta & West Point), the Rome Railroad Company, the Augusta & Waynesboro (later the Augusta & Savannah), the Nashville & Chattanooga, and the East Tennessee & Georgia lines for the specific purpose of garnering the western trade.[32]

Although the Georgia Railroad reaped high returns on its operations, the company's management was cognizant of the threat presented by heightened competition from the Central of Georgia. Despite efforts to diversify its freight business, the Georgia Railroad continued to rely too heavily on the cotton trade. As Superintendent George Yonge noted: "Over 3,000 empty cars are annually carried into Atlanta by the Georgia Railroad, offering the means of transportation for upwards of 20,000 tons of Up Freight . . . [that could] increas[e] our earnings one hundred thousand dollars."[33] Because of this disparity between up and down shipments, the Georgia Railroad's management contemplated a through connection from Nashville or Memphis to the sea. As a corollary to this plan, steamship connections were planned to Northern ports. Since the Georgia Railroad was linked to South Carolina railroads, management assumed that Georgia Railroad freight could be transported to Charleston, where it would be loaded onto steamers bound for New York.[34]

The Georgia Railroad's fiercest competitor, the Central of Georgia Railroad, also moved to tap new areas. President Richard R. Cuyler was particularly attracted to the rich cotton and produce sections of southwest Georgia. Hence the Central subscribed heavily in the Macon & Western (which linked the former city to Atlanta) and the Southwestern Railroad (which proposed lines from Fort Gaines to Columbus and Eufala, Alabama). In addition, the Savannah-based line aided smaller companies building spurs to Milledgeville and Thomaston. By the mid-1850s, the Central's investments—and common interests in these other companies—had produced a system of sorts, virtually controlled by the Central. Moreover, connections to and through Atlanta via the Western & Atlantic gave the Central "737 miles of continuous railroad track with the Mississippi River at Memphis."[35]

The Central also moved to parry the threat posed by the Georgia Railroad's proposed steamship line. Beginning in 1858, the Central began investing in a line of steamers that operated between Savannah and New York and Philadelphia. The road's management justified such actions as productive of state and sectional pride. Fearing that Northern steamers were diverting the road's traffic, the Central decided to transport the road's freight directly to eastern ports and thus undermine the rival Philadelphia and New York steamship companies. From 1858 until the outbreak of the war, the Central's steamers carried the road's freight trade to the Northeast.[36]

Georgia's railroad promoters could take pride in their accomplishments. In 1836, when the first charters were acted upon, 7 miles of rail had been laid. Ten years later, 609 miles were in operation, and by 1860 that figure had more than doubled. Of 9,182 miles of track in the Southern states in 1860, Georgia claimed 1,420.[37] The state, municipal authorities, and private citizens had invested over $26 million in Georgia's eighteen lines. Best of all, the Georgia system was integrated, though some lines varied in rates and through city connections.[38]

The Central and Georgia Railroad systems and the Western & Atlantic formed the backbone of Georgia's antebellum railroad network. Some smaller companies were also chartered, but they did not begin construction until after the depression eased in the mid-1840s. As one scholar has noted, virtually all of the railroads built after 1845 were "complementary additions" to the state road and the Central and Georgia railroads. Many of the new companies, such as the Atlanta & West Point, the Southwestern, and the Macon & Western, were aided or, in some instances, leased by the Central and Georgia systems. The managers of these two dominant corporations used their lines to build up local traffic at their respective termini and to develop the cities and resources adjacent to their roads. Yet these managers were not interested only in the local effect of their lines. Men like King and Cuyler were very much aware of the larger role of the railroad in the state's political economy. Visions of extensive market connections and new commercial and industrial combinations that would benefit the whole state surely played a role in their decision making. By their actions,

Georgia's railroad managers demonstrated an awareness that a diversified economy was the key to future prosperity.[39]

The extensiveness of the Georgia network and its many connections with market centers outside the state altered some of the more provincial motives of Georgia's railroad managers. Indeed, plans to build an air line route through the Carolina Piedmont to the Northeast and another line to the Alabama coal fields in the late 1850s demonstrated that these men had developed a regional orientation. Whereas older lines were conceived on the basis of the state's strategic geographical position and its agricultural commerce, projects advanced at the end of the antebellum era embraced what Milton Heath has called a "new conception—of the dominant roles in the modern economy of manufactures, railroads and inland rail centers." These plans indicated that "a new center of commercial orientation was rising already in north central Georgia."[40]

The "cooperative" nature of Georgia's railroad building may account for this subtle difference. The state's roads were the product of state, local, and individual initiatives. Georgians came, not unnaturally, to assume that railroads were a quasi-public enterprise, an essential component in the state's quest for prosperity.[41]

As might be expected, the expansion of the railroad network created a heavy demand for iron rails, cars, and engines. In the early years of the nineteenth century, Southerners had relied heavily on Northern and European imports to build and equip their roads. As Georgians laid more lines, the demand for iron goods of all sorts increased dramatically. Astute Georgia entrepreneurs capitalized on this demand and worked to tap local resources that would render iron production profitable. As early as the 1830s state and local geological surveys prompted Mark A. Cooper to establish the Etowah Iron Works near Cartersville, Georgia.[42] The Etowah works soon gained a reputation for producing a fine grade of railroad iron which was eagerly purchased by the Georgia railroads. By the 1850s, several furnaces dotted the north Georgia hill country, and they provided the materials—and the incentive—for the establishment of rolling mills and factories to outfit the state's carriers. One of the first such concerns was the Georgia Railroad Company's machine shops. To make their concern self-sufficient, the company's managers built a facility to manufacture its own rolling stock in Augusta in 1848.[43] Not to be outdone, the Central Railroad also built its own machine shops in its headquarters city, Savannah.[44]

With the completion of the Western & Atlantic Railroad, Atlanta entrepreneurs went to work to supply a portion of that road's needs. The city boasted the "very reliable" Winship Machine Shop and Foundry and the Gate City Rolling Mill. The Gate City facility, soon renamed the Atlanta Rolling Mill, was managed by former Northerners considered of "gr[ea]t Integrity & first rate bus[iness] talents." The mill was "regarded with much favor by the RR Cos." that patronized it.[45]

Atlanta's Chattahoochee River counterpart in the southwestern portion of the state, Columbus, also housed three rolling mills. Local credit agents considered the Columbus Iron Works, the Muscogee Foundry, and the Muscogee Railroad Work Shops to be "solid concerns." Each firm played an important role locally by manufacturing railroad equipment and by rolling and rerolling iron rails.[46]

The 1860 census corroborated what Georgia entrepreneurs and boosters already knew: the state had made considerable strides in industrial development and economic diversification in the aftermath of the depression of the 1840s. In 1850, 1,527 manufacturing establishments boasted capital investments of $3,404,917. Those concerns employed 6,600 men and 1,718 women operatives who earned wages of $1,713,304. The total value of products manufactured in the state stood at $7,086,525.[47] Ten years later, there were 1,890 manufacturing concerns—an increase of 24 percent—representing an accretion in capital investment of almost 100 percent. More than 9,500 men and 2,064 women worked in these concerns. The total value of products had more than doubled, to $16,925,564.[48]

A comparison with regional and national trends in capital investment and value of manufacturing output per capita sheds further light on Georgia's development. Georgia's rate of growth between 1850 and 1860 in the former category was nearly 71 percent—a figure that outstrips most state and regional indexes (see Table 1). Moreover, the value of manufacturing output per capita in the state increased 104 percent. Such statistics must be viewed with caution, for though they demonstrate tremendous relative increases, they also show that Georgia, like the South, trailed considerably behind the older manufacturing regions of the United States.

Historians and economists have been apt to dismiss overall Southern manufacturing in the antebellum period because of its agricultural base: the top industries by capital investment in the region were related to agricultural processing. Yet national rankings of capital invest-

Table 1. Regional Patterns of Manufacturing, 1850–1860

Region	Capital invested per capita		Percent gain	Value of output per capita		Percent gain
	1850	1860		1850	1860	
Northeast	$57.96	$82.13	29	$100.71	$149.47	33
Middle States	35.50	52.21	32	71.24	96.28	26
Northwest	11.70	18.95	38	26.32	37.33	30
Pacific	10.39	42.35	307	84.83	129.04	34
South	7.60	10.54	39	10.88	17.09	57
Cotton South	5.11	7.20	41	6.83	10.47	53
Georgia	6.02	10.30	71	7.81	16.00	104
United States	22.73	32.12	29	43.69	59.98	27

Sources: Gavin Wright, *The Political Economy of the Cotton South: Households, Markets and Wealth in the Nineteenth Century* (New York: Norton, 1978), p. 110; and Don H. Dodd and Wynelle Dodd, *Historical Statistics of the South, 1790–1970* (University, Ala.: University of Alabama Press, 1975), pp. 18–21.

ment in manufacturing and value added to product by manufacturing indicate that agricultural processing industries dominated the national economy, too. In 1860, the top three industrial sectors by capital investment and by value added to product in Georgia were cotton goods, sawed lumber, and flour and meal; in the United States as a whole, the rankings were cotton goods, flour and meal, and sawed lumber. In short, manufacturing patterns in Georgia throughout the decade mirrored national patterns, and state, regional, and national manufacturing was characterized by processing industries.[49]

Certain areas within the state benefited more than others from this growth. In particular, the Piedmont region profited from the incipient industrial revolution within the Empire State of the South. No less than 80 percent of all manufacturing establishments in Georgia were located above the fall line. That region, with its excellent rivers, moderate climate, and transportation links, was easily adaptable to manufacturing.[50] In a ranking of counties by value of product produced by manufacturing, only Chatham County (Savannah) lay below the fall line (see Table 2). The other five—Muscogee, Richmond, Bibb, Cobb, and Taylor—were located either on the fall line or slightly inland. A

Table 2. County Rankings by Value Added by Manufacturing

Chatham County	$1,917,357
Muscogee County	1,409,711
Richmond County	1,363,642
Bibb County	1,003,824
Cobb County	676,609
Taylor County	533,435

Sources: U.S. Census Office, *Manufactures of the United States in 1860: Compiled from the Original Returns of the Eighth Census* (Washington, D.C.: U.S. Government Printing Office, 1865), pp. 63–75; *Annual Report of the Comptroller General of the State of Georgia Made to the Governor, October 20, 1861* (Milledgeville: Boughton, Nisbet & Barnes, 1861), pp. 58–62.

similar configuration favoring a fall line location was also manifested in the rankings of counties by capital investment in manufacturing (see Table 3).

The tangible evidence of Georgia's growth reinforced optimism. The *Milledgeville Southern Recorder* argued that "no State in the Union possesses, in so great a degree, the elements of national and individual wealth as Georgia."[51] *DeBow's Review* cataloged the state's strides in railroad building, the erection of textile factories and rolling mills, and the development of mining and asked none too rhetorically: "Is there a State in Christendom in the enjoyment of so many material elements of comfort, prosperity and success as the great state of Georgia? . . . When that day shall come [when all projects were completed and all resources tapped], Georgia will not only be the Empire State of the South, but the Empire State of the World!"[52] Such puffery is all the more striking because it was written immediately after the Panic of 1857. Georgia escaped the woes of many Southern states during that dislocation, and as a result her progress was only marginally checked. Indeed, the state's comptroller general closed his report for the year 1857 by remarking upon "the flattering and prosperous condition of our state at this time, financially and otherwise."[53]

Growth statistics and optimism seem to fly in the face of recent historical analysis. Scholars have devoted volumes to explaining how and why the Southern economy lagged during the antebellum period. Though different historical schools have used different methodolo-

Table 3. County Rankings by Capital Investment in Manufacturing

Richmond County	$1,057,200
Bibb County	955,131
Chatham County	913,400
Muscogee County	808,500
Fulton County	770,600
Cobb County	484,453

Sources: U.S. Census Office, *Manufactures of the United States in 1860: Compiled from the Original Returns of the Eighth Census* (Washington, D.C.: U.S Government Printing Office, 1865), pp. 63–75; *Annual Report of the Comptroller General of the State of Georgia Made to the Governor, October 20, 1861* (Milledgeville: Boughton, Nisbet & Barnes, 1861), pp. 58–62.

gies, they all seem to agree that, in general, the slave-based agricultural system was the main obstacle to capital formation and investment, technological innovation, and entrepreneurial development.[54] Given such arguments, how does one explain Georgia's growth and development in the late antebellum period? Somes clues to a resolution of this paradox may be found in antebellum observers' assessments of the state.

When Daniel R. Hundley traveled through the South during the late 1850s, he was struck by the influence of "Southern Yankees" in the region. Hundley believed that Southern Yankees had become an "institution" in the South. These primarily middle-class individuals were most commonly found in trade and speculative activities. Although Hundley had little good to say about this segment of the Southern population, he did concede that they, in league with other members of the Southern middle class, "contributed no little to the present prosperity of the Slave States." Hundley concluded his discourse by remarking that the "best specimens" of the genus were to be found in Georgia.[55]

Hundley was not alone in seeing Georgia as a haven for a Yankee-like spirit. Frederick Law Olmsted's journeys through the Southern states in the mid-1850s took him into Georgia, where he was as struck as Hundley by what he found. Olmsted realized that Georgia possessed a slave-based agricultural system, but he could not help but notice remnants of Georgia's colonial past. Olmsted found that the state's origins, specifically its philanthropic purpose, its initial prohibition of slavery, and its settlement by tough, hardy Scottish, English, and German pioneers, continued to exert a decisive influence on the current inhabitants. "It is obvious to the traveler, and notorious in the stock market," Olmsted wrote, "that there is more life, enterprise, skill and industry in Georgia than in any of the old Slave Commonwealths." To underscore his observations, Olmsted quoted a letter from an Alabamian to the *New York Times*: " 'Georgia has the reputation of being the *Yankee Land of the South*, and it is well-deserved. She has the idea of doing—the will and the hand to undertake and accomplish—and you have only to be abroad among her people to see that she intends to lead the way in the race of Southern empire.' "[56]

Olmsted's and Hundley's observations were not isolated instances. Numerous other travelers and newspaper correspondents visiting Georgia commented on the Yankee influence in the state, and they did so in positive terms. Southern boosters held up Georgia and particularly its cities, where the Yankee ethos seemed most prevalent, as a worthy example to be followed elsewhere in the region. Even envious competitors implied in their comments that the state and its fast-growing cities and towns possessed elements worthy of imitation.[57]

Justifying Georgia's impressive growth in terms of a distinct and different mentality does not, however, fully explain the state's development during the late antebellum era. Georgia's fertile soil and its location—between the Atlantic seaboard and the lower South—rendered it a veritable "land of opportunity." Liberal land policies, enacted during the early years of the nineteenth century, encouraged farmers and planters from the regions where the soil was exhausted in the upper South to emigrate to Georgia. The opening of rail lines and manufacturing concerns attracted others to the state. The seemingly boundless opportunities in agricultural and nonagricultural pursuits pulled both Georgians and non-Georgians to different parts of the state.[58]

Although locational factors, or what geographers would term environmental determinants, loomed large in Georgia's growth during this period, other equally important elements must be taken into consideration. After all, many states, both North and South, enjoyed similar advantages, but not all partook of these opportunities. In many cases, the difference between change and the status quo was achieved by people. This does not suggest that a few strong-minded individuals were wholly responsible, only that human action and individual decision making made a significant difference. The actions and decisions of particular individuals converted Georgia's resources and fertile valleys into the land of opportunity it became by the late 1850s.

Beginning with Joseph Schumpeter, social scientists have created a theoretical framework to explain the role of the innovator, or the entrepreneur, in economic growth and development. The relationship between the innovator and his society was—and is—complex, but some broad generalizations help to place these theories into perspective. The entrepreneur innovates, he manifests a "creative response" to prevailing conditions. By forming "new combinations," or enterprises, he creates new situations that precipitate socioeconomic change. A prerequisite to such actions is social approval. As Schumpeter noted: "Entrepreneurs will be few and without great importance . . . where this action is despised and frowned upon."[59]

The Georgia experience accommodates such a view. In the beginning, the state government encouraged growth and diversification. Georgia was blessed, almost from its founding, with political leadership that encouraged innovation and diversification. As early as the 1820s, the state's chief executives and General Assemblies had proved more than amenable to policies (such as internal improvement projects and liberal land and tax policies) that aided economic growth. Such policies provided aspiring entrepreneurs with the "external security" they needed to establish their enterprises.[60] In essence, the state's political leadership followed policies that approximated the stance taken by the Whigs in the 1850s. Georgia's Whiggishly oriented politicos forged "a climate of opinion . . . sympathetic to the development of efficient business organization and practice."[61] These political leaders anticipated and indeed implemented the Southern Whig party's "Industrial Gospel."[62] In general, the Southern wing of the party urged that Southerners "stop talking" about lessening economic dependence on the North and "resort to acting. Let the puffing of the locomotives, the busy murmur of factories and the splashing of steam paddles be our eloquence." In Georgia, the Whig leadership acted upon this proposition by passing and successively liberalizing incorporation statutes throughout the 1840s and early 1850s, which allowed individuals to pool their capital to create manufacturing establishments. Because of state legislative aid, the "means of achieving effective entrepreneurship" were encouraged and facilitated. In essence, the state was creating the "minimal conditions" for security in entrepreneurial action. Once such safeguards went into effect, Georgia's entrepreneurs went to work, forming companies to manufacture cotton goods, building railroads, and establishing sawmills and rolling mills. They responded energetically to opportunities to expand business by always keeping an eye to the future. In sum, Georgia's businessmen helped sponsor state and urban growth by responding creatively to the situation.[63]

The vision of a new economic order did not appeal to everyone. Such tangible manifestations of economic change as railroads, factories, and the like informed all Georgians of the transformations that were taking place in their state. Few could remain oblivious, and some became downright apprehensive. Yeoman farmers in particular were unconvinced that increased government activity and corporate growth were unqualified blessings.[64] These individuals found their champion in Joseph E. Brown.

Brown, a staunch Jacksonian from the Georgia hill country, was elected governor in 1857. Although Brown advocated economic growth and continued to sponsor projects begun by his Whig predecessors, he showed his Jacksonian mettle on the subject of corporations, especially banks. Financial panic on Wall Street and the subsequent contraction in credit in 1857 prompted Georgia's banks to petition the state legislature for relief. The General Assembly heeded the plea and allowed Georgia's bankers to suspend specie payments. Brown's response was worthy of Old Hickory: he vetoed the bank relief bill and sent a stern rebuke to the banks and their allies in the statehouse. The legislature overrode Brown's veto but not before a long and heated debate over constitutional prerogatives and individual rights.[65]

The import of the governor's actions went beyond his veto. Indeed, Brown's veto message and his rebuttal to the override of that veto created a popular sensation. Brown argued that the legislature was creating a "privileged" class by allowing the banks to renege on their obligations. Banks had increased in wealth and influence, he said, and hence were attempting to pressure the government to afford them privileges not extended to farmers and laborers. For the governor, the question was "Shall the banks govern the people or shall the people govern the banks?"[66] Brown went on to promise that he would prosecute any "chartered monopoly" that threatened the sovereign rights of the people. Before long, Brown would see danger in all forms of corporate activity. "Corporate power rules the state, and is constantly on the increase. Unless the masses of people can be aroused upon this subject, and induced to take the power into their own hands by hurling corporate *tools* from place and power there is no remedy."[67]

Brown's outbursts found a receptive audience among many Georgians, especially in smaller towns and among debt-ridden farmers. The larger cities and established interests generally supported the legislature—and the bank lobby that exerted such a powerful influence on that body. Though Brown was defeated, his actions did prompt the rise of a decisively anticorporate sentiment in the state. Soon, all large economic concerns were lumped together as a source of evil. Brown issued calls for the stricter enforcement of charter regulations and the implementation of tougher state regulatory laws. Aspiring entrepreneurs felt the impact of this anticorporate outburst. Milton Heath notes that Brown's use of the anticorporate hobbyhorse and the support he received for his corporation baiting "indicated that Georgia already was experiencing some of the problems of industrial growth and concentration that became associated at a later date generally with the growth of the corporation." A sharp decline in the number of incorporations passed by special legislative act from 1857 to 1858 demonstrates how effective the governor was in whipping up anticorporate sentiment.[68] The state that had, in the past, fostered entrepreneurial endeavor and achievement suddenly reversed its policy and created an environment significantly less conducive to innovation and experimentation.

Ironically, the planter class, the group that, according to some historians, would have felt most threatened by the rise of urban-industrial corporations and their capitalist managers, manifested less hostility toward corporate concentrations than did their yeoman counterparts. Large agricultural interests supported the bank lobby. The apparent acquiescence of the large landowners and slaveholders to corporate growth and development seems to undermine the assertion that planters thwarted industrial development through their control of state governments and policy making. Far from opposing such economic concentrations, Georgia's legislators encouraged their creation through the liberalization of incorporation statutes and tax policies.[69] Still, the combination of grass-roots anticorporate sentiment coupled with tightened regulations on the charter of new corporations may have discouraged Georgia's aspiring industrialists from creating additional manufacturing concerns.[70]

Despite Brown's actions, Georgia's manufacturers and managers had achieved considerable results in their drive for diversification. Indeed, the state's push for industry was, for the most part, a reflection of a broad-based commonality of interests. Georgia's slaveholders apparently voiced little concern over the state's strides toward diversification. They leased slaves to the state and to private companies to aid in the building of Georgia's railroad network. Moreover, about 5 percent of Georgia's 462,198 bondsmen were employed in manufacturing establishments.[71] Planters also invested in industrial concerns and supported industrial growth by allowing the corporate form of business organization to take effect. In league with merchants and traders, Georgia's planters worked hard to encourage diversification, internal improvements, and industrial expansion. Only toward the end of the antebellum era, when some influential leaders saw danger in Georgia's economic strides, did the popular climate shift to a more restrained, perhaps even distrustful, view of unbounded and unregulated economic growth. Such concerns and fears, however, grew less immediate as national political questions intruded.[72]

Considering the evidence, Georgia appears to be a novelty in the antebellum era. Its lack of a hostile, hegemonic planter elite, its development of manufacturing, and the growth of urban centers within the state suggest that perhaps Georgia was an atypical member of the Old South. Nonetheless, trends in Georgia such as agricultural improvements, increased investment in manufacturing, the rise of vigorous town centers, and general economic diversification were also evident in other states of the slave South.[73] Georgia's quest for economic diversification created an environment extremely conducive to the rise of a group of entrepreneurs and local businessmen who perceived new opportunities in nonagricultural endeavors and moved to take advantage of state and local aid to internal improvement projects. Canals and railroads, built ostensibly to facilitate commerce, encouraged manufacturing activity. Those individuals who availed themselves of local and state resources reaped financial benefits and further legislative sanction for their endeavors, and they aided Georgia's overall economic growth. Success bred more opportunities and more plans.

Economic change and development are, of course, relative. Despite the tremendous achievements in diversifying the economy, Georgia remained predominantly agricultural: 90 percent of the population was rural, staple crop cultivation dominated, and farm values exceeded the value of goods manufactured by 150 percent.[74] The popular climate, which had so aided the rise of an entrepreneurial group, ultimately hampered its full flowering in the waning years of the antebellum era. Anticorporate ferment and a general distrust of economic concentrations prompted many Georgians to rescind their previous approbation of industrial endeavors. Those who had led the development drive were forced to bide their time until the popular mood again changed.

Still, Georgia was a Southern leader, largely because the state's entrepreneurs had seized the opportunities presented to them. Georgia ranked third, behind Virginia and Tennessee, in capital investment in manufacturing; it possessed the South's second most extensive railroad network; and it maintained an agriculturally diversified economy that supported a heterogeneous population of planters, merchants, yeomen, and industrialists. The state's growth, development, and prosperity in the late antebellum years induced Southern journalists and social critics to hold up Georgia as the model for emulation.[75] It is small wonder, then, that when the national political situation deteriorated in 1860 and Southerners threatened secession, Georgia's actions were closely watched. The Empire State of the South's economic strength and political clout were essential for the consummation of secession and the establishment of a Southern nation.

2 Building a War Economy

The 1860s were crisis years for Southerners generally and for Georgians in particular. The decade brought secession, war, defeat, and dislocation, topped by halting reconstruction efforts. As the new decade dawned, however, all that lay in the future, and although the political situation was undeniably tense, most Georgians hoped that the new year would bring continued economic improvement and opportunity. Such optimism as was found in the Empire State of the South in 1860 cannot be dismissed as mere naïveté or as myopia. Georgians had every reason to hail the new year with confidence and great expectations. Their economy was strong and thriving; the state's agricultural crops portended good harvests and fat profits; the railroad network was, to a large degree, completed; and the state press and public could point with pride to the development of various manufacturing establishments.[1]

The state's growth and diversification had aided the rise of thriving town centers throughout Georgia. In 1860, the largest urban areas were Atlanta, Augusta, Columbus, and Savannah. Individuals in each of those cities had taken advantage of opportunities in the manufacturing and commercial sectors, and the result was a strong urban economy with greater diversity than previously. Savannah, an "economic backwater" and poor relation to rival Charleston throughout much of the antebellum period, reclaimed its third-place ranking among Southern seaports through aggressive boosterism and expanded commercial ties made possible by extensive rail and steamship connections. The city boasted an active commercial elite that used its Chamber of Commerce to promote local internal improvement projects and manufacturing to bolster the port's economy.[2] The town of Columbus owed its growth and prosperity to the rise of the cotton textile industry. Natural resources, convenient rail links to market centers, proximity to the state's cotton belt, and vigorous planter and merchant capitalists had pushed the Chattahoochee River town to the front ranks in cotton manufacturing. The rise of such concerns as the Coweta and Carter factories and the Howard Manufacturing Company had dramatically changed Columbus from a sleepy river town into a vibrant, bustling manufacturing center.[3] Across the state, Augusta duplicated Columbus's achievements. Here, too, natural resources, vigorous entrepreneurs, and a choice location spurred the town's growth and development. Though Augusta registered less important gains than other Georgia cities, it continued to serve as a leader in textile manufacturing and had proved a worthy object of emulation.[4]

The newest and undoubtedly most dynamic and brash town was Atlanta. Not even on the map when Columbus and Augusta were taking their tentative steps toward diversification, Atlanta by 1860 was a bustling, prosperous commercial center of more than nine thousand souls. Led by what one historian has characterized as "innovative and imaginative business leadership," Atlanta displayed none of the trappings usually associated with the antebellum South. Indeed, both contemporary and latter-day historians remarked upon the conspicuous absence of the "planter ideal" so pervasive in Charleston, Mobile, and elsewhere. Instead, Atlanta epitomized an aggressive, "get-ahead" spirit that still evokes comment today. Its inhabitants included former Northerners, hill people, and country yeomen. Whatever their origins, Atlantans had, by 1860, established the foundations of a city that would be more characteristic of the twentieth century.[5]

Many adjectives may be used to characterize the mood and spirit that pervaded Georgia in 1860, but ingenuousness is not one of them. Georgians were not oblivious to the increasingly vitriolic political debates that swirled as the presidential contest approached. They had viewed with alarm the creation of a purely sectional party that claimed as its raison d'être policies inimical to Southern interests. It is no surprise, therefore, that the Georgia press in 1860 trumpeted the state's natural advantages and exhorted Georgians to undertake more investment in the development of local manufacturing.[6] A corollary argument to the push for industrial self-sufficiency was the call for direct trade between the South and Europe and the nonimportation of Northern goods. Such commands were not new; from the first murmurings of sectional division, movements had been afoot to humble Northern entrepôts by inaugurating direct trade with Europe. Predictably, these calls bore an exact relationship to the ebb and flow of sectional relations: as tensions mounted, so, too, did the call for direct trade; as they abated, the grandiose plans were abandoned.[7] Editors argued that nonimportation would cripple Northern merchants and, in turn, expand Southern markets. Moreover, home industry would take root more firmly. The press warned, however, that without a full commitment to the development of manufacturing in the state, all efforts for direct trade and nonimportation were doomed. The *Augusta Chronicle and Sentinel* spoke for most Southern editors when it wrote: "Let us begin to reform it before it is too late; let it not be a spasmodic, tantalizing effort, but a settled, determined purpose upon the part of the entire South to build up and develope [sic] her internal strength."[8]

Although calls for direct trade and industrial self-sufficiency proceeded apace, they were soon overshadowed by coverage of the national political conventions. In Georgia, the three-way Democratic contest reflected both the state's interest in the election and the divided mind of the Georgia electorate. In the end, Democratic divisions nationally proved decisive in electing the Republican Abraham Lincoln president. Lincoln's victory prompted consternation, confusion, and the immediate secession of South Carolina.[9]

Indecision may have prevailed in some quarters, but not in the Georgia governor's mansion. Apparently, Governor Joseph E. Brown foresaw a Republican victory even before election day. Convinced that Lincoln and his party would force abolition and social equality upon the South, he urged that steps be taken to counter such a threat. The day before the presidential balloting, Brown asked the Georgia legislature for a $1 million appropriation to augment the state's defense capabilities. Brown next issued a call for ten thousand volunteers and seized arms and ammunition in United States arsenals located throughout the state to equip those troops. Cognizant of the need for even more weapons, the governor recommended to the state legislature that bonuses be offered to private individuals to establish cannon and munitions factories. Brown also requested and received a $350,000 appropriation for the manufacture and purchase of more arms.[10]

Brown did not stop there. The end of November 1860 found him corresponding with Secretary of War John P. Floyd. To ensure that Georgia was receiving the most up-to-date weapons, Brown requested from Floyd samples of United States Army issue cartridge belts and boxes and Colt revolvers. He also asked that Lieutenant Colonel William J. Hardee, a renowned tactical expert and author of *Hardee's Tactics*, be sent to Georgia to act as the state's purchasing agent for military goods. Since Hardee was a native Georgian, Brown did not think his request extraordinary; what was extraordinary was that the governor would solicit aid from the national government to bolster state defenses in case that government undertook aggressive actions against Georgia.[11]

Somehow, during this flurry of executive activity, Brown found time to schedule 2 January 1861 for the election of delegates to Georgia's secession convention. While Georgians went to the polls on that day, Brown ordered Colonel Alexander R. Lawton to secure Fort Pulaski, a stronghold guarding the approaches to the vital port of Savannah. This bellicose act—undertaken before Georgia seceded—was accomplished without a loss on 3 January.[12]

The governor's actions made the vote in Georgia's secession convention almost anticlimactic. On 19 January 1861, by a margin of 208 to 89, Georgia severed its ties to the national Union and joined South Carolina, Mississippi, Alabama, and Florida in the Southern Confederacy. With the passage of Georgia's ordinance of secession, it appeared as though all previous ambivalence and indecision were forgotten. Throughout the state, rejoicing was the general rule. People fired cannons, lit bonfires, and held barbecues, while artillery companies and volunteer regiments stepped proudly to the "Secession Quick-Step."[13]

The press of eager volunteers and the requests of the Provisional Government of the Confederate States of America overwhelmed any lingering doubts among Georgians. New and important questions and issues demanded attention. How were the state and Confederate governments going to equip the "flower of Southern youth"? How were the troops to be trained? What resources of men, material, and money had Georgia to draw upon? In a word, who was to build and organize the state's war machine? These questions would be answered by Georgia's leaders of the mobilization effort.

No one in Georgia was more aware of its military deficiencies than its governor. Brown realized that purchases of arms and acquisitions from seizures were insufficient for the contest at hand. Accordingly, he appeared before the Georgia General Assembly on 6 November 1861 to suggest "the propriety of either establishing a State Foundry for [arms] manufacture or of guaranteeing to such company as will engage to manufacture them such an amount of patronage as will secure success." Brown also reported that, on the recommendation of a gunsmiths' convention in Atlanta, he had "appropriated a part of the machine shops of the State Road [Western & Atlantic] to the purpose of forging gun barrels" for Harpers Ferry rifles.[14]

Brown's measures pointed up in bold relief the problems faced not only by the state of Georgia but by all the Confederate states. Although the South as a whole, and Georgia in particular, had an established manufacturing base in the antebellum period, it was soon obvious, even to the most ardent Confederate boosters, that this base was totally inadequate for the demands of a large-scale war. There were no small arms manufactories, no ammunition depots, save at the scattered federal arsenals that had been seized, no accoutrements, and no heavy ordnance establishments anywhere in the South. The existing foundries and mills would provide a useful and necessary base for the manufacture of some articles of war, but it was patently clear that more were needed.[15]

Ironically, the deficiencies in the Confederate military-industrial plant proved fortuitous, at least initially. From Fort Sumter on, conventions and meetings of all sorts were held throughout the South. Merchants, planters, established capitalists, and aspiring entrepreneurs all manifested a great willingness to help the Confederacy embark upon its drive for independence—political as well as economic. These convocations received regional press coverage and support. The *Charleston Mercury* pointed with pride to various state efforts to establish arms manufactories, textile establishments, and the like. The *Mercury* concluded its glowing appraisal by stating: "Thus it will be seen that the South is really becoming independent; and if during the prosecution of the war, so much energy is displayed, how much more rapid will be the strides taken after the establishment of our independence."[16] The *Atlanta Southern Confederacy* expressed similar gratification at the sight of manufacturing establishments "springing up as if by magic." The editors urged that "the manufactures extend their limits and facilities, and throw out their branches until every hamlet shall resound with the clack of the water wheel or the puff of the steam engine."[17] Some editors went so far as to suggest that the Union blockade was a blessing in disguise, for it would force local investment and the development of manufactured goods previously obtained from the North. The Southern press perhaps made its greatest contribution to the mobilization effort by linking manufacturing with patriotism. As the *Atlanta Daily Intelligencer* put it: "He who engages in a useful branch of manufacture fights and whips the Yankees as effectually as he that marches to the field of battle. . . . While

bread must be made, clothing and all munitions are equally necessary. Fat stomachs are poor things with naked backs and defenceless
arms."[18] The combination of necessity, exhortation, and patriotic loyalty succeeded in securing not only the commencement of tentative
steps toward broader participation in manufacturing pursuits but in
changing the attitude of Southerners previously unconvinced that
industrial pursuits were desirable.[19]

Georgia's activities in the initial phases of the mobilization effort
were quickly emulated by other states and by the central government
of the Confederate States. In August 1861, the Confederate Congress
empowered the secretary of war, with the approval of the president, to
"make advances upon any contract, not to exceed thirty-three and
one-third percent, for arms or munitions of war."[20] General Josiah
Gorgas, chief of the War Department's Ordnance Bureau, directed the
establishment of government-operated arsenals and ordnance manufacturing centers throughout the Confederacy. These works were usually located near preexisting local facilities, but other considerations
came into play. All ordnance establishments created expressly for the
Confederate war effort had to be placed safely within Confederate
territory, well removed from potential enemy movements; they had to
have ready access to either water or rail transportation to ensure the
conveyance of finished products to the areas where they were most
needed; and they had to have an adequate and convenient power
source.[21] As might be anticipated, antebellum town industrial bell-
wethers proved most able to satisfy those prerequisites. In due course
the government established arsenals, foundries, and other munitions
works from Richmond to San Antonio. Not surprisingly, towns designated as arms and ordnance manufacturing centers welcomed the war
industries because they promised capital inflows and jobs.[22]

As 1861 drew to a close, Confederate leaders looked with pride on
their newborn nation's efforts to build a war machine from scratch.
President Jefferson Davis, in an address to the Confederate Congress,
summed up the achievements of the Confederate States in their first
full year of existence: "The necessities of the times have called into
existence new branches of manufactures and given a fresh impulse to
the activity of those heretofore in operation. The means of the Confederate States for manufacturing the necessities and comforts of life
within themselves increases as the conflict continues and we are
gradually becoming independent of the rest of the world for the supply of such military stores and munitions as are indispensable for
war."[23]

Davis, however, spoke too confidently and prematurely. As he called attention to advances made, others within the War Department and on the state level perceived acute difficulties and weaknesses. It was to these soft spots in the Confederate war machine that Confederate and local military men and private entrepreneurs would address themselves in the new year.

In February 1862, Secretary of War Judah P. Benjamin submitted his report on the status of his department to President Davis. On the positive side, military appropriations had enabled commissioners to travel abroad to obtain much needed arms before the Union blockade had taken effect. Equally important, manufacturing had yielded essential supplies of saltpeter and gunpowder. The Confederate government had entered into contracts with three lead mines, and other agreements promised to produce muskets, rifles, and sabers. Government arsenals, though hamstrung by a dearth of skilled labor, were manufacturing rifles and muskets at a rate of fifteen hundred per day. Benjamin noted that only in the area of small arms production was the Confederacy deficient. In most other sectors, he reported, "Confederate States have, in the brief period which has elapsed . . . evinced the capacity of providing all that is necessary to the maintenance of their independence."[24]

The dearth of small arms was not alleviated as time passed. Just one month later, in March, Benjamin reported that the supply of those articles was "woefully deficient." Benjamin added: "The manufacture of small arms is a slow and tedious process, and the accumulation of supplies necessary for such an army as we now require is the result of the labor and expenditure of long series of years"—years the Confederacy obviously did not have. Legislation, Benjamin argued, would do little good: "Laws cannot suddenly convert farmers into gunsmiths." He concluded that "no recourse remains but importation," an alternative of doubtful feasibility because of the Union blockade.[25]

Although Benjamin contended that legislation would not substantially aid the Confederacy, the Confederate Congress acted anyway. On 12 March 1862 Congress passed an "Act to Organize the Bureau of Artillery and Ordnance," which detailed the reorganization and supply duties of the Ordnance Bureau and its personnel. Of special importance was Section Nine, which designated where armories, arsenals, and depots were to be located. Three of the thirteen projected sites were in Augusta and Savannah.[26] Knowing that these new centers could not function without raw materials, Congress also mandated the creation of a new bureau to collect and distribute iron, copper, lead, and saltpeter and to oversee the production of those articles: the Niter and Mining Bureau.[27] Shortly thereafter, the Adjutant and Inspector General's Office issued a special order directing Niter Bureau officers and military commanders "to seize niter in the hands of private individuals who either decline to sell it or ask more than fifty cents per pound for it." The transportation of commodities seized or manufactured was given precedence "over all other Government stores."[28]

To assist the newly reorganized War Department, the Confederate lawmakers also passed an "Act to encourage the manufacturing of saltpetre and small arms." This legislation promised that any individual or group within the Confederacy who undertook arms manufacturing would "receive from the Government an advance of fifty per cent. of the amount required for the erection and preparation of the works and machinery necessary to such a manufactory." Interested individuals or firms were to submit a plan and a budget to the president. Upon his approval, the government-sponsored portion was to be paid in installments.[29]

Equipped with ample statutory authority, Gorgas moved to make the Confederacy self-sufficient in military supplies. Gorgas worked untiringly to standardize arms and ammunition manufacturing and to create a well-ordered war machine. Although the Pennsylvania-born officer created facilities throughout the South, he found many ready-made ones in Georgia.

His first action was to establish a central laboratory at Macon, Georgia, to ensure uniformity of ammunition.[30] Naturally, a laboratory designed to aid ammunition production was of little use without the production of gunpowder, a commodity that was obviously in great demand. Gorgas therefore instructed his subordinate, George Washington Rains, to choose a suitable location and to oversee the construction of a Confederate powder works.

Gorgas could not have selected a better man for the job. Born in North Carolina in 1817, Rains had attended West Point, graduating high enough in his class to be commissioned in the Army Corps of Engineers. His expertise in engineering was supplemented by a thorough knowledge of chemistry and geology. In 1844, he became assistant professor of those sciences at his alma mater. After serving in the Mexican War, Rains resigned his commission to become president and part owner of the Washington Naval Works of Newburgh, New York. With the outbreak of war in 1861, however, Rains reported to President Davis to offer his considerable skills to the newly formed Confederacy. His assignment to the Ordnance Bureau in July 1861 was to prove a godsend.[31] Gorgas gave Rains virtual carte blanche in establishing a powder works in the Confederacy, and Rains did not disappoint him. After touring the Confederacy to find a suitable spot, Rains chose Augusta, Georgia. It was a fortuitous choice, not just for the city but for the Confederate war effort as well. The outbreak of the war had deranged trade in the black belt town and had led to unemployment in the manufacturing and building sectors. Rains thus found an eager and willing labor supply. Further, Augusta had a firmly established manufacturing sector that had thrived for years because of its proximity to raw materials sources and the water power provided by the Augusta Canal. Augusta lay close to rail lines and enjoyed a temperate climate that would ensure year-round production. The region was also blessed with top-grade soil free from "lime and earthy salts," which assured that top-quality saltpeter could be produced. No other area in the Confederacy satisfied Rains's prerequisites for the establishment of a powder works.[32]

The selection of a site was only one problem facing Rains. Although he obtained a copy of a pamphlet written by the superintendent of the Waltham Abbey Powder Works in England, providing details of the machinery and processes used at that unsurpassed facility, Rains lacked knowledge of building specifications. Nevertheless, he selected the site of the old United States magazine and, tapping the local contracting firm of Denning and Bowe, commenced building the powder works. Rains demonstrated both his resourcefulness and his ingenuity throughout the endeavor. He obtained machinery and materials from other Confederate centers and experimented endlessly with methods to speed up and improve the processing of saltpeter. Under Rains's aegis, the Augusta Powder Works was completed in April 1862, after only seven months, and at the remarkably low cost of $385,000.[33]

In recognition of Rains's accomplishments, Gorgas made Rains commander of the Augusta Arsenal, and Rains immediately began converting the existing facility to produce war matériel of all kinds for the Confederacy. Again, machinery and tools required for the production of gun carriages, artillery harnesses, cartridges, percussion caps, and artillery projectiles were obtained from all over the South. Rains's goal was to create a centralized production center, as existed in Richmond, to supply ordnance materials for the Deep Southern and western theaters. Soon, the Augusta Arsenal was producing 30,000 rounds of small arms ammunition and 125 to 150 rounds of field artillery ammunition daily. These totals were exceeded only by the Richmond establishments.[34] Rains also arranged the purchase of an idle machine shop, a foundry, factories for gun carriage production, and a facility for the manufacture of powder boxes and cartridges. The arsenal, powder works, and their adjunct plants became veritable hives of war-related activity. Indeed, from 1863 to 1865, Confederate-operated concerns at Augusta produced, among other things, 174 gun carriages, 115 caissons, 10,535 powder boxes, 110 bronze twelve-pounder Napoleon field guns, 85,800 rounds of fixed ammunition, 476,207 pounds of artillery projectiles, 4,626,000 lead balls, and 10,760,000 small arms cartridges.[35]

Visitors to Augusta during the war were struck by the city's activity and prosperity. Newcomers and, later, refugees, who arrived in a seemingly constant flow, were quickly absorbed by the booming war industries with their insatiable demand for labor.[36] Augusta's facilities grew to such an extent that the Confederate government determined to increase its stake in the city by establishing a Naval Quartermaster Division and the Confederate States Clothing Bureau and Shoe Manufactory there.[37]

Although government-owned and operated businesses dominated the city's economy during the war, private entrepreneurs also took advantage of the wartime demands of the Confederate government to expand and diversify their own businesses. In part, they were motivated by a desire to support the war effort, but they also saw an opportunity to profit from the crisis. W. C. Jessup, who ran the saddlery and harness firm of Jessup, Hatch & Day, was one such entrepreneur. At the outbreak of the war in 1861 Jessup was running a profitable business that had what one source called "a monopoly of the trade" in saddles and harnesses. When the Augusta Arsenal opened, Jessup, Hatch & Day immediately began manufacturing harnesses for the military. Another example was S. S. Jones, owner of a hardware business, who expanded and diversified his business to meet Confederate demands. By the spring of 1862, Jones & Company was manufacturing canteens, camp utensils, bayonet sheaths, artillery buckets, and up to ten thousand military belt buckles a week. Anxious not to lose his regular customers, Jones assured his fellow

Augustans that articles for domestic consumption could still be obtained.[38]

Other than government shops, however, the most important contributor to the war effort was the firm of Rigdon, Ansley & Company. Charles Rigdon had trained as a smith and operated as a scalemaker in St. Louis before the war. When war came, Rigdon, a Southern sympathizer, left St. Louis and journeyed to Memphis, Tennessee, where he entered into a partnership with former gunsmith and cotton broker Thomas Leech. In 1862, the two men established a sword factory, the Memphis Novelty Works, but they were forced to suspend operations and move the concern to Columbus, Mississippi, when Federal advances threatened Memphis. Rigdon and Leech had no sooner set up shop in Mississippi than they were again compelled to flee from the persistent Yankees. After relocating in Greensboro, Georgia, Rigdon and Leech bought the Greensboro Steam Factory, obtained a government contract, and began to manufacture .36-caliber revolvers. In December 1863, the partnership was dissolved; Leech continued to manufacture on government account on a limited scale, and Rigdon moved to Augusta, where he formed a new partnership with Jesse A. Ansley, A. J. Smythe, and C. R. Keen. After obtaining a lease to operate with the Augusta Canal Company, Rigdon, Ansley & Company, with a capital stock of $160,000, began manufacturing revolvers virtually identical to the highly regarded and much desired Colt (too similar, in fact: after the war, Colonel Samuel Colt sued Rigdon for the illegal use of Colt revolver patents).[39] In Augusta, Rigdon, Ansley & Company produced over twelve thousand of its valuable revolvers; Rigdon subsequently became known as the Confederacy's "ace revolver manufacturer." Local accounts of the firm end in late 1864, but Ordnance Bureau communiqués indicate that Rigdon and his partners continued to manufacture sidearms for the Confederate government until the end of the war.[40]

Other ambitious individuals also participated in the local mobilization effort. Although none of these men left accounts detailing their motivations and aspirations, the evidence suggests that they diversified for both selfless and selfish reasons. For years they had heard state officials and the local press trumpet the importance of economic independence. Wartime needs presented a golden opportunity to achieve those goals. To be sure, these men felt an obligation to the Southern cause, but patriotism was not their only motive. The readiness with which they embraced the opportunities and their willing-

ness to take risks demonstrate that they were fully alert to the prospect of personal gain. For them, aiding the war effort and making a
profit constituted complementary goals.

War-related production promoted prosperity and high morale in the
city, conditions absent in many parts of the Confederacy. Visitors to
Augusta were struck by the activity of the powder works, arsenal, and
private firms that produced on government account. "Personne" reported that such activities "will tend to make Augusta one of the most
enterprising and bustling cities of the South."[41] A British observer,
who was a member of Her Majesty's Coldstream Guards, was so
impressed with the operation of government works in the city that he
deemed them "convincing proofs of the determined energy of the
Southern character, now that it has been roused."[42] The local press
served as the manufacturers' booster by pointing with pride to Augusta's strides and by urging those not involved in war manufacturing
to avail themselves of the opportunities. The editors of the *Chronicle
and Sentinel* castigated those with capital who sought investment in
Confederate and state bonds and securities. More immediate—and
lucrative—returns on investments, the paper argued, were available
in the form of war-related manufactories.[43] Everywhere the call was
the same: invest in manufacturing, aid the Southern cause, and, not
coincidentally, grow rich.

Although the Augusta facilities received the lion's share of attention, other Confederate arsenals in Georgia also contributed greatly to
the Southern war effort and demonstrated the valuable opportunities
for investment that existed. Indeed, Augusta's antebellum textile
manufacturing rival, Columbus, became one of the Confederacy's
most important manufacturing centers in the Deep South.[44] Columbus attracted the notice of government authorities early in the war. Its
location near rail lines and its river connection to Gulf ports made the
town a natural site for the establishment of government works. Moreover, Columbus boasted a wide array of manufacturing concerns.
While the textile establishments caught the eye of the Quartermaster
Department, the Confederate navy claimed the Columbus Iron Works
in June 1862.[45]

William R. Brown established the Columbus Iron Works in 1848. It
was a "modest business," consisting of one forge and one rolling mill.
In 1861, Brown's foundry produced three-inch artillery pieces. Shortly
thereafter, he obtained government contracts to manufacture brass
twelve-pounders. The ironworks continued to produce those field-

pieces for the Ordnance Bureau until it was leased to the navy in 1862. Once the navy took over the ironworks, full-scale production of ordnance began. Under the direction of Major James H. Warner, the former chief engineer of the Gosport, Virginia, Navy Yard, the Columbus Iron Works began manufacturing cannons, ships, and ship boilers. One student estimates that three ships and approximately seventy brass Napoleons were produced at Brown's works.[46] Columbus's facilities also attracted the attention of the War Department, and in June 1862, Captain F. C. Humphreys of the Ordnance Bureau was dispatched to the Chattahoochee River town to oversee the erection of a Confederate arsenal. By November, the Columbus Arsenal was producing ten thousand rounds of small arms ammunition a day and seventy-five to one hundred rounds of artillery shells. Though its output lagged behind that of Augusta, it nonetheless surpassed establishments at Selma, Macon, and Charleston.[47]

The greatest contributions to the Confederate war effort in the city, however, came from private individuals. Local firms, cognizant of the advantages to be gained from the manufacture of arms and military accoutrements, formed the vanguard of Columbus's mobilization drive. They demonstrated a willingness to innovate and a desire to augment the city's industrial base.

As soon as the militia units were called out, Columbus entrepreneurs went to work, turning their peacetime businesses into factories for the production of war matériel. A. H. DeWitt, for example, converted his jewelry shop into a sword manufactory, and local mechanics Madison Barringer and Joseph Merton turned to the manufacture of gun carriages. Such efforts, however, were overshadowed by the achievements of the Haiman brothers.[48]

Louis and Elias Haiman were Prussian immigrants who settled in Columbus in the 1830s. Their father established a small hardware store, and upon his death the brothers took over a business credit agents considered "not . . . of much strength" but "in good repute." When war broke out in 1861, Louis leased additional space to manufacture swords. Confederate authorities proved to be eager buyers: the concern became so profitable that after one year, Louis was forced to purchase the Muscogee Iron Works so as to handle the increased demand for products. Periodic steel shortages induced Elias to travel to Europe to buy raw materials to be run through the Federal blockade. Meanwhile, the sword factory expanded and diversified production to include saddles, bayonets, tin cups, and mess articles.[49]

Louis decided to diversify still further in the summer of 1862. After much trial and error—and expense—he developed a sidearm modeled after the navy Colt. Louis's persistence paid off: in August 1862, the Haiman brothers garnered a War Department contract to produce ten thousand of their Colt-style pistols. While Elias worked overseas, shipping materials through the blockade, Louis continued to work for the Confederate War Department as the Columbus Fire Arms Manufacturing Company. Ordnance Bureau officials estimated that the Haimans' establishment was worth $80,000—a vast improvement over the value of the brothers' old hardware store.[50]

Eldridge S. Greenwood provides another example of the wartime opportunities that existed for those willing to take up the challenge. Greenwood had managed a wholesale and commission house in Columbus for almost thirty years when Georgia seceded. In the late 1850s, he had begun a partnership with William C. Gray, and although credit reporters did not consider the firm to be a "strong" one, it was deemed a "clever bus[iness] house" that had "weathered several storms successfully."[51] Greenwood & Gray demonstrated their cleverness in 1862 when they bought out A. H. DeWitt. DeWitt's initial success as a sword manufacturer had induced him to build an even larger facility. DeWitt failed to produce swords to government standard and was forced to sell his factory to the commission merchants. Greenwood & Gray hired J. P. Murray, an English-born gunsmith and skilled mechanic who had worked his trade in Columbus for several years, to convert the facility into a rifle works. The rifle factory, located about 150 yards from the Haiman brothers' Columbus Fire Arms Manufacturing Company, grew, eventually employing 150 workers. Greenwood & Gray sold most of the rifles to Confederate authorities in neighboring Alabama. Duff Green, the Alabama quartermaster general, estimated that his bureau received 262 rifles and 73 carbines from the Columbus-based firm from October 1863 to November 1864.[52]

Like Augusta, Columbus profited greatly from the war industries in its midst. Yeomen from the surrounding area and refugees from Georgia and elsewhere flocked to the city and found employment in the various manufacturing plants. By 1863, the population of Columbus had swelled to fifteen thousand—a 60 percent increase in just three years. Prosperity and optimism pervaded the city, and with just cause: its abundant resources were being efficiently used, its economic base had expanded, food and jobs were plentiful, and the Yankees posed no immediate threat. Locals would have been hard-pressed to dispute the *Columbus Daily Sun's* contention that the city was almost immune from war-related problems that affected other Southern cities.[53]

Perhaps the greatest beneficiary of wartime demand was Atlanta. The War Department targeted early this up-and-coming interior town of the state as a Confederate support base because of its railroad connections. The government's establishment of military operations in the city created even more opportunities for Atlanta's residents and laid the groundwork for the city's emergence as the major Deep Southern distribution center both during the war and after.

The Confederate government's actions provided the catalyst that sparked local industrial promoters and investors to action. Just before the fall of Nashville, Tennessee, to Union forces in February 1862, the War Department began to search for a suitable site to relocate the Nashville Ordnance and Arsenal works. Prominent citizens in Atlanta petitioned the City Council to approach the Confederate government to obtain government works. Local businessmen were not motivated solely by patriotism. They were fully cognizant of the economic advantages that would follow from trade with the government. Moreover, many Atlanta entrepreneurs, eager to augment the city's commercial base with industries, saw the relocation of war production centers to Atlanta as bringing that dream to fruition. These boosters were gratified when the Confederate government accepted Atlanta's offer and moved the Nashville arsenal facilities to the Gate City of the South. With this acquisition, Atlanta began its rise as the chief manufacturing and supply center for the Southern armies.[54]

Although preeminently a commercial entrepôt, Atlanta did not lack industrial establishments even before the Confederate arsenal was located there. Indeed, a foundry, rolling mill, and various grain mills dotted Atlanta and its environs. Nonetheless, local obstacles militated against the establishment of the kind of industrial base found elsewhere in the state. Because of the city's commercial character, it lacked a large corps of skilled labor to man industrial concerns. Railroads crisscrossed the town, but to reluctant urban investors, urban markets and raw materials seemed too far-flung to justify factory development. Although city ordinances dating back to the early 1850s had exempted capital investment in manufacturing from taxation, only a few entrepreneurs took advantage of the offer. Though some Atlantans were indifferent or unresponsive to calls for industrial development, they never manifested any overt resistance to industrialization.

Rather, as one scholar has written, those "who established industrial plants of all sorts . . . were hailed . . . and their industrial ventures praised as contributors to the prosperity of the city."[55]

Considering the number of firms in Atlanta that obtained contracts from the Confederate arsenal and shifted to war-related manufacturing, the conversion to the "industrial gospel" was remarkably swift. Established concerns were in the vanguard, but new industries, eager to profit from wartime demand, soon joined the effort. The experiences of all these individuals would play a crucial role in shaping the city's later history.

One of the city's first war manufacturing entrepreneurs was John C. Peck. Born and reared in New England, Peck was forced to move south because he suffered from asthma. After settling in Atlanta in 1858, Peck formed a partnership with locals A. H. Brown and Edwin Priest. With the outbreak of war, Peck converted his planing mill into a factory and contracted with Governor Brown to manufacture a thousand "Joe Brown pikes." Peck rendered even greater service to the Confederate war effort when the War Department enlisted him to build the magazine, laboratory, and miscellaneous other buildings for the Confederate arsenal in Atlanta. The various contracts indicate that Peck received substantial remuneration for his services.[56]

Another example of wartime conversion was the rolling mill of Colonel William Markham and Lewis Scofield. Like Peck, Markham had been born in Connecticut, but he had emigrated to Georgia in the 1830s to establish himself in business. Upon his arrival in Atlanta, Markham gave up his career in merchandising to enter into a partnership with fellow Yankee Lewis Scofield. In 1858, the firm of Scofield & Markham purchased Dr. L. A. Douglas's failed Atlanta Rolling Mill. The mill specialized in rerolling iron rails and producing iron bar. Credit reporters noted that in 1860 the concern was worth "at least [$]40,000" and that its new proprietors possessed "such energy . . . [it] is doing better than it ever did." With the onset of war, Scofield & Markham expanded their plant to facilitate the manufacture of iron rails, cannon, and gunboat iron plate. In December 1861, they contracted with Confederate naval agents Nelson and Asa Tift to supply the Navy Department with rolled armor plates of varying sizes. By 10 January 1862, Scofield & Markham had delivered 390,325 pounds of iron plate to the Tifts. Later in 1862, the Tifts reported that Scofield & Markham had supplied iron casings to the Confederate navy in "a most prompt and satisfactory manner."[57] Despite their contributions to the Southern cause, locals continued to distrust Scofield & Markham because of their Northern birth. That factor may explain the sale of the Atlanta Rolling Mill to the Charleston firm of Trenholm & Frazier in 1863. The newly christened Confederate Rolling Mill continued producing on Confederate contract after its sale to the Charlestonians.[58]

Another Yankee-born Southern émigré who joined the city's mobilization effort was Joseph Winship. Winship had left his native Massachusetts in 1820 and settled in Jones County, Georgia. After partnering with his brother in a shoe factory and tannery in Forsyth, he moved to Morgan County, where he established a cotton gin factory. In 1845, Winship moved to Atlanta, and there he built a foundry and rolling mill. Winship's Machine Shop and Foundry, which specialized in railroad car construction, made Winship a pioneer in the development of Atlanta's industrial concerns. Even a devastating fire in 1856 did not discourage Winship: he rebuilt and expanded his foundry's production line into other areas, including bridge casings and boilers. Winship presided over "one of the strongest concerns" in the city, and he was noted locally for his "untiring energy." The Winship works never approached the manufacturing capacity or the output levels of the Western & Atlantic Railroad's machine shops, but the firm did render invaluable assistance to the Confederate war effort by producing freight cars, miscellaneous railroad supplies, and iron.[59]

Northerners who had settled in Atlanta were not the only ones to produce for the Confederate cause. Hammond Marshall, a Kentuckian, founded the Atlanta Sword Factory. Besides producing about 170 swords weekly for the War Department, Marshall's establishment also manufactured carbines. McNaught and Ormond's Novelty Iron Works manufactured various ordnance supplies. Although these private firms and individuals rendered valuable skills and products to the war effort, their initial efforts were largely piecemeal.[60] With the establishment and full-time operation of the Atlanta Arsenal, however, these men and their expertise contributed mightily to the city's mobilization drive.

Colonel Marcus H. Wright, commander of the Atlanta Arsenal, began soliciting local firms for government contracts in May 1862. The combination of military necessity and local ambition required that government operations be supplemented by private effort. Interested parties submitted bids for contracts, and the lowest offers received government approval.[61] Close scrutiny of the contracts and records of the Atlanta Arsenal indicates that Atlanta businessmen seized the opportunities offered by the Confederate government. Brady & Solomon and Scofield & Markham sold iron; H. Marshall & Company furnished swords. S. A. Durand promised two thousand haversacks; J. B. Langford & Son contracted to manufacture cavalry saddles; E. E. Rawson and McNaught and Ormond's company produced pistol caps; and other firms contracted to manufacture complete accoutrement sets. Even firms as distant as Rome, Dalton, and Gainesville, Georgia, received Confederate sanction to manufacture everything from cotton webbing for accoutrements to horseshoes and twenty-pound Parrott guns. In addition to heavy ordnance and arms, local contractors produced 8,500 sets of accoutrements, 3,000 sabers, 7,000 haversacks, 3,500 canteens, and 5,000 knapsacks.[62]

The flood of new business redounded to the benefit of the city. The short business depression between secession and the onset of armed hostilities ended with the establishment of the various war industries and the production of war goods. From 1862, the city experienced a boom that was widely reported and wildly applauded. The *Atlanta Daily Intelligencer* rhetorically challenged Atlanta's urban rivals elsewhere in Georgia to equal the Gate City's growth, wealth, prosperity, industrial prowess, and commitment to the cause.[63] A South Carolina correspondent commented favorably on the "warlike aspect" of the city and its great contributions to the "establishment of our independence." Another reporter complained that he could not possibly keep track of all of Atlanta's manufacturing establishments because they increased daily. The city's growth as a manufacturing center did, however, produce some unfavorable reviews. One Charlestonian remarked that "the bustle and whirl of business speak of naught but gold, gold, gold! Everybody seems hurrying on, intent upon acquiring a fortune by the quickest mode which his active brain can suggest." That observer was more perceptive than he knew: what he described was the "Atlanta Spirit," a concept that would be a potent rallying cry in the future.[64]

Local editors pointed to the town's boom to illustrate again and again the need for Confederate self-reliance. Public notices brought attention to local concerns and urged Atlantans to patronize them. The exigencies of war were extolled as positive benefits, for they forced diversification and industrial development, which together would assure prosperity and independence. Some editors went so far as to state that greater benefits would result if the war proved to be a protracted affair. A speedy resolution of the crisis was potentially dangerous, for it held out the possibility that old patterns of economic "vassalage" to the North would be resumed.[65]

The city of Savannah did not share in the growth and prosperity of the state's other military-industrial centers. Residents had eagerly welcomed secession and war and had, initially at least, enjoyed commercial prosperity. As Georgia's chief port city, Savannah quickly became a blockade-running hub. Local individuals petitioned the Confederate State Department for letters of marque and reprisal. Savannah's wartime boom was further enhanced by the establishment of a Confederate arsenal in the city. According to local observers, the combination of military contracts and military demand in the city had produced a veritable hive of activity. As one Savannahian noted approvingly, "Every paper contains notices of some new branch of manufacture springing up in our midst: cannon are cast and ball and shell made in various places—numerous powder mills have been established . . . Southern industry and ingenuity are being largely developed."[66]

Jubilation and confidence in Savannah quickly gave way to fear. Northern naval attacks on Hilton Head Island and Port Royal, South Carolina, in November 1861 prompted the flight of many residents. With the establishment of a Federal navy base on Port Royal, Savannah military officials scrambled to bolster the city's defenses. Under the direction of General Henry Wayne, local troops erected redoubts, dug entrenchments, and mounted heavy siege guns to protect all avenues to the city. Confederate leaders asked planters to volunteer to lease their slaves to aid the defensive effort, but they were eventually forced to impress slave labor because of the planters' intransigence.[67]

Meanwhile, Commodore Josiah Tatnall did his best to defend the river approaches to Savannah. His "mosquito fleet" of riverboats patrolled the waters around Cockspur Island, where Fort Pulaski, the strongest point guarding the Savannah River's entrance to the city, was located. Fort Pulaski had stood as sentinel since colonial days, and its seven-and-one-half-foot-thick masonry walls, built in 1812, were considered in 1861 to be "impregnable by all known standards."[68]

Federal naval raids continued along the South Carolina–Georgia coast during 1862 and resulted in the establishment of a Federal naval base on Tybee Island, which faced Fort Pulaski on the Atlantic side. Colonel Charles H. Olmstead, the twenty-four-year-old commander of Fort Pulaski's 385-man garrison, directed the construction of embrasures and the location of gun emplacements in expectation of an attack that the Confederates knew would come. On 10 April 1862, Olmstead received a communiqué from Union commander Major General David Hunter demanding the capitulation of the fort. Olmstead refused, stating that he had been placed there to defend, not surrender, the fort. Shortly thereafter, the Federal bombardment from Tybee Island commenced, and the power of the Federal guns surprised, dismayed, and terrified Southern observers. As one resident noted, "Nothing could withstand their tremendous force; the heavy timber placed against the casemate doors offered no resistance at all. The whole system of warfare is revolutionized; brick is no longer of any avail; we must have *iron forts* and *iron clad ships*. Fort Pulaski has been made the victim of a new mode of laying siege."[69] This resident voiced a conviction many must have felt by 1862. In a sense, the Federal assault on Fort Pulaski demonstrated in microcosm the capability of a more mature industrial base. The superiority of the rifled guns and their seemingly inexhaustible supply of ammunition betokened not only the future magnitude of the struggle but also the power of the Union's manufacturing sector. Despite valiant achievements in the military-industrial realm, Georgians and other Southerners could not have been oblivious to their industrial inferiority or to the consequences it portended.

On 11 April 1862, Fort Pulaski fell to Union forces. Not only did the Confederacy lose provisions, ordnance stores, and prisoners, it also lost a valuable port. With the fall of Fort Pulaski, Savannah began an economic decline. The Confederate arsenal was moved quickly to the safer interior town of Macon. The tightening of the Union navy's cordon around the port city brought blockade running to a virtual halt. Enterprising locals either moved their blockade-running operations to Wilmington, North Carolina, or Charleston, South Carolina, or took up other endeavors. Savannah continued to be an important Confederate navy yard after the loss of Pulaski, but all other war-related operations ground to a halt. Business and trade fell off drastically, and Confederate conscription and the threat of a Yankee invasion substantially winnowed the city's population. Visitors were struck by the "strange, mysterious . . . quietude" that reigned in Savannah.[70]

Those who remained in Savannah experienced problems that soon plagued the entire state—and nation. The tightening of the Union blockade led to shortages of food and clothing. Although such wants were initially "welcomed" because they fostered home manufacturing and hence true "independence," they soon bred disaffection and demoralization. One man noted that "there is nothing in the stores." Shoes cost over $30 a pair, and a bushel of sweet potatoes commanded $16.[71] Currency depreciated and housewives were urged to economize. Soon, however, complaints of high prices gave way to charges of extortion. Many acknowledged that "the great mass of people exhibit the most sublime virtue and patriotism." A pernicious minority, however, "monopolize[d] everything and resell at enormous profit." The "rapid thirst for wealth" had taken over those not actively engaged in the cause. For most city dwellers, those individuals formed an insidious fifth column: "Their nefarious practices . . . inflict more injury upon us than the Yankees themselves." Jews, aliens, former Northerners, and blockade runners were especially targeted as causing popular suffering and generally undermining the war effort. Evidently, these rapacious speculators, "intent only on gain! gain! gain!" precipitated a sort of social "revolution" in the city. As one resident noted, "The rich are ruined, the poor can now grow rich. . . . Anyone who is willing to buy, keep, and resell at a profit can now grow rich; the recipe is simple—the practice successful."[72]

Savannah's experience demonstrates that not all Georgia cities were able to capitalize on the war. Besieged from the beginning of hostilities, Savannah's businessmen never had the opportunity to use war-spawned demands to enhance the city's economy. Elsewhere in Georgia, war-related activities produced an optimistic, determined spirit that fostered innovation and diversification. In Savannah, the absence of those opportunities yielded popular demoralization and economic decline. Never given the chance to mobilize, Savannah stagnated, its entrepreneurial spirit stifled.

As Emory M. Thomas has argued, by 1863 the Confederate South was at "full tide"—at the height of its power and strength. The untiring efforts of ordnance chief Josiah Gorgas had produced impressive results. The War and Navy departments had erected or refurbished arsenals, supply depots, and arms and munitions factories. Local firms throughout the South had entered into contracts with the Confederate War Department to augment government production of war matériel. In sum, mobilization had fostered the development of a military-industrial complex.[73] Hence Gorgas did not engage in hyperbole when he wrote of Confederate achievements: "Where three years ago we were not making a gun, pistol, nor a sabre, no shot nor shell (save at Tredegar)—a pound of powder—we now make all these in quantities to meet the demands of our large armies."[74]

The demands of the Confederate war machine produced other results. Sleepy towns and established urban centers were transformed into bustling centers of industrial and commercial activity as war agencies were created in their midst. Demands for manufactured goods and labor swelled urban and town areas—often beyond their physical capacity to accommodate the newcomers—and hastened the urbanization process.[75] Opportunities in the military-industrial sector provided new and nontraditional chances to achieve wealth and status. Indeed, the transformed pattern of Southern society during the war was not, as Blaine Brownell points out, "so new as it was freed from many of the social and political barriers to the unfettered entrepreneurial spirit that had emerged in the late 1850s."[76]

Unfortunately for the Confederate cause, the clock did not stop in 1863. Even at the height of its power and strength, the Confederate military-industrial complex manifested fissures that would become irreparable chasms as greater demands were placed on it. As Gorgas was all too aware, the industrial base of the Confederacy suffered from two persistent lacks: skilled mechanics and raw materials. Iron, steel, and saltpeter had been obtained from foreign sources, but as the Union blockade stiffened, these supplies were cut off. The Niter Bureau succeeded in establishing artificial niter beds in South Carolina, Georgia, and Alabama, but these plants were inadequate to meet the demand, as were private contracts to produce that necessary commodity.[77]

Diminished supplies of iron and steel also hampered Confederate efforts. Several states tried to duplicate Georgia's efforts to foster iron manufacturing within their borders, but these endeavors bore little fruit. The central government was forced to confiscate iron. This policy proved more deleterious than beneficial because seized iron usually came from the overburdened railroad system. This "robbing Peter to pay Paul" policy perhaps initially aided ordnance manufacture, but in the long run, it wreaked havoc with the ill-equipped and overused Confederate transportation system.[78]

If and when raw materials were obtained, the Southern Confederacy still needed to find a sufficient number of workers to manufacture those products into articles of war. Conscription, instituted in

April 1862, took many able-bodied laborers from the factories and foundries, and battlefield deaths further winnowed the ranks of would-be mechanics. The Georgia and Confederate governments attempted to remedy this problem by exempting mechanics and arms manufacturers from the draft, but even that did not supply all the labor required.[79]

Although all these problems were apparent by 1863, the Confederacy fought on. Gorgas and his subordinates marshaled the resources at hand and continued to produce arms and ammunition for the armies in the field. Yet in galvanizing the military-industrial sector, the Ordnance Bureau was forced, because of shortages in materials and labor, to assume almost total control over the allocation of resources and the manufacture of military hardware. Gorgas and Secretary of War James Seddon well knew that a more efficient use of the articles available was of paramount importance. They reasoned that with greater centralization of authority, ordnance production could be enhanced and overall logistics improved. Thus temporary measures of government control became permanent: the government implemented strict oversight of munitions facilities and established price schedules for the various commodities needed. As Herman Hattaway and Archer Jones have observed, "Though it fell short of adequacy, the Confederate government's centralizing . . . activities wrought a veritable revolution" in the management of the economy.[80] By the end of the war, the Confederate war bureaus exercised a monopoly in many sectors of the economy.

The Confederacy's control of the war industries had serious consequences for establishments in Georgia. In Atlanta, government seizures of plants and materials produced inflation and speculation, which led to popular demoralization. The implementation of martial law aggravated the situation and strained, almost to the breaking point, relations between the city and the Confederacy.[81] Similar conditions prevailed in Columbus and Augusta. As shortages and inflation fostered speculation, and as government controls tightened, prosperity faded and morale declined. Although the people of these cities tended to blame the government's policies for the changes in the general welfare, disaffection never reached the level found in Atlanta.

Despite government controls, war production was strained by 1864. Impressment, speculation, shortages, and criticism of Confederate domestic policies soon gave way to a more immediate and dangerous problem: the Federal advance out of Chattanooga, Tennessee, and the invasion of north Georgia. Suddenly, it seemed to most Georgians, the war that had touched them only peripherally threatened to engulf them. To be sure, Yankee cavalry raids had been a persistent threat and, often, a wretched reality. But campaigns begun in the spring of 1864 portended more ominous consequences. The Federal high command had determined to cut through the Confederate "heartland" of Georgia and to reduce the government citadel in yet another "On to Richmond" campaign. Rebels and Yankees alike realized that though the Confederate capital was an important political and industrial center, Georgia, with its factories and farms, was the nation's economic backbone. If Georgia fell, the collapse of the Confederacy would not be long in coming.

There can be no denying that the Confederate mobilization effort in the armament industries was seriously handicapped by failures to develop adequately raw materials sources and recruit labor. Yet, for all the deficiencies, the Southern states fielded an army and supplied it with arms, ammunition, and heavy ordnance for four years. Existing facilities were converted to war manufacture, and private and government establishments were brought into being virtually overnight. Northern invasions of key manufacturing and raw materials sectors took their toll, and the Federal blockade eliminated alternative sources, but still, the South produced, supplied, and fought. Emory Thomas is correct when he concludes that "the degree of industrialization achieved by the Confederate South was phenomenal. The Confederates sustained themselves industrially better than they did agriculturally, and far better than they had any reason to expect in 1861."[82] The War Department and private contractors continued to produce war goods despite increasingly insurmountable obstacles. In the end, it was the inadequacy of the raw materials supply and not the war-spawned industrial superstructure that proved to be the decisive factor in the Confederacy's collapse. As one scholar has noted, "the superb élan of the Southern fighting man could compensate for only so much hard iron."[83]

One reason the Confederacy was able to attain such an impressive level of industrialization was Georgia. The strong base it had established in the antebellum period was, from the beginning, called upon to produce for the war effort. The Empire State of the South did not disappoint the Confederate government. Rolling mills and foundries in Atlanta and Columbus turned to war-related manufacturing; government installations in Augusta, Columbus, and Atlanta, as well as Macon, Athens, Rome, and Dalton, were materially aided by private individuals who produced ordnance, ammunition, and arms or who supplied raw materials to fuel those establishments. By 1864, the investment in manufacturing in Fulton, Muscogee, and Richmond counties had increased fourfold. Inflation, impressment, and in some instances, government takeover, could not diminish the revolution in heavy manufacturing.[84]

Some historians have acknowledged that Southern industrialization was catalyzed by the requirements of Confederate mobilization, but they have dismissed the idea that Southern manufacturing made absolute gains. War-related manufacturing, they argue, was of a temporary character.[85] Such a contention is in need of qualification. In many cases—and Georgia provides some key examples—war manufacturing was superimposed upon an established base. Moreover, other enterprises were created outright to meet the demands of war. The insatiable demand for military hardware and the Confederate government's offer of lucrative contracts and cash advances impelled established manufacturers to move swiftly to seize the opportunities for increased production—and profits. Others were prompted to embark upon manufacturing pursuits for the first time to meet the army's urgent need for rifles, ammunition, and heavy ordnance. Untried and established industrial entrepreneurs were presented with the chance to create, maintain, and expand the manufacturing sector. They seized the chance, and their successes enabled the Confederate government to equip an army for four years. In the end, Southern military failure resulted not because the Confederacy lacked a capacity to manufacture, nor because it lacked experienced industrial managers, but because it could no longer fuel its industrial establishments with raw materials and labor.[86]

The experience of Georgia during the war demonstrates that there was success in the midst of failure. Georgians such as the Haiman brothers, Jesse Ansley, Joseph Winship, and others proved adroit at industrial pursuits. They exhibited ingenuity, resourcefulness, and resilience in meeting the new demands of their country. Their experiments, successes, and contributions proved what could be accomplished in manufacturing, even under the most adverse circumstances. At the same time, they proved that there was money to be made in industrial pursuits. Such actions portended great things for the future development and diversification of the state and the region. It remained to be seen, however, how those innovating entrepreneurs would employ their skills in the postwar world.

3 Building a Supply Economy

Mobilization for war in the South entailed far more than raising and arming troops. Confederate and state authorities were fully aware that the eager recruits who flocked to the Stars and Bars in the early days of 1861 would need far more than enthusiasm and bullets to face the Yankee legions. Domestic production of muskets, sabers, pistols, and other accoutrements of war was essential. But no less essential were the uniforms, shoes, blankets, tents, and forage necessary to an army's survival in the field. Such demands required planning and the husbanding of raw materials to ensure that the gray army was well clad and well supplied when it marched to battle. Both contemporaries and historians have criticized Confederate supply efforts, but the success in galvanizing these sectors of the economy must be accorded more than passing marks: distribution and organization may have failed, but Southern manufacturing did not. Private entrepreneurs and government agents worked tirelessly to manufacture goods for the armies in the field.

To address these mobilization efforts, General Orders No. 1, dated 25 March 1861, created the Quartermaster Department, which, under the provisions of the directive, was empowered to "give effect to the movements and operations of the Army, prepare quarters, hospitals, camp and garrison equipage, transportation and all military stores and provisions . . . [and to] furnish storage for all military supplies; provide fuel, forage, and straw; [and] supply blankets, shoes and clothing."[1] Abraham C. Myers became "Acting Quartermaster General of the Confederate States," and on him fell the burden of clothing, feeding, and supplying the Southern armies.[2]

At the time of his appointment, Myers was serving as quartermaster general of Louisiana. A native of Georgetown, South Carolina, Myers had attended West Point and graduated thirty-second in the class of 1833. Commissioned a second lieutenant, Myers had served at army posts throughout the South until tapped for service in the Mexican War. While in Mexico, he compiled an impeccable record of service in the quartermaster corps and rose to become chief quartermaster for the U.S. Army in Mexico. After his tour of duty there, he served under the United States quartermaster general, Joseph E. Johnston. Upon the outbreak of sectional hostilities in 1861, Myers resigned his post and tendered his services to the Confederate government. Myers ardently desired the nascent Confederacy's top quartermaster position, and he lobbied hard to get it. His letter writing to influential South Carolinians paid off, for he received his plum in March 1861. No one would deny that he brought a wealth of experience to the newly created post. Yet that experience, born of his military training, would ultimately doom his efforts. Myers always acted according to military regulations as delineated in the *Quartermaster Manual* of the "Old Army." Because of his rigid adherence to military protocol, he lacked the inventiveness and flexibility needed for his post.[3]

Myers threw himself into his new duties with vigor. His primary task was to clothe and equip the army with the standard-issue uniform of blue flannel shirt, gray flannel pants, wool stockings, boots, blankets, and cap. The small stock of these and other items, however, was soon exhausted by the seemingly endless stream of would-be soldiers eager to "whip the Yankees."[4] Because of the failure to keep uniform and accoutrement supplies abreast of demand, the Quartermaster Department was forced to adopt a policy in the spring of 1861 whereby prospective enlisted men were required to provide their own clothing in return for a $21 commutation fee that was to be paid semiannually.[5] But Myers was aware that such a policy could not continue indefinitely, for many of the enlistees did not have the means to provide themselves with the standard issue. Consequently, he placed advertisements in the Southern press for contractors to manufacture tents and equipment for the department. Myers also made overtures to Southern textile mills to obtain contracts for uniforms and blankets. To facilitate the collection and dispersal of articles he hoped to obtain from regional mills, Myers established quartermaster depots in Montgomery, San Antonio, Charleston, New Orleans, Mobile, Nashville, Richmond, and Lynchburg.[6]

Myers's efforts during the first year of the war were aided inestimably by private concerns. Heeding the exhortations of the Confederate press, individuals and towns "rediscovered" home spinning and cottage production.[7] Of even greater assistance were the contracts effected between Confederate authorities and Southern textile factories. These contracts proved a boon to both parties: the Quartermaster

Department was guaranteed a relatively constant supply of clothing, blankets, tents, and other supplies, and Southern mill owners, freed from Northern and European competition, found a ready-made market for their goods.

When Georgia seceded from the Union in 1861, she brought with her the solidly established manufacturing base in textiles that led the South in the number of mills, spindles, and looms in active operation. Georgia's cotton mills were widely scattered throughout the midsection of the state, but two cities in particular were renowned for their establishments: Columbus and Augusta. Each river town housed old and respected concerns that had been in continuous operation for close to thirty years. Textile entrepreneurs of the Confederacy's Empire State moved quickly to consummate agreements with the Confederate and state governments to manufacture troop clothing and camp equipage. As might be anticipated, the mills of Columbus and Augusta proved to be eager Confederate suppliers.

Columbus's Eagle Manufacturing Company entered the war era as the largest and most prosperous textile establishment in the city. Local demands and products furnished to the Confederate government boosted the annual product value of the Eagle Company's goods and its profits. Apparently, not even the disruption of trade with the North—the source of the company's antebellum wool supply—stalled production. Tapping Georgia and Florida wool sources, the Eagle Company continued to produce two thousand yards of gray tweed daily. By the end of 1861 and into 1862, the factory's owners moved to diversify production. Citing the Union blockade and the loss of Northern goods, the Eagle mills promised to add domestic articles to their production list so as to meet the needs of both civilians and soldiers. Moreover, the mill owners assured interested observers— and government agents—that their machinery had been "adapted" to facilitate the manufacture of tent cloth, India rubber cloth for haversacks and capes, and mariners stripes for shirts.[8]

The Eagle Company's local rival, the Columbus Factory, also responded to wartime demands. In 1861, the firm employed 110 operatives who produced three hundred thousand yards of cotton cloth, seventy-five thousand yards of woolens, and forty thousand pounds of yarn and thread annually. Yet, as government orders poured in, the Columbus Factory increased production threefold in an effort to keep pace with the seemingly insatiable demand for its products.[9] Although the Eagle Mills and the Columbus Factory garnered the lion's share of the attention—and the government's contracts—smaller establishments in the city also shared in the early wartime manufacturing and production boom. Those local concerns provided tangible evidence that a vibrant entrepreneurial ethos was abroad in the city.

Columbus merchants and storekeepers proved to be ready and willing suppliers of war goods. J. W. Sappington and his brother operated a small grocery store in Columbus dating from the 1850s. The firm had a local reputation for honesty and enjoyed good credit, despite its lack of "means" outside of the brothers' stock-in-trade. In 1861, the great demand for soldiers' shoes prompted Sappington to change his line of business, and he converted the grocery store into a shoe factory. In the spring of 1862, *DeBow's Review* called attention to Sappington's new factory, noting that it had the capacity to produce eight thousand pairs of shoes a year. In time, Sappington's concern became the largest privately owned shoe factory producing for the war effort in the Confederacy.[10] Similarly, the partnership of Manly & Hodges had built up a sizable trade in "fancy dry goods" before the war. Beginning in 1861, the firm became a regular supplier of tents for the Confederate army and the Georgia militia.[11]

Another dry goods merchant, Simon Rothchild, had a more checkered career. He and his brother had settled in Columbus after having failed in business in Griffin, Georgia. Rothchild and Brother began as peddlers in dry goods, but after five years in Columbus they claimed capital worth $30,000 and a stock of goods that included the desirable labels on New York City concerns. With the commencement of hostilities, however, Simon turned his talents to the manufacture of army uniforms. In less than a year, Rothchild provided the local Confederate quartermaster with four thousand complete suits of clothing; he furnished Georgia militia companies with another fifteen hundred.[12]

Between firms that supplied the Confederate Quartermaster Department and firms that produced arms and ammunition for the South's army and navy, Columbus became a vital war production center. Before the war ended, Columbus was destined to become one of the Deep South's largest manufacturing cities. Foreseeing extensive Confederate wants, Columbus businessmen worked ceaselessly to provide war goods. They demonstrated a heightened awareness of their city's potential, and they labored tirelessly to realize that potential. Their willingness to experiment and innovate proved that they were alert to the opportunities the war presented.

The energy and initiative of Columbus entrepreneurs and the city's proximity to railroads and natural resources were not lost on Quartermaster General Myers. Late in 1861, he established a quartermaster depot there, and he commissioned a local merchant, F. W. Dillard, to supervise construction of the Columbus depot and to manage the depot once it became operational. Dillard proved to be a remarkably able choice. Before the establishment of the quartermaster depot and shops, war-related production in Columbus was marked by its independent, bordering on haphazard, nature. Under Dillard's firm direction, "piecemeal" production became orderly and regular. Major Dillard worked closely with such local concerns as the Eagle Company and Manly & Hodges and contracted for almost the full output of all firms.[13]

It soon became apparent to Dillard, however, that private manufacturing, though prodigious, was inadequate to fill the voracious demands of the army. To augment local endeavors, Dillard established government clothing shops for the manufacture of uniforms. He also created Confederate tanneries to work in conjunction with local shoemakers.[14]

Augusta, Columbus's textile manufacturing rival, did not initially manifest the same enthusiasm for war-related production. Secession and the disruption of traditional trade channels led to local shortages and speculation. Charges that merchants and manufacturers were creating artificial scarcities in goods dampened the zeal for war and led to a waning of patriotic fervor. Local industrialists and the city's press attempted to arrest the incipient demoralization by stressing the need for Southern self-sufficiency. Their exhortations carried little weight throughout 1861. The push to make Augusta a manufacturing center for the Southern Confederacy appeared doomed. Many merchants and planters insisted on continuing their prewar practice of investing in commerce. Since those individuals controlled the bulk of liquid capital for investment purposes, they stymied local industrialists' plans to expand factory production to meet the increased demand for manufactured goods occasioned by the war.[15]

This preference for commercial as opposed to industrial investment was curious: the city possessed a substantial manufacturing base, yet commerce, especially trade in cotton, continued to hold an enduring attraction. The divided mind of the city was graphically evident in the local press. For most of 1860 and 1861, the *Augusta Chronicle and Sentinel* had appealed for the development of local resources and the opening of direct trade with Europe. The populace was urged to

support measures that would encourage manufacturing and economic diversification because such endeavors would foster true independence: "The Southern manufacturer in every department must be
encouraged—home industry patronized in every branch. Southern
clothes [and] Southern shoes . . . must be worn, and those who can't
dispense with silks and broadcloths must get them no longer from
Yankeedom. . . . In a word, let us no longer consider anything useful
or indispensable unless it be a Southern product."[16] The *Chronicle and
Sentinel* concurred with the *Savannah Republican* in its call for a protec-
tive tariff. One can envision the response of Augusta Calhounites
when the paper asked, none too rhetorically, "Shall we . . . not take
the same steps to protect ourselves that have made New England so
powerful? Shall those enterprising spirits which have already taken
the lead in manufacturing in the South be sacrificed to the dogma of
free trade?"[17]

Yet such pleas for energy, the encouragement of Southern enterprise, and the cultivation of industrialism were undermined by appeals to local merchants to curtail the workday because of hot weather
and by warnings that manufacturing centers were "nurseries of aboli-
tionism."[18] The press voiced the convictions of many when it argued
that self-sufficiency and the manufacture of goods previously obtained from the North had to be achieved, but in the drive for economic and political independence, "we never expect or desire our
country to become a great manufacturing country. We want no im-
mense Lowells, Manchesters [or] Birminghams, for they suit not the
genius of our people, our institutions or our government."[19] At this
early stage in the war, many Southerners generally, and Augustans in
particular, hoped to meet the demands of full-scale war without having to surrender their long-held convictions about the evils of a manufacturing society. In short, they wanted the matériel of war but not the
industrial society that was capable of supplying it.

The desire to achieve economic self-sufficiency without industrialization and its attendant ills proved a quixotic hope. Under the pressure of the Union blockade and the exigencies of war, the established
pattern broke down. Augustans were forced, unwillingly perhaps, to
come to terms with the new order the war with the Yankees created.
Before the ink had dried on antimanufacturing editorials, pioneering
locals moved forward to lead the mobilization drive.[20] Entrepreneurs
who had fought the antimanufacturing mind-set found in war demands a release from their shackles. Led by the city's textile entrepre-

neurs, Augusta embarked upon a belated effort to supply the Confederacy's Quartermaster Department.

One of the first firms to tender its services to the Confederacy was the Augusta Factory. Mill improvements and plant expansion in the late antebellum years made it one of the two largest such establishments in the Confederacy. The factory's 15,000 spindles and 462 looms possessed the capacity to produce 20,000 yards of cotton cloth daily, no inconsiderable amount given the demand for uniforms.[21] Augusta's other major mill, the Belleville Factory, resumed production after a devastating fire just as the war commenced. Belleville contained one-third the spindle capacity of the Augusta Factory; nonetheless, it still produced 3,000 yards of cloth a day. Moreover, Belleville had 1,200 wool spindles, which were capable of producing between 800 and 1,000 yards of woolen goods daily.[22]

Throughout 1861 and well into 1862, the textile mills of Augusta churned out cotton and woolen goods for the Confederate Quartermaster Department. Disaster struck the Belleville Factory in February 1862, when an accident in the oilcloth department started a fire that consumed most of the mills. As owner George Schley and other interested parties well knew, the "loss [was] irreparable . . . a public as well as a private calamity. It . . . not only deprives the Government of [a] manufactory much wanted, but throws out of employ a great number of industrious poor, who were dependent on its successful operation."[23] After the loss of the Belleville Factory, the Augusta Factory was the city's largest independent textile producer for the Confederate cause. The demands placed on that concern increased dramatically, and although the Augusta Factory continued to produce almost exclusively for the Confederate government, its output could not keep abreast of demand. As a result, the Confederate Quartermaster Department established the Confederate Clothing Bureau in Augusta late in 1862. The next year saw the Confederacy increase its stake in Augusta still further with the construction of cotton presses to augment private and government cloth manufacture.

Although mills in cities such as Augusta and Columbus operated incessantly, they could not keep pace with the demands of both the military and the civilian population. The Quartermaster Department was particularly frustrated in obtaining needed supplies because of the nature of its contractual agreements. Initially, Southern mills operated under a competitive bidding system. The curtailment of Northern and foreign sources and the consequent high prices on the open market, however, encouraged Southern cloth and clothing manufacturers to renege on government contracts to meet civilian needs. As early as October 1861, Quartermaster General Myers was complaining to Secretary of War Judah P. Benjamin that material costs for clothing had gone up 100 percent. Moreover, clothing importers, basing their prices on prevailing Southern market values, were demanding substantially higher amounts for blockade-run goods to cover both risk and Southern demand. Even had prices remained stable, and if Southern manufacturers had stayed faithful to their contractual obligations, the supply situation was bleak. "The resources of the Southern States," concluded Myers, "cannot supply the necessities of the Army of the Confederate States with the essential articles for cloth for uniform clothing, blankets, shoes, stockings and flannel."[24]

The poor supply situation and high costs of manufactured articles did not escape government notice. A congressional committee investigated all the supply bureaus to determine how to ameliorate problems.[25] Before the committee could begin its inquiry, however, the country was rocked by the news of serious military reverses in the western theater of the war. The fall of Forts Henry and Donelson on the Tennessee and Cumberland rivers and the subsequent evacuation of Nashville were not just stunning blows to Confederate morale; Southern retreat from that area meant the loss of large quantities of arms and supplies at the key Nashville quartermaster depot. The nation had barely digested that news when word came that the vital port of New Orleans was threatened by Union forces. Seemingly overnight, two major supply centers were lost to the Confederate war effort. Quartermaster General Myers did little to reassure panicky Southerners. In his report to the Committee on Military Affairs, Myers stated bluntly that Confederate reverses and retreats had seriously impeded quartermaster supply efforts. With domestic production "limited," Myers predicted that it would be a "positive impossibility" to supply all Confederate troop wants for the year.[26]

The bleak situation of late winter 1862 was even more dire by spring. To counter the loss of manpower occasioned by the expiration of the initial twelve-month enlistments and to bolster the fighting effort, the Confederate Congress passed, at President Davis's urging, a comprehensive conscription act in April. All able-bodied men between the ages of eighteen and thirty-five were required to shoulder arms in defense of the cause.[27] Although subsequent legislation allowed exemptions from conscription for those employed in crucial war industries, the draft took its toll.[28] The Southern textile industry was especially hard hit by the new draft law, for exemptions did not initially include mill operatives. Quartermaster General Myers complained to the War Department that quartermaster supplies remained inadequate largely because of "the interference of the conscription act with the arrangements of the manufacturers with whom contracts have been made. Under [the act's] operations, [mill owners] have been deprived of the services of their employés [sic] to such an extent that they have been rendered incapable of complying with the contracts made with this department for a continual supply of various articles absolutely essential for issue to the Army." The only remedy to this deplorable situation, Myers maintained, was to exempt or detail from the ranks the requisite number of workers to ensure the resumption of factory production at full capacity.[29]

While waiting for a response to his plea for more operatives, Myers worked to relieve the pressing shortage of raw materials. Confederate quartermaster depot officials in each state were instructed to buy up or impress all local supplies of wool and leather to manufacture into clothing and shoes at government shops and private establishments. Shortly after gaining this virtual monopoly on raw material sources, Myers was given another weapon to keep textile manufacturers faithful to government contracts. In October 1862, the Confederate Congress repealed the April exemption acts and extended the exempted categories to include cotton and wool factory operatives, mechanics, skilled tradesmen, shoemakers, and tanners—but with a certain condition: "The profits of such establishments shall not exceed seventy-five per centum upon the cost of production." Should profits of mills and factories exceed that percentage, all exemptions were to be revoked. Such a requirement indicates that the government was aware that many businessmen were involved in the war effort for reasons not entirely patriotic. Another indication of continuing suspicion is that workers were detailed from the ranks for only sixty days at one time. Their details were renewed "only if the supply officials were satisfied that the companies were discharging their responsibilities to the government."[30]

The government's attempts to monopolize raw materials and mill production for the war effort inevitably created inflated prices and civilian shortages. Several states passed laws making it a misdemean-

or to speculate in or monopolize essential articles, but such initiatives did little to arrest the speculation and profiteering that seemed to increase with each passing day.[31] As shortages and speculation continued, popular indignation and unrest grew. Speculators were deemed little better than treasonous extortionists. As the *Atlanta Southern Confederacy* saw it, the speculators' "ruling passion is a lust for gain; and their sordid souls care naught for the miseries of their fellow mortals, and [they] have no interest in the good of the country, if its ruin would advance their own personal aggrandizement." Before long, industrialists were lumped with speculators as the cause of all ills on the home front. Many believed manufacturers were amassing great wealth at the expense of those who had made the supreme contribution to the war effort by serving at the front. "Is it right that war . . . with its carnage and woe, should work an absolute benefit to one class, while it ruins the rest? Shall those who are permitted to . . . be exempt from service on account of these employments [tanning, shoemaking, cotton manufacturing, and so on] out of which they are making such fortunes, amassing such wealth and splendor, in full view of want, poverty and destitution which has been brought by men leaving home . . . not be required to contribute a portion of these gains for the benefit of the sufferers by the war?"[32]

Given the tide of public opinion, it was obvious that something had to be done. The state of Georgia moved swiftly and decisively to counter this threat to both civilian and military supply—and morale. In November 1862, the Georgia General Assembly passed legislation giving the governor power to seize "Factories, Tanneries, and Manufactured Articles."[33] Factories were required to present proof of their contracts with the Confederate government. Concerns not exclusively engaged in Confederate production were required to give their surplus goods to the state's quartermaster agents for distribution to the Georgia militia and Confederate soldiers serving in Georgia. The state promised to reimburse those factories for goods bought or seized at a rate of 10 percent over invoice; for contracts that were made with the state, the rate would stand at 25 percent over the cost of production. This legislation gave Georgia much greater control over manufacturing and helped check profiteering.[34]

Such actions did not escape criticism. If there was still latent hostility to business enterprise and suspicion of the motives of businessmen, there was even more hostility to the idea of state-managed businesses. The *Atlanta Southern Confederacy* argued that legislating to control prices and profiteering was "notoriously unsuccessful" and that seizures of goods were unwarranted—and unjustifiable—unless an emergency situation existed. If clothing, shoes, and other manufactured articles were needed, bounties and tax breaks should have been implemented to encourage capitalists to undertake manufacturing projects. "The State has enough to do to take care of its legitimate business," argued the *Southern Confederacy*, "without taking control of and conducting private men's business. The State can't run a factory as well and as cheaply as the man who owns it."[35]

Governor Brown, however, believed Georgia could operate a factory as well as a private owner could. His motive was not only to support the war effort but to ensure that manufactured goods were available to the civilian population of the state. In December 1862, at Brown's urging, the state House appropriated $100,000 "for the erection of machinery to manufacture [cotton] cards for the people of Georgia, the works to be established in the Penitentiary" at Milledgeville. The House bill also provided for the purchase of a half interest in the cotton card factory of Messrs. Divine, Jones & Lee, at Cartersville, Georgia. Cotton cards produced at both facilities were to be sold to needy Georgians at cost. "No profits to the State are intended, the object being to supply the people with the means of making their own apparel at home."[36]

Georgia's actions in late 1862 underscored in bold relief the problems facing the Confederate Quartermaster Department. Up to that time, procurement and manufacturing policies operated in a vicious circle. Government pressure on private mills and the virtual monopoly exercised on raw materials denied noncombatants adequate stocks of material necessities. Charges of profiteering and persistent scarcities produced disillusionment and demoralization. Governor Brown and the Georgia General Assembly enacted drastic measures in an attempt to break the cycle. State regulation and oversight of government contracts were initiated to ensure that Georgia militiamen and Confederate soldiers in the state had adequate clothing and camp supplies. State manufacturing and the sale of cotton cards were designed to meet civilian needs.

Quartermaster General Myers was not oblivious to the supply problem. Throughout 1862, local quartermasters warned that supplies of clothing and raw materials at depots were reaching dangerously low levels. The Confederate Congress again enacted legislation to ease the Quartermaster Department's problems. "An Act to encourage Manufacturing of Clothing and Shoes for the Army" empowered the president with the authority to use government funds to purchase, through Confederate agents, finished goods, machinery, and raw materials from abroad. Myers urged that the government go one step further and provide his department with impressment powers should individuals or firms holding necessary commodities "not sell them to the Government, or ask extortionate prices."[37]

Supply problems, expanded operations, and the enlargement of the Quartermaster Department's bureaucratic apparatus prompted Myers to undertake the reorganization of his department in the spring of 1863. The quartermaster general divided the Confederacy into quartermaster purchasing districts. Each district, which in most cases comprised a single state, was to have a chief purchasing officer who was to exercise "exclusive control over purchasing and contracts in each district and to regulate prices for buying army supplies." Once a store of supplies was accumulated, the purchasing officer would forward it to one of several designated depots located near Confederate field armies. When supplies were needed, the army would send requisitions to the area quartermaster, who would distribute supplies from the local depots. The only articles exempted from this plan were leather goods. Major Dillard of the Columbus, Georgia, depot had total control over all leather supplies in Tennessee, Alabama, South Carolina, and Georgia. Under Dillard's direction, those leather supplies would be manufactured into shoes for the army at the Confederate Shoe Factory in Columbus.[38]

Myers's reorganization scheme proved effective, and it eliminated many of the problems that had plagued the department. State-level quartermaster depot agents efficiently collected supplies and made contracts with local firms which usually stipulated that the government receive two-thirds of the output. Equipment and clothing were received from the factories at the designated depots and then channeled to the armies.

Unfortunately for Myers, he could not enjoy his accomplishment. President Davis's refusal to promote Myers to brigadier general, the rank required of a quartermaster general by act of Congress, effectively ousted him from the top quartermaster post. Davis then offered the position to Georgia politician Howell Cobb, but Cobb refused the honor. Davis's second choice, Brigadier General Alexander R. Lawton, did not have the luxury of declining: on 7 August 1863, Special Order No. 187 appointed Lawton quartermaster general of the Confederate States.[39]

The appointment proved a happy one. Lawton's elevation from field command to supply chief owed in large measure to his antebellum career. Although he had not been Davis's first choice, Lawton possessed the credentials that made him a logical choice. His West Point training and service in the United States and Confederate armies made him familiar with army routine; his experience as president of the Augusta & Savannah Railroad (1849–54) had given him valuable experience in administrative duties.[40] Lawton brought new energy to the reorganized Quartermaster Department. Although he continued procurement policies Myers had established, Lawton worked to tighten the controls on department contractors. Diligence, however, could not compensate for the dearth of materials. Though Lawton worked tirelessly to remedy persistent problems, he met with little success.

Lawton was not allowed the luxury of a leisurely study of quartermaster organization, duties, and supplies on hand. He had barely assumed his new position when he was confronted with a major supply crisis. Stores of blankets, shoes, and miscellaneous camp equipment, enough to outfit the armies through 1864, were lost with the capture of two blockade runners in September and October 1863. Lawton scrambled to accumulate supplies for the winter, but he ran into the same problems that had plagued Myers. By the fall of 1863, the War Department had overspent its budget for the year. Money was exceedingly tight, and funds that were pried loose were earmarked for the Ordnance Department. Secretary of War Seddon and Secretary of the Treasury Christopher Memminger refused to assign Quartermaster Department requisitions to a high-priority status. Apparently, those gentlemen believed bullets were more necessary than shoes and blankets in a fight with the Yankees. Displeased but undaunted, Lawton sent an endless stream of dispatches to agents in the Bahamas and Bermuda to arrange for the shipment of new stores. He also clamped down on domestic sources by detailing inspectors to factories under government contract, and he arranged for the establishment of a new Confederate shoe factory in Montgomery, Alabama.[41]

Though Lawton's efforts were admirable, they failed to produce the supplies needed for the winter. Confederate commanders complained to the quartermaster general throughout the fall that their troops were ill-equipped to face another winter—let alone a Yankee attack.[42] In

December 1863, the situation brightened when several successful blockade runs enabled the Quartermaster Department to provision the armies. The failure of the Federal campaigns to capture both Charleston and Wilmington meant that foreign supplies could again stream into the South in the holds of blockade runners. Nevertheless, Lawton's baptism by fire proved to him that regular supplies of clothing and camp equipage were not merely a desired goal but an absolute necessity. Vagaries in domestic sources and production and problems with importation had to be rectified.[43]

Lawton tackled domestic suppliers first. Under Myers, contracts with textile manufacturers were based on either a "fixed amount" of cloth or "a certain proportion of the factory's monthly output." Lawton abandoned this procedure. He began a systematic renegotiation of all contracts held by manufacturers and ensured that his department would garner maximum productivity from all firms, using as a "lever government controls over raw materials, transportation and manpower." In effect, Lawton promised Confederate capitalists that they would receive needed raw materials and workers if their firms supplied the Quartermaster Department with two-thirds of their output. The 75 percent ceiling on profits was cut considerably: firms with government contracts would now realize 33.3 percent profit over the cost of production.[44] The new quartermaster general did not end his reorganization drive there, however. In the spring of 1864, he ordered Major G. W. Cunningham of the Atlanta quartermaster depot to take "charge of the Factories of . . . South Carolina, Georgia, Alabama, Florida & Mississippi." Cunningham was to "introduce some uniform system in connection with the Factories in the States referred to. You are charged with the sole power to contract with the same & will regulate the price, proportion of product to be delivered on Govt account & other matters connected with their establishments."[45]

The reorganization of the Quartermaster Department undertaken by Myers and Lawton directly affected establishments in Georgia. The Columbus quartermaster depot, under the direction of Major Dillard, became the chief source of shoes for the Confederate army. Dillard's monopoly of all leather and hides in the surrounding country enabled him to consolidate local shoe shops into one centralized establishment. Problems with the quality of the shoes manufactured caused Myers and Lawton not a little concern, as did the chronic leather shortage. Nonetheless, the Columbus shoemakers kept producing and succeeded in correcting previously shoddy production. The leather shortage, though never totally resolved, was eased somewhat by Dillard's exclusive control over all hides in the six-state region. All tanners and commissaries were required by military order to supply Dillard with hides for the manufacture of shoes. The Quartermaster Department also made arrangements to ensure that Dillard had adequate machinery to conduct his business.[46]

The Columbus mills continued to produce on government account, and Confederate and state legislation virtually removed them from participation on the open market. The Eagle Manufacturing Company manufactured daily several thousand yards of cotton duck, oilcloth, osnaburgs, heavy gray tweeds, and sheetings. Two-thirds of their output went to locally established government clothing shops, where a predominantly female work force transformed the cloth into suits of clothing for the army. Each operative made, on the average, four suits a week and was paid two dollars per suit.[47]

Precise statistics on the output of the Columbus Factory do not exist. Given congressional regulations, however, it is safe to assume that the Columbus Factory also provided the Confederate Quartermaster Department with two-thirds of its output. The goods not contracted for by the government were taken by the Georgia Quartermaster Department to supply state troops and militia.

The war industries located in Columbus produced an economic boom that overshadowed the most prosperous years of the antebellum era. Men and women from the surrounding countryside flocked to the town to obtain employment in government and private shops. Though Columbus did not escape wartime inflation, wages kept pace with the cost of living, and hence real suffering was averted. Before the government and the state assumed their monopoly over local production, residents of Columbus enjoyed a supply of cloth and yarn at retail prices. Indeed, charges of speculation and profiteering, so common elsewhere in Georgia, were conspicuous by their absence in Columbus. The press called attention to the "patriotic" deeds of the owners of the Eagle Manufacturing Company. Not only did those capitalists sell directly to consumers at reduced rates, they also established mill schools for local children.[48]

The *Columbus Daily Sun* did not engage in hyperbole when it declared, in 1863, "There is perhaps no city in the Confederacy that has felt less the deprivations and inconveniences of war than Columbus." The demands of established concerns and the needs of newly created war industries had made the city a poor farmer's or refugee's dream.

Full employment, relatively good wages, abundant stocks of food and clothing, and the city's isolation from the terrible battles that ravaged other areas fostered optimism, prosperity, and an intensified commitment to the cause.[49]

Events in the summer of 1863, however, slowed the economic boom. Army demands for subsistence reduced considerably local stocks of provisions. Inflation, which had been held in check, suddenly surged out of control. The constant stream of refugees seeking to share in Columbus's boom and to escape Yankee advances swelled the town's population to over fifteen thousand and created additional shortages in housing, food, and other goods. Battlefield deaths and conscription winnowed the work force, and although women and slaves more than adequately filled the void, the scarcity of menfolk brought the cost of war close to home. When word of the twin debacles of Gettysburg and Vicksburg reached the town, morale began a slow but inexorable decline. A former hotbed of Confederate loyalty, Columbus became, by late 1864, the center of despondent and embittered criticism of Confederate actions and policies.[50]

Augusta enterprises also acceded to the government's new regulations in the wake of the Quartermaster Department's administrative and organizational shake-up. Unfortunately, surviving contracts between the Augusta and Belleville factories and the Confederate Quartermaster Department are fragmentary for the period before 1863. Goods produced and received by the Augusta firms in December 1862 appear, however, to be illustrative of the former system. According to those contracts, the Augusta Factory's four mills produced 2,400 yards of wool yarns, 10,000 yards of hickory striping, and 42,500 yards of osnaburgs at a cost of $28,500 to the government. Smaller concerns in the city contributed virtually their entire month's production of osnaburgs and sheetings to the government.[51]

The implementation of revised government regulations apparently did not significantly change contractual terms. By the summer of 1862, locals were complaining that factory-produced cloth and thread in the city were exceedingly scarce because "the factory is so much occupied with government orders."[52] Indeed, by the middle of the war, factories were producing almost exclusively on government account. The *Augusta Chronicle and Sentinel* praised the growth and development of the Augusta Factory and drew special attention to the improvements its directors had initiated to ensure continued production. The factory sold goods to the Confederate government, the state of Georgia, and "benevolent associations" at government-established prices, which, from 1863 on, were set at fifty cents a yard. That figure, the newspaper reported, was one-third the prevailing market price. Mill improvements had boosted productive capacity to 20,000 yards a day. The Augusta Factory's 15,000 spindles employed 750 operatives. In less than one year, workers had produced 4,200,384 yards of assorted cloth of which 3,132,997 yards went to the Confederate government. That amount testifies to both the insatiable demand for such goods and the Quartermaster Department's success in obtaining, through regulation, such a large percentage of the firm's output.[53]

The boom created by war-related industries in Augusta dispelled much of the antebellum uncertainty about—and opposition to—enlarging the city's manufacturing base. The Augusta Factory endeared itself to locals by providing employment to "needy" women, devoting attention to the development of their "moral character," and selling provisions to workers at the low prices charged the government.[54] The establishment of the Georgia Clothing Bureau in the storerooms of local clothier J. K. Hora also provided employment for women, who produced five hundred sets of garments a day for state recruits. Government-owned and operated cotton presses and shoe manufactories supplemented private production and also provided employment for locals and the never-ending stream of refugees who were attracted by Augusta's prosperity, proximity to rail connections, and reputation for adequate housing. A visitor to the city during the height of the war was astonished by the activity and prosperity he saw: "No place that I have seen in the Southern States shows so little of the traces of the war, and it formed a delightful contrast to the war-worn, poverty-stricken, dried up towns I had lately visited."[55]

Time—and the Union army—however, continued unimpeded. Federal invasions of the South Carolina and Georgia coasts and movements out of Tennessee into northern Georgia swelled the stream of refugees. Soon the city's heretofore adequate housing vanished, and overcrowding pushed rents up to exorbitant levels. The influx of people also produced shortages and higher prices, which fueled an inflationary spiral that appeared, by late 1863, to have no end. Shoes sold for $30 a pair—when they could be had; butter cost $4 a pound; and a dozen eggs commanded $2. Merchants and speculators were again publicly excoriated, but such outbursts did little to stop the squeeze most Augustans felt. Disaffection spread like wildfire as civilian authority broke down under the pressure of scattered mob activities, high prices, and grim news from the battlefields.[56]

Galloping inflation and recurring shortages of food and clothing

prompted Governor Brown to urge the passage of measures that
would alleviate suffering on the home front. The establishment of the
cotton card factory at the state penitentiary in Milledgeville and the
continued state investment–part-ownership in the Pioneer Card Factory at Cartersville had yielded no inconsiderable results. Despite
persistent shortages of wire, used to produce the cards, approximately one hundred pairs of cards were produced daily at each establishment. The governor appointed T. T. Windsor sales agent of the
cards produced at the state-operated facility. Aware that demand for
the cards exceeded the number manufactured, Brown instructed
Windsor to distribute the cards as equitably as possible among the
counties. People wishing to purchase them could do so at cost. As
an added inducement, the state promised to give individuals who
brought animal hides to the card distribution center priority over
others wanting to buy cards. State officials hoped that through that
exchange, leather, another desperately needed commodity, could be
obtained.[57]

Georgia legislation empowered state agents to purchase all textile
manufactures not consigned to the Confederate government. Again,
the object of this action was to relieve shortages in cotton and woolen
goods and more adequately to equip Georgia militia, home guards,
and Confederate troops stationed in Georgia. Georgia Quartermaster
General Ira Foster supervised the collection and distribution of all
factory output not earmarked for Confederate government service.
He paid special attention to the procurement of yarn for the state's
needy: yarn obtained was to be funneled to county-level inferior
courts, and, after presenting evidence of need, families were entitled
to purchase it at $6 a bunch.[58]

Quartermaster General Foster assessed state supply efforts in 1863.
Under the terms of the 1862 legislation, contracts with the state's
factories and tanneries had garnered many needed supplies. Experiments with cotton duck had produced an "admirable" substitute for
leather. The Georgia Clothing Bureau at Columbus was producing for
Georgia soldiers at full capacity, and state agents were actively engaged in the procurement of raw materials to supply state and private
manufacturing concerns. Despite such efforts, however, Foster was
forced to conclude that supplies and state quartermaster appropriations were insufficient for the approaching campaign season.[59]

The cause of the shortages in supplies was not hard to find. As
Foster told Confederate Secretary of War James Seddon, "the suffer-

ings of Georgians in Confederate State service" were occasioned by the "extensive operations of the Confederate Government" in the state. Foster urged that he be allowed to obtain goods outside of Georgia "to relieve the necessities of Georgia soldiers when the Confederate Government should be unable to do so." Foster's request was shifted to Quartermaster General Lawton, and there it remained. Lawton argued that he had no authority to allow states to purchase goods outside their borders and declined to interfere in the matter. Apparently, Foster made do with the resources in Georgia and received goods from neighboring states. His *Annual Report for Fiscal 1864* recorded terms of contracts with scattered Georgia mills and clothing manufactured at the Georgia Clothing Bureau. He also reported that agents dispatched to Texas and Alabama had obtained supplies of wool and leather.[60]

The Georgia quartermaster general was not the only one stymied by shortages of raw materials and a lack of money. The entire Confederate States Quartermaster Department suffered from these same ills. Quartermaster General Lawton struggled to alleviate the desperate situation, but he worked against heavy odds. A tax levied on manufacturers, wholesale dealers, merchants, and brokers that was designed to raise revenue "to provide for the common defense" raised only a fraction of what was required in 1864 to keep war production up to the levels demanded. Purchases from abroad slowed to a trickle as the Union cordon tightened around key blockade-running entrepôts. As a result, persistent shortages in raw materials hampered factory output and led to an increased reliance on impressment. Private firms, mistakenly believing that public authorities could more easily obtain raw cotton, wool, and leather, sold out to the government. Other manufacturing concerns, victimized by high inflationary costs for labor and materials, defaulted on contracts. Charges of fraud in the Quartermaster Department and profiteering by manufacturers further undermined the department's efforts to procure supplies and added to popular unrest with heavy-handed government policies. When it seemed as if the situation had reached its nadir, the Confederate Congress, in the face of military manpower shortages, began revoking draft exemptions for mechanics and mill workers.[61]

Lawton continued to demonstrate his resourcefulness in addressing obstacles that must have seemed overwhelming. He empowered local quartermasters with sweeping impressment warrants to obtain needed raw materials and notified army commanders that "mechanics employed on Govt contracts in Wool & Cotton Factories" would be detailed from active duty to the mills. "Upon the product of the labor of these men," Lawton wrote, "the Armies of the Confederacy depend, almost exclusively, for many indispensable orders of supply." Lawton anticipated protests and tried to forestall them by informing the various Confederate commanders that the operatives "render more service to the cause employed in the Factories, than they possibly can in the field."[62] He also moved to augment shoe supplies by approving a plan to establish a shoe factory at the Andersonville, Georgia, prison. Columbus Quartermaster Dillard and G. W. Cunningham in Atlanta were to provide hides and machinery to the Confederate commandant at the stockade. Lawton predicted that great results would attend the use of skilled labor among the Federal prisoners of war.[63]

Lawton's exertions eased the tight quartermaster supply situation, momentarily at least. Early in 1865, he reported to Secretary of War John C. Breckinridge and the Special Committee on Troop Clothing that all troops were adequately clothed and supplied with camp equipment for the winter season. Some shortages did remain, and Lawton was forced to concede that many private soldiers lacked overcoats and flannel jackets. He maintained, however, that "manufacturing facilities [for clothing production] are ample" and predicted that shipments of wool and cotton from the Cis-Mississippi region would furnish the mills with the necessary raw materials. Lawton was forced to conclude his report on an ominous note, however: the government had an outstanding debt in excess of $5 million to the textile factories under Confederate contract. More distressing still was the current dearth—nonexistence might be a better word—of Quartermaster Department funds. The department not only lacked the means to retire that debt, but it was doubtful, bordering on impossible, if the mills could be provided with raw materials and the goods produced could be paid for. The whole system, Lawton warned, was "about to crumble in for want of funds, the factories being without means to meet current expenditures."[64]

The system did crumble. Federal invasions of the Confederacy's heartland eliminated the few remaining sources of raw materials and curtailed factory output. The Confederate fiscal system, long operating on the brink of disaster, was crushed by inflation and a lack of revenue. As Richard Goff has observed: "At the end, abundant crops and idle factories attested to the Confederacy's productive potential, but there were no factory workers, no money and no transportation to turn that potential into supplies for the army."[65]

The leading authority on the Confederate supply effort maintains that several key factors accounted for the failure of the supply bureaus to equip Confederate forces adequately. Chief among these factors was the government's reaction to events: the government never formulated a long-term policy of supply but merely acted when crises arose. Failure to implement plans in anticipation of future emergencies led to destructive competition between the various bureaus and to an inefficient allocation of resources and funds. Had centralization of supply functions taken place at the top of the government's organizational hierarchy—such organization as the bureau chiefs themselves implemented—overall inefficiencies might have been corrected. Moreover, civilian resistance to supply initiatives such as impressment and government price setting (created in no small measure by popular perceptions of incompetence, greed, and corruption) could have been eased through better organization and communication.[66]

Though generally accurate, this chronicle of deficiencies tends to overlook the positive achievements of the Quartermaster Department. That Southern soldiers were provisioned with clothing, blankets, shoes, and camp equipage for four years demonstrates unequivocally that the Quartermaster Department, for all its shortcomings, did meet most basic needs. More important still, domestic sources of goods—cotton and wool factories and tanneries—under private initiative at first and under government fiat later—met the challenge of equipping troops. In the face of dwindling resources, losses in manpower and machinery, and a dearth of funds, the Southern textile industry continued to operate, albeit with imperfections, until burned to the ground or forced to suspend operations because money, men, and materials could not be had. Those mill entrepreneurs and their actions in relation to the Quartermaster Department must be assessed before a final verdict is delivered on the supply effort.

In contrast to their civilian government overseers, textile entrepreneurs manifested organizational efficiency and interstate communication and cooperation. From the beginning, the Manufacturing and Direct Trade Association of the Confederate States took an active lead in the coordination of Southern manufacturing activities. Meeting annually in Georgia, the association provided Confederate industrial leaders with a forum to discuss the establishment of direct trade with Europe, the procurement of machinery, and the impact of government policies on their concerns. Led by such antebellum advocates of Southern industrial development as William Gregg and Daniel Pratt, the Manufacturing and Direct Trade Association sought improved production and more equitable government remuneration and control through a united front. Indeed, at the 1862 and 1864 gatherings, Southern industrialists used their organization to unleash salvos against government price policies and output controls and to counter allegations that they were profiting unduly at civilian and government expense.

The association's arguments demonstrated a combination of patriotism and self-interest. Low government prices forced manufacturers to operate at a loss. To compensate, manufacturers were compelled to charge consumers higher prices in the marketplace. Higher prices fueled inflation and, more serious, bred unwarranted allegations of profiteering. Such sentiments, these entrepreneurs feared, would dampen enthusiasm for manufacturing in the Confederacy and dissuade potential capitalists from embarking upon similar ventures.[67] Military reverses and chronic shortages toward the end, however, induced many factory owners to place self-preservation ahead of patriotic service. As capital dried up, textile manufacturers refused to accept the government's payment for war goods in worthless Confederate bonds and notes. They also demanded that contracts be renegotiated on a monthly basis so that increased production costs could be adequately remunerated. The manufacturers were not oblivious to the protests such actions elicited, but, as in the past, they met opprobrium with coordinated action.

In assessing constant supply problems and government policies, the manufacturers possessed more insight than did their military contractors. The association's president, William Gregg, articulated the concerns and complaints of factory owners and manufacturers throughout the Confederate South when he stated that supply problems were a consequence of antebellum attitudes. Indifference on the part of many Southerners had discouraged able entrepreneurs from undertaking manufacturing endeavors. Those who had established factories had suffered from a want of patronage. When war demands shook Southerners from their lethargy and apathy, budding capitalists and established entrepreneurs were stymied by government interference and "the odium attached to selling domestics . . . at market value." Both factors had discouraged profit-making to reinvest in the operation and the expansion of production. Had Confederates invested in and encouraged manufacturing pursuits with the same level of commitment they did will-o'-wisp blockade runners, Gregg asserted, adequate supplies and manufacturing self-sufficiency could have been attained.[68]

The manufacturers' criticism of government policies was warranted. Increased controls on materials and production had not significantly increased the effectiveness of quartermaster supply. Further, such policies had heightened speculation and created even greater popular disaffection. Such an atmosphere could have suffocated entrepreneurial endeavors. Fortunately for the Confederate supply effort, it did not.

The association's views and, more important, its activities, cast doubt on Emory M. Thomas's assertion that government control of war industry was required because "there was too little time for a class of industrial entrepreneurs to ripen and flower 'naturally.' "[69] Thomas's further claims that industrialization directed by the military and the government made the "profit motive" an "inconsiderable factor" are also subject to criticism in light of the association's lobbying activities on behalf of a relaxation of government controls on profits.

Manufacturers in general, and the association in particular, were fully aware that several states—not the least of which was Georgia— had an established industrial base and a corps of experienced entrepreneurs. It was those firms and those individuals who, before the government became involved in manufacturing, kindled the mobilization effort with arms and supplies. Indeed, those capitalists provided role models for others to embark upon war-related manufacturing. The demands of the Confederate war machine provided entrepreneurs with a golden opportunity to increase and diversify production, garner profitable new contracts, and formulate plans for the extension of the Southern manufacturing base. These factors are amply borne out by contemporary actions. How else can one explain popular and press hostility to perceived manufacturers' self-aggrandizement at the expense of the cause and the entrepreneurs' subsequent defense of their activities? In what manner may one view the actions of smaller firms and scattered individuals in converting existing facilities into ones more suited to war-related manufacture? How does one account for the emergence of firms created solely to aid the war effort? Finally, how can one reconcile tightened government controls and legislative enactments on individual and corporate income and profits if profit-seeking did not exercise a predominant influence? Manufacturing concerns established by the government may have been directed by "preindustrial men" with "traditional outlooks," as Thomas maintains, but government controls on profits and on private concerns testify to the existence of aggressive entrepreneurs with "acquisitive instincts."[70]

Statements by historians and contemporaries may exaggerate the bias against manufacturing in the South during the Civil War era, the extent to which manufacturers were held as "contemptible extortioners," and the degree to which entrepreneurship of the "Yankee" variety was stunted. Still, strains of both Yankee entrepreneurship and traditional hostility toward manufacturing pursuits are to be found in Georgia during its experience with supply mobilization.

Augusta harvested the fruits, both bitter and sweet, that war mobilization sowed. Throughout the experiences of boom and bust, euphoria and demoralization, many Augustans never totally reconciled their encouragement of manufacturing with their antipathy toward industrial excess. Indeed, while they applauded increased production, full employment, and the humanitarian efforts of the local factories in meeting the needs of the poor, they never got over their fear of a Manchester arising in idyllic Augusta.[71] Toward the end, that specter loomed uncomfortably near, as undesirable refugees and restive workers inundated the town. Fortunately for the war effort, Augusta entrepreneurs were not so torn nor so fearful of the consequences of industrialization. They used the stimulus of war to expand production and to experiment in new lines of goods.

Residents of Columbus apparently never wrestled with the implications of increased industrial production. For that city's capitalists, the war created nothing but opportunity: the chance to build on antebellum accomplishments in textile manufacturing by garnering lucrative government contracts.

Factory entrepreneurs in Augusta and Columbus seized the challenge a state of war provided. They worked energetically to supply Confederate, state, and local demands and, coincidentally, to advance their own interests. Mill owners such as George Schley, William Howard, George Jackson, and others brought a wealth of manufacturing experience to the mobilization and war efforts and aided those efforts tangibly and intangibly as a result. They incurred heavy physical and financial losses as a consequence of their activities. They adapted to tightened government controls that could have stifled their entrepreneurial energies. In spite of such adverse conditions, they augmented their base of operations and attained added expertise that would prove invaluable in the future. Most important, the successes of their enterprises and their demonstration that manufacturing was not only essential but profitable helped chip away at any lingering doubts about the efficacy or feasibility of Southern manufacturing.

Georgia's mill entrepreneurs also served as role models for smaller concerns. Grocers, merchants, and clothiers emulated the example of larger firms and diversified production or undertook entirely new lines of business with an eye to obtaining government contracts. J. W. Sappington, Simon Rothchild, and countless others risked time and money in pursuit of personal gain and a contribution to the war. They, too, suffered physical and financial reverses as a consequence of their involvement, but they gained new skills and experience.[72]

Patriotism, the opportunity for individual and corporate gain, and the sheer adventure of embarking upon new careers in a society made fluid by war all played a role in motivating Georgians and other Southerners to take up the burden of Confederate supply. Grandiose dreams of Confederate manufacturing self-sufficiency, individual wealth, and state and national prosperity foundered on the realities of insufficient funds, scarce materials and labor, and bureaucratic inefficiencies. Nevertheless, some could foresee a bright future, based on war-established foundations, amid the wreckage of the Confederate supply effort.

4 From Entrepreneurs to Managers

Georgia's Railroads and the War Effort

A key component of the Confederate mobilization effort was the Southern rail network. Politicians, bureau chiefs, and commanding officers could wax poetic about the Confederacy's capacity to gear up for a war, but a stark reality remained: all the troops mustered and the munitions, arms, and accoutrements manufactured would prove of little worth if they could not be transported expeditiously to the front. Despite a severe inferiority to Northern railroads—both in total mileage and in the nonconformity of gauge—the Confederacy's railroad managers did meet most of the demands placed on them. Their inability to adapt fully to changed conditions during the war, however, handicapped transportation efforts and ultimately contributed to Southern defeat. Southern railroaders in general and Georgia railroaders in particular were innocent accomplices to the Confederacy's downfall. The railroads were different than any other sector of the war economy. By 1860, as several scholars have pointed out, railroads manifested all the characteristics of modern business corporations.[1] Innovation and risk-taking had characterized the initial stages of railroad building and growth, but the completion of the lines necessitated a more conservative, managerial approach. Innovation or entrepreneurialism continued to play a role periodically, but in general, managerialism, which required attention to profits, dividends, and stockholders, became the key principle that guided railroad operations. Because of this emphasis on the managerial, not all of the South's railroad men were able to respond creatively to the challenge of wartime mobilization.

Southern boosters pointed with pride to the achievements the region had made in railroad construction in just over two decades. Beginning in the 1840s, after the worst effects of the depression had worn off, regional capitalists had moved swiftly to join the nationwide railroad boom. Southerners perceived that the lucrative commerce of the West needed only to be tapped to pour riches into their laps. Consequently, a fit of incorporation seized the region and produced railroad companies that laid nearly nine thousand miles of track by 1860.[2]

Impressive as it was, this railroad growth was by no means uniform. Virginia and Georgia (which together accounted for roughly one-third of all Southern trackage) contained extensive systems that linked major commercial centers; Louisiana, by contrast, possessed only 328 miles and Alabama and Mississippi barely double that figure. Not only were there gaps in the Southern rail network, but the Southern system was hampered by parochialism. Many companies refused to allow through traffic on their lines for fear it would enrich rival towns. Compounding this problem was the lack of a uniform gauge. Most lines used a five-foot gauge, but Virginia, North Carolina, Kentucky, Mississippi, and Alabama used the four-foot-eight-and-one-half-inch "standard" gauge used in most of the Midwest and Northeast.[3] Finally, Southern railroad entrepreneurs purchased their hardware outside the region, preventing the development of a support industry. Locomotives, cars, and railroad iron were usually obtained from Northern or European dealers. Only three Southern companies—Richmond's Tredegar Iron Works, the Nashville Manufacturing Company, and the Augusta, Georgia, Forest City Foundry—produced railroad equipment. Problems such as these were to loom large during the course of the war, but in the postsecession glow, few perceived how troublesome they would prove.

Despite such inherent disadvantages, the South did derive benefits from its railroad system. Some companies, including several in Georgia, were run by extremely able men, who had long experience in managing railroads. The railroad boom of the 1840s and 1850s had led to the establishment of a few rolling mills and foundries. Regional capitalists had invested extensively in rail projects, and local capital and talent had been used to the fullest. Though many Northerners had found gainful employment on the engineering and road crews of the various Southern lines, the majority of Southern railroad entrepreneurs were born and bred south of the Mason-Dixon line. Indeed, the domination of Southern railroads by local entrepreneurs with local interests was probably the principal factor in preventing the development of a unified interstate system.[4]

With the notable exception of the Brunswick & Florida, Georgia's railway companies were directed by native Southerners and, more often than not, by born-and-bred Georgians. The Georgia Railroad and Banking Company was begun under the aegis of James Camak of Athens. In 1841, the man most prominently associated with the Georgia Railroad, John P. King, was elected president, and the next year, the company's headquarters was transferred to Augusta. King was a well-known and respected member of the Augusta community. Born in 1799 in Glasgow, Kentucky, he had journeyed to the Savannah River town in 1817 to attend the prestigious Richmond Academy. In 1819, King was admitted to the Georgia bar, but he retired from his practice after a decade to attend to private business. He served as a judge of the Common Pleas Court beginning in 1833 and then was appointed to the U.S. Senate. King resigned from the Senate in 1837 after he made a speech critical of the Van Buren administration that rankled some Georgians in official circles. King returned to Augusta and was engaged in private business until he was tapped for the Georgia Railroad presidency in 1841.[5]

King's election to the presidency proved fortuitous for the company. When he assumed his duties, the Georgia Railroad was nearly bankrupt—the depression of the late 1830s had rendered the cost of labor and materials beyond the means of the young company. Using his personal assets, King pushed the work ahead, completing the road to Atlanta in 1845. By 1846, the company was again paying dividends to its stockholders.[6]

King used his position as railroad president to boost the general economic development of Augusta. For King, railroads were but one medium to achieve economic diversification: he also perceived that manufacturing was a requisite for balanced economic growth. Consequently, King became one of the founders of the Augusta Canal Company, which was chartered by the Augusta City Council in 1845. Indeed, King's private contributions helped fund the preliminary surveys for that canal. King and other Augusta merchants and capitalists believed that the canal would serve as a catalyst to local cotton manufacturing. Mills located on small creeks had proved profitable; hence the increased power of a canal virtually ensured further manufacturing successes. During the late antebellum period, King agitated constantly for the establishment of manufacturing enterprises. His efforts did not go for naught: on the eve of the Civil War, Augusta boasted a substantial manufacturing base in cotton textiles. Moreover, the city had extensive rail connections to other interior market centers. Much of the credit for Augusta's successful diversification of its economic base in the prewar years properly belongs to John P. King.[7]

King's counterpart on the rival Central of Georgia was Richard R. Cuyler. A native Georgian, Cuyler had assumed the reins of the Central in 1842, but unlike King, he devoted himself almost exclusively to railroad work. Cuyler was an aristocrat, and he oversaw the business of the Central from his offices in Savannah and from his plantation, located near the outskirts of the city. The Central's extensive investments in and virtual control over the Empire State of the South's expanding rail system were largely the result of Cuyler's energy as president. He ran an aggressive, solid concern, and he enjoyed the backing of some of Savannah's most prominent merchants and businessmen.[8]

Cuyler was also blessed with competent subordinates. None, however, was as able as William M. Wadley, who became superintendent of the Central in 1849. Wadley was born in New Hampshire in 1812 and had trained as a blacksmith in his father's shop. Like many other Yankees, he had journeyed south in the early 1830s to work on that region's railroads. Wadley settled in Savannah in 1833 and signed on with the Central of Georgia. He rose rapidly, moving from laborer to "railroad troubleshooter" to superintendent in just sixteen years, taking time to marry a Savannah belle on his way to the top. He left the Central in the late 1850s to oversee the construction of the Southern Railroad of Mississippi and the Vicksburg, Shreveport & Texas Railroad. By the time his adopted state of Georgia seceded, he was considered one of the most knowledgeable railroad men in the South. He took those formidable credentials back to Savannah and threw his lot with the South.[9]

During Wadley's stint in Mississippi and Texas, he may have made the acquaintance of another Yankee-bred Georgian destined to play a major role during the war, Lemuel P. Grant. Grant hailed from Maine, but he had moved to Pennsylvania in his teens to do engineering work on the Philadelphia & Reading Railroad. In 1840, Grant moved to Georgia and assumed the post of assistant engineer on the Georgia Railroad. He supervised the grading and laying of track to Terminus until 1841, when the depression halted work on that line. He was then hired by the rival Central Railroad, but by 1843 Grant was back with the engineering corps of the Georgia Railroad. He became, in succession, chief engineer of the Montgomery & West Point and the Atlanta & West Point railroads. In 1853, Grant resigned from the Georgia

Railroad and moved to the Southwest to oversee railway projects in Louisiana, Mississippi, and Texas. Five years later, Grant was presiding over the Southern Pacific Railroad of Texas, but he remained at that post for only one year. By 1859, Grant was back in Georgia, promoting the Georgia Western Railroad, a project designed to link Atlanta with the rich coal fields of Alabama. The Georgia Western scheme did not come to fruition before secession, but Grant remained hopeful. With the breakup of the Union, however, Grant shifted his attention to the needs of the Confederacy.[10]

Georgia's principal railroad men differed little from their counterparts elsewhere in the South—and the North. Some, like Cuyler, were part of the Southern elite, but a larger proportion were "self-made men of superior capacity"—men such as John P. King, William Wadley, and Lemuel Grant. They were not wedded to vague principles or abstractions, nor were they actively involved in the vitriolic political debates that swirled about them in the late antebellum period. These Southern railroad entrepreneurs were businessmen first and foremost. If politics and talk of secession came to dominate their thoughts by 1860, it undoubtedly stemmed from a pragmatic concern: how would secession affect business? With the fall of Fort Sumter, they would have an answer to their query.[11]

When war became a reality in April 1861, the Provisional Government of the Confederacy was ensconced in Montgomery trying to create a nation out of seven Southern states. Disorganization reigned in most departments, but Postmaster General John Reagan attempted to bring some order to his bureau by making mail contracts with Southern railroads. Reagan's desire to coordinate railroad activities led him to invite representatives of the leading Southern carriers to Montgomery in April. By the time these Southern capitalists reached the Confederate capital, the War Department had entered the picture by seeking a hearing at the convocation.

The railroad meeting proceeded swiftly and smoothly. The secretary of war, Leroy P. Walker, issued a statement on the military's railroad needs, and that proposal gained first hearing. Walker's plan was accepted without prolonged debate or discussion. Convention secretary Daniel H. Cram conveyed the meeting's resolutions to Walker on 30 April. The representatives of the railroad companies (including all major lines except those in Virginia and Texas) resolved to "transport troops and munitions, upon the plan indicated . . . at the following rates . . . : Men, two cents per mile; munitions, provisions, and material, at half regular local rates." The companies also agreed to accept payment for services in Confederate bonds or treasury notes in the event "that the money at the command of the Government may be required for other purposes, and particularly to provision and keep in the field the troops required for the defense of the Confederate States."[12] The assembled capitalists also proved amenable to Reagan's proposals to regulate the mails and adopted them without dissent. With such amity prevailing, the remainder of the convocation was devoted to meeting Confederate government officials and selecting a central committee empowered to call similar gatherings when conditions warranted. Two of the three men elected to the central committee were Georgia railroad managers John P. King and R. R. Cuyler.[13]

Written agreements and verbal assurances of unflinching patriotic service were one thing; the realities of troop supply transport and regular passenger and freight service were quite another. As mobilization proceeded, rail traffic became increasingly disrupted. Troops inundated cities and towns in search of transportation to the front— wherever it might be. Provisions stockpiled to feed the Confederate legions rotted at depots for want of an adequate number of freight cars. More ominous still, railroad companies that possessed machine works and car shops found a fertile field for extra profits in government contracts. Military authorities, anxious to arm all able-bodied males who flocked to the Stars and Bars, discovered that locomotive manufacturing facilities could easily—and graciously—be converted to the production of ordnance. The Central of Georgia and the Georgia Railroad shops churned out their share of gun mounts and gun carriages for state and Confederate authorities, as did other companies. But though they aided the shooting, they neglected the maintenance and routine upkeep of their engines and cars. This failure would, in the not too distant future, prove enervating.[14]

Victory at the Battle of Manassas on 21 July 1861 precipitated the drive to reorganize the Confederate transportation system. While Southern patriots danced in celebration, more sober souls in Richmond realized that the battle could have been a great victory and ended the conflict. Numerous reserve regiments that could have followed up the Federal retreat were left idle, miles from the front, because adequate rail transportation could not be found.[15]

President Jefferson Davis moved quickly to remedy the problems exposed at Manassas. He appointed William Shepperd Ashe, president of the Wilmington & Weldon Railroad, assistant quartermaster of transportation in Virginia. It was a wise choice. Ashe and his subordinates traveled extensively throughout Virginia and adjacent states surveying the condition of all the roads. Ashe made recommendations to the Richmond authorities on significant gaps that needed to be filled. He also worked to obtain iron, engines, and cars from other lines to bolster the transportation network in and into the Old Dominion. Unfortunately for the Confederacy, Ashe's recommendations were largely ignored, and his overall efforts foundered on insufficient government support and self-interested railroads. A proposal to begin an inquiry on "the necessity of further legislation to insure the more speedy transportation of troops and military and naval supplies" was tabled in the Confederate Congress because it was "reported that no further legislation was necessary."[16] In December 1861, President Davis reported to Congress on Ashe's proposals to build connecting links between the major lines in the Confederacy, but he concluded that a lack of funds militated against such construction at that time. Davis did, however, urge that the Congress take some steps to extend government aid to Southern railroads. Already the dearth of manufacturing facilities was being felt as ironworks and machine and car shops found it increasingly difficult, if not impossible, to produce iron rails and cars, as well as ordnance and munitions. The president was understating the case when he remarked: "If the railroads should be generally disabled from transporting troops and military supplies for the prosecution of the war, the result would be most disastrous." He urged Confederate lawmakers to consider ways to encourage the establishment of additional rolling mills and furnaces. For Davis, at least, the exigency of war justified government aid to the railroads.[17]

The situation did not improve with the new year. Civilian traffic on the various railroads began to fall off as military shipments increased. The boom in government business, however, did not yield the grand profits that had been expected, for military rates, established at the railroad meetings, were almost 50 percent below normal passenger and freight rates. The nature of government shipments also affected the carriers. Heavy weaponry and supplies carried on lines made of flimsy rails in some portions of the Confederacy contributed to numerous delays and breakdowns. As materials and facilities for upkeep grew increasingly scarce, the railroad managers determined that extraordinary steps had to be taken to remedy the situation.[18]

Top government officials began to receive entreaties from railway executives asking for government aid or proposing plans by which service could be rendered more efficient. Walter Goodman of the Mississippi Central presented a plan to Davis that was to serve as the frame of reference for the Richmond railroad meeting, scheduled for February 1862, and for subsequent congressional debates and inquiries on government aid to the railroads. Goodman argued for set contracts between the carriers and the Confederate government. He felt certain that legal and binding contracts would ensure that the various railways served the government first. Goodman further urged that government-appointed agents be detailed to oversee the shipment of troops, arms, supplies, and ammunition. He concluded that all plans for increasing the efficiency of the railroads were contingent upon the government's establishment of ironworks and rolling mills devoted exclusively to railroad maintenance. Railroad shops at Savannah, Augusta, Atlanta, Charleston, and Nashville, Goodman argued, could be contracted to provide exclusively for the Southern carriers. Further, those shops could be supplied by "two or three rolling mills erected in as many sections of the Confederacy."[19]

Davis had no sooner received Goodman's communiqué than he was handed a report from a special committee appointed to investigate the Quartermaster Department—the agency responsible for railroad affairs. Chairman T. N. Waul reported that it was imperative to increase the effectiveness of railway transportation. To that end, the Waul committee recommended "that military control be taken of the principal railroad routes terminating or passing through Richmond, Nashville, Memphis, Atlanta, and all routes leading to the headquarters of our several army corps, which should be placed under the direction of an efficient superintendent, free from local interests, investments, or connection with special railroads."[20]

The Waul committee report and Goodman's letter touched off debates in various quarters of official Richmond and formed the backdrop to the railroad meeting that convened in the capital city in February 1862. The assembled railroad executives concurred with Goodman's plan to locate government-established rolling mills in various quarters and to have the government offer subsidies to encourage the development of mineral resources and ironworks. The Congress and Quartermaster General Myers also voiced approval of such arrangements. All disagreed, however, with the proposal for government control of certain railroad lines. Myers protested that government railroad agents would interfere with the carriers' operations, and rail-road executives refused to consider a plan that threatened the sanctity of private property. In addition, numerous congressmen vociferously objected to the concept of government confiscation and to the principle of government aid for the construction of railroad lines, even for lines deemed essential to military operations.[21]

Railroad matters, therefore, remained at an impasse until March 1862, when Representative Peter W. Gray of Texas offered a resolution "that the Committee on Military Affairs be instructed to inquire into the expediency of the Government taking absolute control and management of all railways and their rolling stock during the war." Again, debate raged until the House and Senate finally produced a watered-down bill "to provide for the safe and expeditious transport of troops and munitions of war by the railroads." As originally framed, the bill could have eliminated most of the problems that plagued railroad transport. Unfortunately, it was subjected to numerous amendments. By the time the final vote was taken, the bill provided for little more than consultation between railroad executives and a government-appointed railroad superintendent.[22]

It was painfully evident that railroad affairs were operating in a haphazard—and deleterious—manner. Secretary of War George Randolph reported to Davis in August that some order had to be effected "to insure . . . a proper state of efficiency." Randolph urged that a head of transportation be appointed "to harmonize the operations of the roads and to maintain their efficiency." Davis duly reported Randolph's recommendations to Congress and blandly asserted: "I trust you will be able to devise satisfactory measures for attaining this purpose."[23]

Meanwhile, railroad executives met again to discuss common problems and to formulate some plan of action. At the Columbia, South Carolina, railroad convention of September 1862, the delegates decided to divide military shipments into four classes and to increase rates charged for freight and troop transport. The railroad executives also voted to petition the government for aid in procuring iron, copper, tin, and other raw materials, and they recommended that government authorities establish rolling mills to ensure railroad mainte-nance. Their final request was most telling: they urged government authorities to refrain from interfering with their operations.[24] Patriots they may have been, but they were still businessmen.

The Georgia carriers were well represented at all the railroad meetings convened during 1861 and 1862. Delegates John P. King, R. R. Cuyler, Western & Atlantic superintendent John W. Lewis, and Macon & Western president Isaac Scott were all concerned by the way the war had affected the functioning of their respective lines. With the commencement of active hostilities, freight and passenger traffic fell off, and normal lines of communication with western and northern markets were suspended. The Georgia Railroad reported regular traffic "deranged": passenger traffic was confined to troop transport and refugees, and freight consisted almost exclusively of arms, munitions, and military supplies. Although net earnings for 1861–62 were quoted at $431,540, the figures were inflated because they were based on depreciated Confederate currency. Even without taking into account the depressed nature of Confederate notes, the decline in earnings was severe: in 1860, the Georgia Railroad had netted $528,044.[25]

R. R. Cuyler reported that the Central, too, had suffered a decrease in earnings. Though the road had recorded a sizable increase in passenger freight, military transport at reduced fees and the increased costs of materials for routine maintenance rendered the future earning capacity of the railroad doubtful. Cuyler subsequently ordered that wages and salaries be cut to offset future losses of the road. Cuyler's Southwestern Railroad was also the victim of a "sharp falling off" of earnings. In 1860, the Southwestern had netted $423,521 and had paid a substantial 13 percent dividend to stockholders. August of 1861 found the Southwestern's earnings decreased almost by half—to $280,463. The road determined to pay a 3 percent dividend but notified stockholders that the reserve fund and bonds would be kept "in hand" and that "strict attention" would be paid to future expenditures.[26]

Reports from the Western & Atlantic Railroad were no more encouraging. Superintendent John W. Lewis reported reassuringly that the state road was in excellent physical shape. Forty-nine new miles of T-rails had been laid and extensive bridge work had been built. Moreover, the Western & Atlantic had paid $438,000 into state coffers during 1861. Lewis tempered his optimism, however, when he discussed the future prospects of the road. "Of the future, I will only say, that the present prospect is very gloomy, as to its making much money; railroad supplies are enormously high, and still advancing and difficult to get at all. Labor is high; trade and commerce nearly destroyed by our political troubles so it would be expecting too much . . . to suppose that its income should be kept at what it has been, or now is."[27] Such reports were duplicated throughout the state and the Confederacy. Problems evident as early as the fall of 1861 did not disappear as the nation settled down to a protracted conflict. Indeed, Southerners would soon look back on 1861 as the halcyon era of the Confederate railroads. After that year, incipient problems would grow to overwhelming proportions.

Confederate policies hampered the operations of all roads, but no road in Georgia was more profoundly affected than the state-owned Western & Atlantic. In the early days of the war, government authorities were scrupulously attentive to the private, corporate nature of railroad companies. The press of events, however, soon induced the Richmond authorities to interfere more and more. Particular lines, especially those linking the southeastern Confederacy with the western agricultural and manufacturing heartland, became hard-pressed to transport goods from the Deep South to the Virginia front: the railroads did not have enough engines and cars to move the vast quantity of goods needed. Secretary of War Judah Benjamin informed Quartermaster General Myers that six twenty-six-ton engines and seventy boxcars were required to render the East Tennessee & Virginia Railroad serviceable to Virginia, and that because the Western & Atlantic and the Mobile & Ohio railroads possessed the requisite means, Benjamin instructed Myers to "obtain from those companies . . . the engines and cars thus imperatively required for the public service." Moreover, he told Myers that if he was not able to obtain the needed rolling stock by contract, "you are authorized to impress them."[28] Such a move was sure to rouse the ire not only of strict states'-rights advocates but also of the businessmen who had invested their lives as well as their money in Southern railroads.

Benjamin informed Governor Joseph E. Brown of his intentions to seize the needed equipment, but the governor proved less than amenable to his request. Brown stated that there were no extra cars and that the threat of impressment clearly violated the sovereign rights of the state of Georgia. The secretary ignored Brown's lectures and seized the desired number of cars and engines. The debate did not end there, however. Less than a fortnight elapsed before Brown was again protesting the government's heavy hand on his state's railroad. Because the East Tennessee line had abused the cars it had received, Brown reported, the Western & Atlantic was "hard-pressed" to conduct "winter business." The governor politely suggested to the secretary that the War Department look to the better-equipped lines, such as the Central of Georgia, for needed cars. Brown assured Benjamin that had the Western & Atlantic the materials to repair the broken engines and cars that filled its Atlanta shops, he would gladly have tendered them to the government.[29] This would not be the last time that the Confederate government saw fit to seize railroad property belonging to the Western & Atlantic. Soon it would confiscate rolling stock on Georgia's other lines as well.

That Governor Brown did not practice what he preached to the War Department was evident a short while later. The Northern-controlled Brunswick & Florida Railroad refused to continue operations because of the war. Such conduct was unconscionable to the governor, especially since it was a Yankee-dominated concern. Accordingly, Brown seized the road "as a means of public defense" and appointed Georgians Charles L. Schlatter to the superintendency and George Hazelhurst to the posts of treasurer and auditor, "until such time as I may think proper."[30]

Brown's motives were not purely ideological; he was determined to keep the state road functioning. He obtained eleven hundred tons of new iron rails, a great boon, and contracted with the Etowah Iron Works, near Cartersville, Georgia, for additional amounts. Although Western & Atlantic Superintendent John S. Rowland reported that "fabulous prices" were demanded for any and all railroad supplies, repairs were being made on bridges and tracks. The Western & Atlantic also expected the return of 180 cars lost to other Southern lines.[31]

Despite problems of maintenance, Georgia railroaders and Confederate officials seriously considered the completion of projects begun before the war and even contemplated new projects considered to be of military value. The president of the Pensacola and Georgia Railroad, E. Houston, wrote to Secretary of War Walker that a connection between his road and the Savannah, Albany & Gulf would greatly benefit the war effort. The proposed 176-mile road would not only unite the Florida system but would also enable the through passage of "cannon and other heavy material" to the Georgia roads and hence to Richmond. Houston told Walker that iron was available in Savannah and that if the government would contract for its purchase, construction could begin at once.[32] Another proposed railroad in the early days of the war was a connection between the Alabama and Georgia Railroad at Blue Mountain, Alabama, and a spur of the Western & Atlantic in Rome, Georgia (see Map 1). The Confederate House gave Davis statutory authority "to provide the means of [military] transpor-

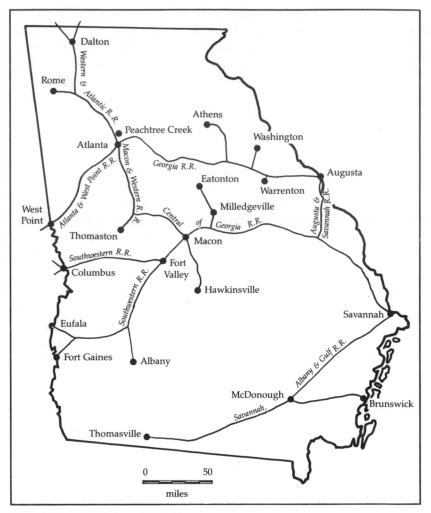

Map 1. Georgia Railroads, 1860

tation by the construction" of the railroad in October 1862. The act appropriated a $1.12 million loan in Confederate bonds and stipulated that the work had to be completed in six to ten weeks and that military transport would receive first priority or the mortgage would be foreclosed. Chief engineer Jeremy F. Gilmer appointed Lemuel P. Grant, chief engineer at Atlanta, to oversee the road's construction.[33]

A local project also received considerable attention in 1862. In the late 1850s, ambitious capitalists in Atlanta had promoted a scheme to connect that city with the major cities of the Northeast via an air line railroad. Internal squabbling and a rival project, the Georgia Western, had prevented the Atlanta Air Line from moving beyond the planning stages. With the onset of the war, the plan was revived. Atlanta citizens held numerous meetings to discuss the feasibility of building the air line to Richmond. They agreed that such a direct link with the Confederate capital was of "incalculable importance" as a "military line": it would shorten the route to Richmond by one hundred miles and be located deep in the interior and thus safe from Federal raids. Committees were duly formed to discuss financing and the like, and all present at the meetings remained confident that the project could be launched.[34]

Plans to build new lines or extend existing ones demonstrate that many Southern railroad managers were aware of the possibility of capitalizing upon war demands to benefit their respective companies. Indeed, statements about the military advantages of a projected road were in reality euphemisms for future profits and development. Promoters, managers, and citizens could not help but see that new undertakings would have both an immediate and long-term effect on the local and perhaps even regional economy.[35]

Still, none of these ambitious schemes of railroad expansion, in Georgia or elsewhere, ever came to full fruition. Some companies did garner contracts; indeed, connections were made between Meridian, Mississippi, and Selma, Alabama; Greensboro, North Carolina, and Danville, Virginia; and Lawton, Georgia, and Live Oak, Florida. But schemes to build lines deemed militarily imperative usually died aborning. The reason for the disparity between plans and accomplishments was not hard to find. All the Confederate and local aid rendered could not produce the amount of iron, rails, machines, and cars needed to build additional railroads. The existing carriers could barely supply their own needs from the available resources; hence it was well-nigh impossible to undertake new building projects, however modest in design. President Alfred Shorter of the Alabama and Georgia Railroad spoke for all Southern railroad managers when he wrote President Davis of the "serious difficulties" that attended railroad construction in the South. Problems faced by the executive of the road directed to build the Rome & Blue Mountain connection were symptomatic of the dilemma facing Southern railroad companies: "You are aware of the many obstacles which may render our efforts fruitless in obtaining iron rails, spikes, chairs, &c, by the usual mode of purchase, and unless that authority which had declared the road to be a military necessity also declares that iron shall be furnished, I know not how to proceed."[36]

As the second winter of the war approached, it became increasingly obvious to all Confederates that better management and use of the Southern railroads was necessary. Government bureaucrats fretted endlessly about how to provide for the troops, given the irregular nature of transportation. Military leaders asked, pleaded, and demanded that supplies and additional troops be funneled to the front. Confederate editors condemned the government for contributing to civilian suffering by monopolizing the railroads for government service. Charges of "bad management" and "recklessly wasteful" use were bandied about in the Southern press. As one editor stated bluntly—and correctly: "We have been killing the goose which laid the golden eggs, and we hope we shall not feel the present inconveniences more severely. It were better to husband carefully and judiciously what remains of our railroad facilities than to be deprived of them altogether, which we fear will be the case if a more careful management is not adopted."[37]

In the face of such concern and unrest, Richmond acted. On 3 December 1862, General Orders No. 98 provided that a railroad bureau chief was "to take supervision and control of the transportation for the Government on all Railroads in the Confederate States." The man tapped for this new post was, as the *Savannah Republican* characterized him, "that Napoleon of railroad managers," William M. Wadley. Wadley's extensive experience in railroading—he had served in every capacity from construction to management—made him one of the preeminent railroad men in the South. Finally, an overall head of Confederate transportation was to take charge, and an effort was to be made to refurbish and reinvigorate the Confederate railway system. Wadley's orders gave him the right to contract and negotiate with the railroads "to secure efficiency, harmony, and cooperation." He was to oversee all government agents and employees working on the various lines and was empowered to "take charge of and employ all engines, machinery, tools, or other property, of the Government owned or used for railroad transportation; and may exchange, sell or loan such machinery with or to any railroad and company to facilitate the work of transportation."[38]

Wadley's appointment elicited opposition from one side. Quartermaster General Myers hardly gave Wadley a chance to move into his office before he began to inundate Secretary of War James Seddon with complaints. Myers, a self-proclaimed authority on military regulations, protested that creating a separate railroad bureau violated accepted army regulations, which stipulated that all transportation be under the control and supervision of the Quartermaster Department. Railroad executives were accustomed to dealing exclusively with his department, Myers argued, and changes in that arrangement threatened to produce delays and confusion. Myers entertained "grave doubts" about the "propriety" of such a policy change and urged that the railroads remain under the purview of the Quartermaster Department. Lest he be accused of insubordination, Myers hastily added that he did not oppose Wadley personally, nor did he disagree with the proposal to centralize railroad operations. Myers only wanted to keep the railroads running—on his terms and under his jurisdiction.[39]

Oblivious to the tempest his appointment created for the quartermaster general, Wadley went to work in earnest. His first act was to call for a meeting of all Southern railroad managers. The convention met in Augusta, Georgia, on 15 December 1862, and Wadley presented his plan for Confederate railroad management. Wadley suggested that the various railroads select superintendents to work with him for the duration of the war. He also proposed that railroads allow cars to transport goods and troops over adjoining lines and that the government aid in constructing connecting links where and when deemed necessary. Government agents were to superintend the loading of all freight to provide the roads with supplies and slave labor when needed. Wadley's plan received the approval of one committee, but it ran into a stone wall when presented to the entire convention. The assembled railroad managers endorsed Wadley's appointment and pledged their cooperation. That cooperation, however, was contingent on certain conditions. The Augusta delegates had their own ideas as to how to remedy the chronic problems that plagued the Confederate transportation system. They recommended and adopted a plan to raise rates charged for government transport. Under the new plan, troops would be transported at the rate of two and a half cents per man and powder and ammunition at sixty cents per one hundred pounds per one hundred miles. Each item in every class was subject to increased tariff charges. Delegate Samuel L. Fremont authored the written justification of the changed tariff schedule: "In view of the greatly enhanced value of every article entering into the consumption of railroad companies . . . [the] committee can see no reason or justice for retaining the present rates for carrying for the Government." After adopting the new charges, the convention resolved that Wadley should return all cars and engines seized by the government "at the earliest practicable moment to the roads to whom they belong." Their business concluded, the assemblage voted to adjourn.[40]

If Wadley was chagrined or disgusted with the aborted railroad convention, he did not evince it officially. Indeed, he demonstrated little emotion when he filed his report of the meeting with Adjutant and Inspector General Samuel Cooper on 31 December 1862. Wadley dispassionately told Cooper that his plan had been tendered to committee and had been rejected. Wadley refused to endorse the railroads' plan to increase tariff schedules. He did offer Cooper an assessment of the causes of the transportation snarl. Wadley believed that army officers randomly impressed railroad equipment, interfered with railroad personnel, and generally manhandled rolling stock. Not only did these practices discourage railroad employees from taking "a proper interest in conducting a business which invests them with no responsibility," but they also fostered distrust among railroad owners and contributed to the destruction of engines and cars. He concluded his report on a note of concern for the future. Rolling stock and machinery were deteriorating daily because of the wear and tear of service. Supplies for repair were scarce or unavailable, and when they were found, they remained unused for want of trained mechanics. The government, Wadley added, could render some "relief by permitting the iron foundries and rolling mills now engaged wholly in Government works to furnish . . . the necessary materials and by permitting the detail of men." Wadley did not exaggerate when he added: "Those difficulties must be remedied or the roads will very soon be quite unable to meet the requirements of Government."[41]

Wadley's concerns did not fall on deaf ears. Just three days later, Cooper issued General Orders No. 2, which endeavored to change government railroad practices. Military personnel were prohibited "from interfering with the engines, cars, running of trains, or with the control and management . . . of railroads." Only quartermasters or commanding officers were to requisition the engines and rolling stock needed for troop and freight transport, and a strict accounting of both time and equipment used was to accompany all such requisitions. Wadley was instructed to oversee the detail of conscripted railroad employees to the various lines. Not long afterward, President Davis reported to Congress that the "embarrassments" of the transportation problem made it essential to place the railroads under "some general supervision."[42] The president added teeth to this directive by sanctioning impressment of railroad lines when deemed necessary.

As a result of these decisions, Secretary of War Seddon instructed Wadley to meet again with the railroad executives to arrange for the more expeditious transport of freight on through schedules. Seddon expressed surprise and consternation that after two years no such policy had been implemented: "The least calculation will show that if the railroads will in good faith give preference to Government freight and steadily . . . run their freight trains by through schedule[,] more than all the supplies needed for the Government can be transported on the leading lines."[43]

Before attending this railroad meeting, Wadley surveyed the status of the various railroads from the Carolinas to Mississippi. His findings did not reassure anxious bureaucrats and harried military commanders. Wadley reported to Seddon that 31 engines and 930 cars were needed to provide efficient transportation for the coming campaign season. The major lines, he continued, had deteriorated nearly 25 percent since the beginning of the war, largely because of the paucity of materials and mechanics. Wadley concluded that, given the inability of the railroads "to meet promptly the requirements of [the] Government[,] Can we expect any better result in the future without some change in their condition?" The railroad chief answered his own query in the negative. It was imperative, Wadley stated, that the "restoration of the principal roads in the country to the best possible condition" be undertaken at once.[44]

The railroad managers convened in Richmond on 20 April 1863 just as Wadley returned from his fact-finding mission. They recommended that an independent railroad bureau be established under Wadley's direction and that all carriers be supplied with tools, machinery, and other supplies from government shops. The managers also urged that the Confederacy establish ironworks and rolling mills devoted solely to railroad production and that steps be taken to obtain additional machinery and mechanics from Europe. The executives completed their work by endorsing the increased tariff rates agreed upon at Augusta in December 1862.[45]

The Confederate Congress met concurrently with the Richmond railroad convention and considered Senator Louis T. Wigfall's "Bill to facilitate transportation." By a vote of eleven to six, the Senate passed the bill, enabling the president to require the railroads to serve army needs and provide through freight service. It also gave the Quarter-

master Department the power to impress any railroad or its appurtenances if the road refused to cooperate or if deemed a military necessity. The bill was duly signed by Jefferson Davis.[46]

The provisions of the railroad act were obviously inspired by Wadley. From the beginning of his tenure as railroad supervisor, he had
endeavored to achieve cooperation with individual railroad companies while providing for Confederate military needs. Wadley had received some cooperation, but he had been frustrated by more than a
few railroad managers who, in his opinion, failed to show "a disposi-
tion to meet the necessities of the Government in this particular."
Wadley did not question their patriotism. Rather, he attributed their
dilatoriness to "demoralization . . . which induces some to make all
manner of excuses rather than take hold honestly to do the work." He
fully realized that his idea of government supervision of rail lines
when necessary was extreme and would undoubtedly raise a chorus
of protest. But he found no other option realistic. Wadley believed that
the threat of seizure would produce results: "To those meeting the
requirements of the Government this law would have no terror, while
to laggards, it would act as a spur."[47]

Wadley believed the new railroad law had two fundamental flaws: it
did not recognize the Railroad Bureau, and it lodged the enforcement
of its provisions with the Quartermaster Department. Alas, Wadley
did not have the opportunity to appeal for the rectification of such
oversights. On 26 April 1863, he was relieved of command because of
a technicality. Though Davis had appointed him, his commission was
subject to Senate approval. Apparently, Wadley's appointment had
been buried under routine business. When it finally came to the attention of the Senate in April 1863, it was rejected.[48] Politicians and
railroad executives who loathed Wadley's plans for centralization
must have been delighted. Quartermaster General Myers finally had
the Confederate carriers back where, in his opinion, they belonged.
But at a single stroke, the Confederacy deprived itself of the most
knowledgeable railroad man in the country.

Although there is little evidence that Southern and especially Georgia railroad managers viewed Wadley's departure with relief, they
were probably glad. Wadley's plans gave the managers everything to
fear. Though they endorsed his recommendations for government aid
to their enterprises, they could not in good conscience accept his
schemes for centralization or nationalization. Such proposals deviated
too radically from accepted management policies and procedures con-

cerning the private character of railroad corporations. In essence, Wadley demanded a national Confederate railroad network; the various railroad managers demanded the status quo antebellum, when each line operated independently within its own region.

Those who supported Wadley's ideas could take comfort in the fact that the Railroad Bureau would continue to operate. Moreover, the man commissioned to replace Wadley was a Wadley appointee and protégé. Frederick W. Sims assumed his former chief's duties by Special Order No. 133, promulgated 4 June 1863.[49] Sims was a native Georgian and had grown up in Macon, where his father had served as mayor. During the 1850s, Sims had served as chief accountant for the Central of Georgia Railroad, and during his service with the road he had become acquainted with his future superior, William Wadley. In 1856, Sims left the Central to become publisher and owner of the *Savannah Republican*. While in Savannah, Sims became something of a society man. He was active in the city's Union Society, an old and highly regarded philanthropic organization. Sims also became interested in politics and was an ardent booster of the nativist American party, serving as vice-president of the Savannah Fillmore Club. With secession, Sims followed his state and enlisted in the Oglethorpe Guards, the military organization of the Savannah elite. Sims served with the Guards until he was captured after the fall of Fort Pulaski in April 1862. After his release from an Ohio prison camp, he joined a Georgia volunteer regiment. When Wadley became Railroad Bureau chief, he brought Sims to Richmond with him. Sims worked tirelessly under Wadley and learned a great deal about the problems and needs of Southern railroads.[50]

Like his predecessor, Sims traveled extensively throughout the Confederacy and dispatched his assistants on similar missions. He, too, met with railroad executives—at a conference in Macon, Georgia, in late 1863—and he, too, was disappointed with the results. Not only did few Southern railroaders attend the meeting, but those who did were more interested in boosting charges on government transport than in efforts to coordinate or centralize the system any further.[51] Though stymied, Sims remained optimistic—and sympathetic to the plight of the Southern railroad companies. Sims argued convincingly that the carriers had been early and innocent victims of the war. "Their incomes had been realized from commerce," he wrote, "and when trade was so suddenly cut off, and before our contest had assumed its present gigantic proportions, a period of inactivity in transportation took place which justly alarmed these managers." Contrary to popular belief, Sims contended, the railroad corporate managers were as patriotic and devoted to the war effort as the rank-and-file soldiers. Those capitalists had selflessly encouraged their employees to enlist and had cut rates to serve government needs. The companies had learned, albeit at enormous cost, that inattention to routine maintenance produced most of the delays and problems that hindered the transportation effort. Sims concluded, however, that it was militarily imperative that the authorities in Richmond aid the carriers by furnishing iron ore and by enabling foundries and car shops to manufacture railroad supplies. He also urged that trained railroad mechanics be detailed from the ranks.[52]

Sims's new boss at the Quartermaster Department was his fellow Georgian and good friend Alexander R. Lawton, who endorsed Sims's observations to the War Department. In turn, Secretary of War Seddon reported to Davis that the combination of the federal blockade, heavy use of existing lines, and the continued government monopoly of rolling mills, foundries, and raw materials threatened the operation of the Southern carriers. Though Seddon praised the railroads' "patriotism" in supplying government needs, he noted that "the delusive expectation of the early termination of the war" had led the companies to neglect the augmentation of their stocks. Seddon added that lately, "with more experience, a wiser prescience guides their management and . . . they are sedulously engaged in endeavoring to increase their stock, and to provide for the contingencies of future service." The secretary concluded that to ensure the railroads' cooperation, they had to be required by law—not contract—to give first priority to government freight. He also recommended that Confederate aid to the roads continue and suggested a policy that had been considered several months previously: "Some of the minor roads will have to be sacrificed to keep up the tracks of the leading lines."[53]

Seddon's recommendation that some of the Confederate railroads would have to be abandoned to allow others to continue functioning underscored the status of the rail network at the midpoint of the war. The monopolization of the few extant rolling mills for ordnance production virtually shut off the railroads from domestic sources of iron goods. Disruption of trade with Northern manufacturers, who, before the war, had provided many companies with their engines and rolling stock, compounded the problem. To the officers of the Quartermaster Department and the Railroad Bureau, there was only one avenue left to continue the decrepit Southern railroads in operation: maintain and conserve "by destroying its substance." Such an option was really no option, for the individual companies were not willing to see their lines sacrificed to benefit others, even if it was for the cause. Indeed, suspicious managers probably viewed the government's policy as designed to aid their competitors. But the government had no other choice. The Confederacy's few rolling mills were working overtime for the Ordnance Bureau. In fact, after 1861 the Confederacy did not produce one iron rail for its transportation network; instead it rerolled old iron rails and cannibalized.[54]

Nowhere were the effects of the use and abuse of railroads more evident than in Georgia. As might be anticipated, the large, well-equipped, and well-managed Georgia carriers were tapped early for government use—and mistreatment. The breakdown of the Georgia railroad network began as early as 1862. Conscription, instituted in April of that year, winnowed the ranks of railroad employees and laborers, and the tightening of the Union blockade shut off supplies from abroad. The railroad car shops of the Central and Georgia railroads had shifted their efforts to fulfill government orders for ordnance. Still, the railroads of Georgia chugged along, carrying troops and provisions to the field armies. The constant wear and tear, however, took its toll, and the lines steadily deteriorated.

On paper, the Georgia railroads appeared to be prosperous and strong. John Screven of the Atlantic & Gulf and Savannah, Albany & Gulf railroads reported that those lines together had earned over a quarter of a million dollars during fiscal 1863. The Georgia Railroad paid two dividends of 6 percent and 8 percent, and net profits stood at a hefty $1,042,965. The Western & Atlantic recorded a gross income of $2,186,869, with expenses of only $688,171. The Central Railroad, too, posted large profits and paid stockholders substantial dividends. It is significant that these managers endeavored to protect their stockholders' interests—as good managers were supposed to—but failed to reinvest profits or suspend dividend payments to aid the upkeep of their lines during this period.[55]

As impressive as such reports appeared, the railroad presidents knew better. All voiced concern over the inability to obtain needed supplies and skilled labor to keep the roads in working condition. The increased cost of available supplies was also cause for consternation.

The superintendent of the Western & Atlantic, George Yonge, noted that a ton of pig iron cost $25 in 1860; that same ton in 1863 commanded $225, and by 1864, it would cost $350. Railroad iron had tripled in price from 1860 to 1863, from $50 a ton to $150. That same ton would command a whopping $500 by 1864. Similar increases were to be found on everything from nails to railroad spikes.[56]

Earnings and profits were also reduced by the method of payment. From the beginning, the Georgia railways, in conjunction with other railroads throughout the Confederacy, had resolved to accept payment for government transportation in Confederate bonds and treasury notes. Since the Confederacy was forced to resort to the printing press to obtain adequate monies to keep the government and the general war effort functioning, the plethora of notes in circulation, without sufficient specie to back them up, fueled inflation and rendered due bills, notes, and bonds almost worthless. Some of the Georgia railroads (the Western & Atlantic most consistently) demanded payment in greenbacks or gold. All such entreaties, however, were politely rejected, and the Georgia railroads were forced to accept remuneration in nearly worthless bonds and interest-bearing notes.[57]

When John P. King and the other Georgia railroad executives commented on the run-down condition of their lines, the deterioration of their rolling stock, and their fears for the future, they were not being overly alarmist. The government was fully cognizant of the situation, and even the general population was beginning to appreciate that conditions on the railways were not up to par. The *Augusta Chronicle and Sentinel* expressed "apprehension" over the condition of Georgia's and the South's railroads. The editors of that paper feared that if the war continued for one or two more years, the railroads of the state and region would collapse, noting that "they cannot be expected much longer to be serviceable without extensive repairs."[58] The *Atlanta Southern Confederacy* viewed the deterioration of the railroad network from a different perspective. Planters and farmers had been induced to plant crops to feed the armies in lieu of cotton, yet the derangement in railway transport had made huge surpluses of foodstuffs a financial burden to the growers: produce rotted at depots or in the countryside for want of transportation to the front. Similarly, able-bodied enlistees and conscripts failed to reach battlefields because there were not enough passenger trains. The *Southern Confederacy* acknowledged that seemingly fabulous railroad profits masked "the wear and tear and incessant expense" of operations but added that "[railroads, as] corporate bodies . . . will attend to their individual interests . . . [and] may not feel called upon to go to the extraneous outlays the exigencies of the service require without aid from the Government." The paper went on to castigate the Georgia railroad executives for pursuing shortsighted policies and for failing to anticipate wartime demands more fully. "We call on Messrs. King . . . Scott . . . and Rowland to wake up. Throw off your old fogy notions and come up to the requirements of the times. Infuse a little life and spirit into your offices—quit counting your baskets full of Confederate notes . . . and bring in a cargo or two of railroad supplies, so that your roads may not *run down.*"[59] Such sentiments demonstrate that many Southerners were becoming aware that the railroad managers were more inclined to pursue self-interest—and self-preservation—than patriotic service, especially as the tide of war turned against the Confederacy. In short, pragmatism would prevail over patriotism.

Despite the bleak situation, the Georgia railroads struggled on, attempting to maintain their lines and rolling stock while serving the needs of the civilian and military populations. To remedy the persistent lack of material, the railways in the state organized the Railroad Steamship Company, chartered to run the blockade from Savannah to obtain supplies from Europe. The Central of Georgia went further and established a new machine shop in Macon in 1862 to replace its Savannah facility, which had been taken over by the War Department for the manufacture of ordnance.[60]

Laudable as such efforts were, they failed to remedy an increasingly desperate situation. As the Georgia carriers struggled to sustain themselves, the demands of the government intensified. In the winter of 1863, the Western & Atlantic was threatened with seizure to aid General Braxton Bragg's retreat from middle Tennessee; the Confederate Navy Department decided that the iron on the Atlantic & Gulf would be put to better use in the construction of ironclads; and Federal raids into north Georgia had frightened Governor Brown into petitioning President Davis for a detail of front-line troops to protect the Etowah Iron Works, the Atlanta Depot, and the Western & Atlantic Railroad from damage. By the end of the summer, R. R. Cuyler of the Central of Georgia was functioning as railroad "czar" of Georgia. Secretary of War Seddon had decided that only the Georgia rail system was sufficiently equipped to carry provisions, troops, and supplies to all Confederate forces in Virginia, Tennessee, and South Carolina.[61]

While Cuyler attempted to marshal south Georgia's supplies and funnel them northward to the war theater, Governor Brown was again fighting off the Confederate high command's efforts to impress the state road and its equipment. Brown complained that the periodic impressment of the Western & Atlantic's rolling stock for use on other roads had left the line unable to support the Army of Tennessee's movements in Tennessee. He alternately apologized for his inability to render more aid and condemned those same officials for policies that had produced such a state of affairs. By the end of 1863, the governor was threatening to stop all Western & Atlantic service on government account unless payment for service was received and cars seized and sent elsewhere were returned.[62]

The new year did not witness any appreciable change in the physical condition of the Georgia railroads. Though the press reported that the railways were "sedulously engaged in endeavoring to increase their stocks and to provide for the contingencies of future service and loss," railroad managers were aware that the roads would be hard-pressed to meet the demands of the spring campaigns.[63] The situation was especially ominous in Georgia. After a decisive Confederate victory at Chickamauga in September 1863, the Army of Tennessee had placed Union forces in Chattanooga under siege. Then a dramatic Union assault up the rocky face of Missionary Ridge had forced Confederate commander Braxton Bragg to retreat into northern Georgia. The defeat at Chattanooga was a twin blow to the Confederates: they had frittered away the fruits of Chickamauga, and now, with their retreat from Chattanooga, they had given up twenty-five important miles of the Western & Atlantic Railroad to Federal control.

With the Union army poised at the gateway to the Deep South, Georgians grew uneasy. The Western & Atlantic became the pivotal railroad for the Confederate supply effort in the western theater. Provisions from the rich agricultural regions of the southwestern section of the state were funneled to the Army of Tennessee via the Southwestern and the Western & Atlantic railroads. Those same lines, in conjunction with the Georgia and the Central of Georgia roads, provided the troops with guns, ammunition, and artillery. If the army was forced to retreat from its base at Dalton, Georgia, down the Western & Atlantic, the other Georgia railroads would be threatened. Moreover, the substantial productive capacity of the state's manufacturing and agricultural sectors would be open to Federal destruction.

Governor Brown and the new Confederate commander, General Joseph E. Johnston, were fully aware of the dangers of the situation.

Unfortunately, policies the government had pursued with regard to the Western & Atlantic—the seizure and dispersal of engines and rolling stock to other roads—came back to haunt the Confederate general and the Georgia governor. Beginning in January 1864 and continuing through July and the Atlanta campaign, Johnston complained unceasingly to Brown and to Richmond authorities that the Western & Atlantic was so badly mismanaged that his troops were not adequately provisioned. The railroad's superintendent, George Phillips, assured Brown that all the supplies requisitioned had been transported to the Army of Tennessee as expeditiously as humanly—and mechanically—possible. Brown, in turn, defended his state's road and informed both Johnston and Confederate Quartermaster General Lawton that supplies could have been transported had it not been for "military orders" that had "carried off rolling stock and engines till we have not enough to meet a heavy demand for transportation." Brown even petitioned Jefferson Davis for the return or replacement of the impressed Western & Atlantic cars and engines. "If you deprive me of the engines and cars of the road," Brown warned, "and do not replace them, I cannot be responsible for a failure to transport supplies to the army."[64]

Charges of mismanagement and negligence continued to be bandied about in Georgia and in Richmond. Allegations that "there seems to be a desire to work for the road's interest rather than sacrifice all for the country's cause," though accurate, were in some ways off the mark.[65] The Georgia railroads, like their counterparts elsewhere, were being called upon to render service that was impossible to provide in 1864, given the broken-down condition of the cars and locomotives. Davis, Lawton, and others might plead, exhort, and demand that the major lines devote time, money, and attention to railroad repairs and reconstruction, but words alone would not produce iron and skilled mechanics to attend to such repairs. Governor Brown came to the crux of the problem when he responded to one of Davis's appeals to "heal thyself": "You do not mention where the *material* to be used in 'repairing and building new Engines and Cars' is to be had. Confederate officers have the control of almost all the iron mills in the Confederacy, and it is next to impossible for the railroad superintendents to get . . . from the mills, the smallest amount of materials with which repairs, absolutely necessary to the present use of the Roads can be made."[66] In a similar vein, President John P. King of the Georgia Railroad spoke for all the state's railroad executives when he considered the deterioration of equipment to be a clear loss and that the "more business it does the more money it loses, and the greatest favor that could be conferred on it—if public wants permitted—would be the privilege of quitting business until the end of the War!"[67]

Unfortunately, "public wants" and government requirements would not allow the Georgia Railroad or any other state or Southern line to "quit business." The War Department and Quartermaster Department did, however, attempt to alleviate the crisis. Railroad Bureau chief Sims pleaded with Quartermaster General Lawton to impress upon the Richmond authorities the need for mechanics to be detailed to the principal lines and for raw materials to be supplied to the roads. The War Department promulgated special orders to the effect that military transport was to receive top priority on all lines. Other officials again advanced recommendations to nationalize Southern carriers, and the War Department again determined to sacrifice secondary connections to maintain the functioning of the Confederacy's main carriers in Virginia and Georgia. This latest flurry of activity, however, could not ease the chaos that characterized the Confederate transportation system.[68]

While the Georgia roads struggled to continue service, the Union army under the command of General William T. Sherman was poised to knock to pieces what little life was left in the Georgia network. For months, Johnston's Confederate army tried to delay the Federal advance but could not. Johnston was relieved of command 17 July 1864 and was replaced by Lieutenant General John B. Hood. Hood's ill-fated offensive outside the city led to his decision to evacuate Atlanta on 31 August. The fall of Atlanta on 1 September produced severe repercussions. It was not just a psychological blow; the city had been the Confederacy's "turntable," its chief production and distribution point for the western armies. Moreover, Hood ordered that all the provisions, rolling stock, and war matériel that could not be moved be destroyed. This was a severe blow, for the goods lost in the evacuation and surrender of the city represented sources of transportation and supply that were desperately needed by Confederate armies in both the eastern and western theaters of the war. Hood absolved himself of all blame for the debacle and charged the Atlanta quartermaster with "wanton neglect." According to Hood, Lieutenant M. B. McMicken "had more than ample time to remove the whole . . . I am reliably informed that he is too much addicted to drink of late to attend to his duties."[69]

Regardless of who was responsible for the failure to remove all the quartermaster stores, the damage was severe. Governor Brown reported that three engines and eighteen cars had been destroyed at the Atlanta roundhouse; seventeen passenger cars, thirty freight cars, and four engines were consumed in the raid at Gordon and Griswoldville. The other major lines reported similar dire news. The majority of the equipment of the Atlanta & West Point Railroad had been moved when Sherman invaded Georgia. Still, one engine, fifty-five cars, and eighteen miles of crucial track were lost with Hood's evacuation. The Georgia Railroad's machine shop, roundhouse, cars, and engines went up in flames, and bridges on the line in the vicinity of Atlanta were wrecked. The litany could be repeated for the Central of Georgia and the Macon & Western. A Georgia newspaper, after assessing the fall of Atlanta and the heavy loss inflicted on the railroads, offered a classic understatement when it observed: "A few more losses of this kind will pretty well use up our means of transportation."[70]

The loss of Atlanta was a severe blow, but Sherman's March to the Sea knocked the Georgia railway network out of the war. Intent upon "making Georgia howl," Sherman destroyed what remained of Atlanta in November 1864, severed his lines of communication, and advanced, virtually unopposed, to Savannah. The Federals lived off the land and destroyed any supplies, factories, and railroads that would aid the Confederate war effort. As one historian has aptly concluded, Sherman's march, "not Appomattox, was the Confederate Götterdämmerung."[71] Federal troops pried railroad tracks loose and heated and twisted them into "Sherman's hairpins." They torched idled rolling stock. They left nothing but smoldering ruins and blackened chimneys to mark where depots and water towers once stood.

As Sherman's "bummers" eviscerated the Confederacy, the Richmond government struggled to maintain what remained of the Southern railroads—and the Confederate war effort. It was a perilous situation. Lee's army, huddled in the trenches around Petersburg, was in desperate need of supplies, but in 1865, one of its chief sources of provisions, the rich agricultural region of southern Georgia, appeared lost forever. Trains did rumble in sporadically from Augusta, but their cargo was insufficient to meet the army's needs.[72]

Meanwhile, the railroad executives were informing Railroad Bureau chief Sims that government transportation charges were being increased to offset continued losses. The government also made efforts to construct short connecting lines that would tap the Deep South's agricultural regions to supply the troops. Moreover, various bureau chiefs were lobbying to have engineers and railroad workers detailed from the front lines to aid the transportation effort.[73] The *chef d'oeuvre* of this flurry of official activity, however, was the proposal of a "Bill to increase transportation efficiency." Beginning in January 1865, the Confederate Congress began deliberations on legislation to "facilitate Government transportation." In February, the bill passed the House and Senate and was forwarded to the president for his signature. Its provisions suggested that Congress finally had seen fit to invest the War Department with the power to regulate the railroads: the secretary of war was allowed to seize any line if the company refused government transport. Where rolling stock was idled, the War Department was empowered to impress it and send it where needed; government freight was considered top priority, and all railroad personnel became government employees. The Congress also appropriated a nonexistent $21 million for railroad rehabilitation and reconstruction.[74]

The passage of the 1865 railroad law marked a decided but belated shift in government policy. Central authority and direction were finally to be vested in one branch of the government. Unfortunately for the Southern war effort, it was too little, too late. Indeed, any effort to remedy the railroad transportation situation in 1865 was doomed, for the keystone of the Confederate transportation system, the Georgia railroad network, had been shattered.

There can be no doubt that the collapse of the Southern railroad system contributed significantly to the final defeat of the Confederacy. Lacking raw materials and skilled workmen to maintain the rail lines and rolling stock that the South did possess, the Confederacy was forced to destroy its substance to maintain itself.[75] For that failure, government officials and railroad executives must shoulder the blame. Military and civilian authorities committed repeatedly what one scholar has termed the "cardinal sin" of logistics: they refused to countenance the centralization of authority over the various railroads. Perhaps the dogma of states' rights and the spirit of John C. Calhoun haunted them; perhaps the idea of private property was so paramount that any suggestion of nationalization and government control was tantamount to heresy. Whatever the reason, the Confederacy's railroad managers were unwilling to place Confederate concerns over private interests: pragmatism and self-preservation eventually transcended devotion to the Southern cause. Moreover, official Richmond evinced little willingness to compel railroads to give military needs consistently top priority. Those who argued for the implementation of such a policy (and William M. Wadley comes to mind immediately) were dismissed outright or relegated to a department in which they could do little harm.

The government and the railroad managers also contributed to the demise of the transportation network through their failure to adopt long-range plans for the principal carriers. The Quartermaster Department and the railway presidents refused to plan ahead. In the early days, when arms and ordnance were deemed top priority, company rolling mills and car shops contracted to manufacture gun carriages and field artillery. Sensing lucrative profits, railroad managers who possessed such facilities welcomed government orders. But as they manufactured armor plate for ironclads and cast twelve-pound Napoleons, the rolling stock of the major lines deteriorated and replacement cars were nowhere to be found. Apparently, it never dawned on official Richmond that ordnance would serve little purpose if it could not be transported to the front.

Georgia railroads provide a microscopic view of the experience of Southern carriers during the war. The major Georgia lines entered the war in a prosperous condition. The Central of Georgia and Georgia railroads each maintained its own car shops so they were less dependent on outside sources for rolling stock and engines than were other lines in the South. The managers of those roads acted in concert with their counterparts from other companies at the various railroad conventions held throughout the war. The Georgia executives denounced government control but welcomed government aid; they "donated" their car shops and rolling stock to military service but demanded greater remuneration for their contributions. Finally, they saw the roads they guarded so fiercely from government monopoly destroyed by the invading Federal army.

Although it is easy in retrospect to condemn railroad officials such as John P. King and Richard R. Cuyler for the policies they pursued during the war, it is also necessary to evaluate those policies according to the prevailing standard of railroad management. Those railroad managers continued to operate their companies in conformity to antebellum notions of the railroad's function in the area it served. Although such strategies had worked well in the past, they proved inadequate in a time of war.

Georgia's railroaders were professional managers whose income and reputation depended upon the successful operation of their companies. They had established solid and profitable concerns because they knew "when to be conservative and when to push for change."[76] Each executive was well versed in railroad management; each chose able subordinates to survey, construct, and maintain his road; and each realized the innovative potential the railroad possessed. Georgia's extensive railroad network was tangible evidence of their success.

Yet those very successes often led railroad managers to a limited outlook. In part, this was a consequence of their achievement. Until 1860, most managers believed that a railroad's function transcended state boundaries only when far-flung markets justified such a move. After the completion and consolidation of their lines, Georgia's railroad managers became *managerial* rather than *entrepreneurial*. They operated their roads with a view to increasing the wealth and standing of their respective local communities and to ensuring profits and dividends for the road's directors and stockholders. The entrepreneurial function of railroaders gained ascendance only when competitors threatened to divert goods and hence profits from the company.[77]

When war came in 1861, Georgia's railroad managers were forced to adopt a less parochial and conservative management policy. The Confederate government's desire to coordinate Southern railroad operations brought Georgia's railroad managers into intimate contact with their counterparts from other companies. Through the medium of railroad conventions, Georgia's railroaders gradually expanded their notions of railroads to an industrywide focus. Acting in concert with their counterparts from other states, they offered their service to the Confederacy. Moreover, they became aware of railroad problems and needs and attempted to solve those problems with a unified, industrywide plan. Implicit (and often explicit) in that plan were the railroad managers' notions about the government's role in the economy. Like their counterparts in the North, Southern railroad managers continued to subscribe to classical economic ideas that viewed government action with suspicion. Confederate railroaders saw the government's role as one of aid, not control. They reaffirmed that unspoken credo at the various railroad meetings held throughout the course of the war. As one scholar has observed, for them, "what business did was economic and developed the country while government action was usually negative and parasitical."[78] Government centralization and control were anathema to them as a radical deviation from accepted notions of government-business relations and the role of the government in the economic life of the country. Because of these ideas, Southern railroad managers failed to convert their industry-wide focus into a broader national focus that could relate railroad strategy and decision making to Confederate national wants. Georgia and the South's railroad managers failed to sustain the war effort adequately because their conception of the managerial function was at variance with military needs. Similarly, the Confederate government failed because it accepted those prescribed managerial functions until it was too late. Although Richmond possessed the power to force drastic departures in railroad management and control, to force a national as opposed to an industrywide orientation, it failed to use those powers in regard to the railroads. Richmond's policy was curious in light of its exercise of centralized, regulatory control in other realms of the mobilization. Indeed, Emory Thomas is correct when he argues that "in the name of wartime emergency, the Davis administration . . . all but destroyed the political philosophy which underlay the Southern republic." Ironically, the administration would embrace such a revolutionary turn only in the areas of ordnance production and quartermaster supply. The railroads would remain exempt from that policy, and the failure to subject those companies to the same oversight as munitions makers and uniform suppliers would prove disastrous to the Southern cause. In this case, consistency would not have been the hobgoblin of a small mind.[79]

The failure of railroad managers to adapt to the changed circumstances of war was not unique to the Confederacy. Northern railroad leaders demonstrated a similar intransigence to government efforts toward centralization and control. They increased tariff schedules at government expense, resisted the establishment of a railroad bureau, and protested any suggestion that the government should seize and manage the roads. William Wadley's Northern counterpart, Herman Haupt, also recommended the organization of a central railroad bureau to coordinate all military transportation and management of the roads, the use of trained railroad men to oversee railroad operations, and the exercise of broad powers to compel private railroad companies to accede to the military's demands. But Haupt's recommendations were never put into practice, and, like Wadley, he was dismissed from office. Wadley's and Haupt's ideas were so alien to accepted attitudes concerning railroad management that they were either rejected or ignored. Only at the very end, when war had altered many ideas and institutions, could such ideas of centralized control be countenanced. By that time, it was too late for the Confederacy. The Confederate railroad managers' limited focus and their adherence to laissez-faire doctrines rendered the railroads impotent in meeting Southern military needs.[80]

Any evaluation of the Georgia railroad managers and their peers is necessarily mixed. They did sustain the troops, but not as efficiently as possible. They did offer their services to the Confederate government, but at an increasingly high cost as the war progressed. They failed to husband adequately the resources at hand. They refused to countenance strict government oversight of their operations. Perhaps it is the ultimate irony that the Georgia railroad managers failed because they exercised their managerial function so effectively: they refused to allow the government to play the role of manager, to centralize managerial functions in Richmond, and to run all Southern railroads. But the Confederate government, imbued with similar notions about the railroads, manifested neither the interest, nor the desire, nor the capacity, once Wadley was dismissed, to assume that function.

Notwithstanding their lack of supplies and labor, the Georgia railroads rendered noteworthy service to the Southern war effort. Despite its ultimate failure, the Georgia transportation system did sustain the field armies, however imperfectly, for four years. When the Confederate cause went down to defeat in April 1865, those railroads were part of the demise. Yet those Georgia railroad managers who had presided over one of the South's most comprehensive networks were not destined to stay defeated. Even as the Confederacy writhed in its final stages, railroad engineers were at work. The men who had built the Georgia system were determined that they would rebuild.

Peachtree Street, Atlanta, 1864 (National Archives)

Ruins of Confederate engine house, Atlanta, 1864 (National Archives)

Ruins of Confederate rolling mill, Atlanta, 1864 (National Archives)

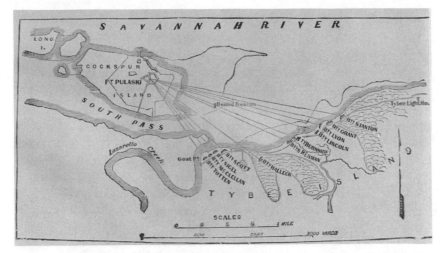

Map of Fort Pulaski, 1861 (Paul F. Mottelay and T. Campbell-Copeland, *The Soldier in Our Civil War: A Pictorial History of the Conflict . . .* , 2 vols. [Boston: Thompson, Brown & Co., 1885].)

Augusta Powder Works (Library of Congress)

Confederate evacuation of Savannah, 1864 (Paul F. Mottelay and T. Campbell-Copeland, *The Soldier in Our Civil War: A Pictorial History of the Conflict . . .* , 2 vols. [Boston: Thompson, Brown & Co., 1885].)

5 *Defeat and Rebuilding*

People in Georgia and elsewhere in the South greeted the fourth year of war with uncertainty. The bravado and gaiety of 1861 had vanished as the demands of the Confederate war machine grew. By 1864, the conflict had become total: every available resource of men and matériel had been tapped, and no sector of Southern society had been left untouched. Yet, in spite of the sacrifice and innovation, defeat seemed likely. Many had grown fainthearted, for the cost of mobilizing and continuing the contest seemed inordinately high. Others were determined to fight on to the bitter end. When it came, those who had stepped forward to mobilize Georgia would be called upon to reconstruct the state.

Both Southerners and Northerners generally acknowledged that the military campaigns begun in the spring of 1864 would be decisive. Georgians, however, had little idea of how those campaigns would affect them. The state had become the Confederacy's economic backbone. Established manufacturers and aspiring industrialists had created a substantial military-industrial complex, particularly in Atlanta, Augusta, and Columbus. Entrepreneurs had produced everything from bullets to buttons, and the output of the various firms had been carried to the troops on Georgia's railroads. It is not an exaggeration to say that Georgia's military centers and its railroads permitted the South to continue the fight. Their destruction formed the keystone of the Federal high command's strategy in 1864.[1]

On 1 May 1864 the army of General William T. Sherman just south of Chattanooga began to move against Confederate General Joseph E. Johnston's Army of Tennessee, which was bivouacked in northern Georgia near Dalton. For the next two and a half months, these adversaries fought and maneuvered their way through Dalton, Resaca, Calhoun, Adairsville, and Cassville. By the middle of July, Johnston's army had been forced into the outer defenses of Atlanta. Sherman's rapid advance and Johnston's apparent inability or unwillingness to stop him led President Davis to respond to pressure from Governor Brown and others. Davis had been dubious about the military prowess of Joe Johnston since the summer of 1861, and now he decided that the general had to go. On 17 July he relieved Johnston of his command and replaced him with General John Bell Hood, the crippled veteran of the Army of Northern Virginia, who had been serving as a corps commander under Johnston.

Hood's reputation as a fighter was well earned, and his brilliance as a divisional commander under both Lee and Johnston had led to his elevation to overall command in the West. He did not disappoint his Richmond superiors, who desired a more aggressive commander. Hood immediately launched a series of attacks that failed to dislodge Sherman but so crippled Confederate strength that the Army of Tennessee had to withdraw into Atlanta's inner defenses. From that moment, it was only a matter of time before Atlanta succumbed to the Federals.

The Confederate army's appearance in the city and the commencement of Federal shelling produced panic among the citizenry. All seemed thunderstruck that the war had come to Atlanta. One merchant noted, "All the Govt stores and Hospitals are ordered away and . . . the citizens . . . have left . . . [or] are leaving." Another resident wrote his wife that "the military situation is a grave one and . . . our State is in great peril—if the army allows itself to be . . . besieged. . . . For the first time since I came up here I feel low spirited and despondent."[2] It seemed clear to all that Atlanta could not long withstand a siege by a force that outmanned and outgunned the defenders.

Hood apparently came to the same conclusion. Unwilling to surrender his army, and mistakenly believing that Federal movements toward Jonesboro, to the south, presaged a Union withdrawal, Hood ordered the evacuation of Atlanta and the destruction of military stores and equipment that could not be transported to safety. The retreat and destruction commenced 1 September.[3]

Hood's troopers proved adept at their demolition duties. Storekeeper Samuel P. Richards, an eyewitness, reported their work in his diary on that fateful September day:

This was a day of terror and a night of dread. About noon came tidings of a severe fight on the Macon RR and that our forces were worsted and the city [was] to be evacuated at once. Then began a scramble among the inhabitants thereof to get away. . . . If there had been any doubt . . . that Atlanta was about to be given up it would have been removed when they saw the depots of Govt grain and food thrown open and the contents distributed among the citizens . . . gratis. . . . The RR cars and engines were all run up to one place in order to be fired just as the army left. Five locomotives and 85 cars . . . were to be burned.[4]

What mobs did not seize and destroy the Confederate army did. One observer noted that the city appeared an "inferno" when the Confederate cavalry blew up the railroad shops. The foundries and ammunition depots were also put to the torch to avoid Federal capture. Citizens not scampering off in search of "hams, side-meat and sacks of provisions" were appalled by the Confederate-directed destruction, as "the tumult and wreckage was not expected."[5]

Atlanta Mayor James M. Calhoun's formal surrender of the city on 2 September and the arrival of the dreaded Yankees shortly thereafter were almost anticlimactic. Sherman and his subordinates restored order to the mob-ridden city and set up camp for their occupation. Atlantans who had not fled from their homes during the initial bombardment grew accustomed to seeing "only Yankee uniforms" on the streets. A Union officer observed, however, that "the streets are empty. Beautiful roses bloom in the gardens of the houses, but a terrible stillness and solitude cover all, depressing the hearts even of those who are glad to destroy it."[6]

Residents of Atlanta did not have the opportunity to get acquainted with their captors. On 11 September, Sherman issued Special Orders No. 70, which tersely stated that the city was to be vacated of all except those associated with the United States Army.[7] Within a fortnight, 446 families were moved about twenty miles south of Atlanta to Rough and Ready, Georgia. Their removal prompted a bitter exchange between Generals Sherman and Hood about the nature of war and prompted more than one Southerner to exclaim: "The fiend Sherman has done what not even the Czar of Russia has done in Poland—. . . the entire population of Atlanta [evicted] from their homes to . . . live as they may. . . . The wretch[,] after raining shot[,] shell & fire among them for 50 Days, now drives them forth like the people of Israel."[8]

The Federals' sojourn in the city ended in mid-November, when Sherman determined to strike into the heart of the state. On 11 November, Sherman directed chief engineer Orlando Poe to destroy all matériel that might be salvaged to aid the Confederate war effort. Sherman saw simple justice at work in the Federal demolition of Atlanta: " 'This city has done and contributed more to carry on and sustain the war than any other, save perhaps Richmond. We have been fighting Atlanta all of the time . . . and have been capturing guns, wagons, etc., etc., marked "Atlanta" and made here all of the time: and now since they have done so much to destroy us and our government we have to destroy them.' "[9]

Destroy them he did. Fifteen fires were set to complete the destruction begun by the Confederates just two months previously. As Sherman's troopers marched out of Atlanta to the strains of "John Brown's Body," the proud Gate City lay in ashes. Railroad lines were torn up, factories and storehouses were gutted, and all but about four hundred private residences were in ruins. As Poe reported, "For military purposes, the city of Atlanta has ceased to exist."[10]

Georgians and Confederates could not bewail the loss of Atlanta for long because the Federal juggernaut was still abroad in the state. More frightening still, no one—Federal or Confederate—knew where Sherman's troopers were headed next: south to Macon or Columbus, southeast to the state capital at Milledgeville, or east to Augusta.

Augusta was thrown into a panic. That city, with its arsenal, powder works, and a multitude of other ordnance-related establishments and factories, seemed an inviting target for the fast-marching Yankees. General George Washington Rains sent numerous and persistent pleas to Richmond urging the necessity of Augusta's defense. Augusta, Rains argued, "cannot be lost without the loss of Georgia, and that would be fatal to the Confederacy." Rains led local efforts to bolster Augusta's defenses, supervising the placement of obstructions in the Savannah River and organizing local home guard units, composed largely of factory workers. To deceive the enemy—and protect the city—news accounts purposely and erroneously reported that all machinery and stores from the powder works and arsenal had been packed up and sent to Columbus, Georgia. By the end of November 1864, the *Augusta Chronicle and Sentinel* reported: "AUGUSTA . . . the great commercial centre of the Confederacy, now has the appearance of a vast military camp. The stores are being closed and their owners are shouldering their muskets. . . . Everything betokens a united and determined . . . resistance."[11]

Sherman's swath of destruction did not include Augusta. After taking the state capital at Milledgeville (the Federals tarried long enough to "convene" the legislature to repeal Georgia's ordinance of secession) and feinting toward Macon, Sherman's army concentrated and headed for the sea. On 13 December, Fort McAllister, on the Savannah

River, fell, forcing Confederate defender General William Hardee to abandon Savannah and evacuate his troops to the north. On 21 December, Sherman telegraphed President Lincoln to present Savannah and all its wares as a "Christmas gift."[12]

The Union army of occupation found Savannah to be a "magnificent prize." The city contained thousands of bales of cotton, a "complete arsenal," steamboats, railroad cars and engines, hundreds of field guns, and powder magazines full of ammunition.[13] As one historian has noted, "Savannah yielded all too graciously." One Union officer remarked that "[a] foreigner visiting the city would not suppose that it was so lately a prize of battle." Most citizens who had fled had left in 1862, when Federal forces had first threatened the city. Those who remained had struggled through lean times; hence an army that could pump money into sagging businesses was not totally abhorrent. A visitor, unfamiliar with Savannah's prosperous economy before the war, wrote to a friend that "the effects and ravages of war are noticeable everywhere . . . this is a most miserable hole." Another remarked that all the residents he encountered believed that the fall of Atlanta and the March to the Sea had "closed the war so far as they are concerned. They hope and pray that our army will march through South Carolina, which region they denounce . . . as being the cause of the war."[14]

They got their wish. On 1 February 1865, Sherman moved out of the city and headed for the cradle of secession, South Carolina. The Union general left behind a state cut in two, its industrial centers either reduced to rubble or under Federal occupation. Union efforts to cripple the Empire State of the South did not, however, end with the March to the Sea. The vital city of Columbus, in the southwestern quadrant of the state, continued to churn out guns and munitions and hence was targeted for destruction by Union cavalry under the command of Brigadier General James Wilson.

Wilson began his campaign by launching an attack at Selma, Alabama, and his troopers then advanced virtually unimpeded to Montgomery. The Columbus press and citizenry expressed little concern as the Yankees approached, for all believed they would strike south toward Mobile. Once Montgomery fell, however, the popular mood changed. On 16 April 1865, Wilson was at the gates of Columbus, determined to "destroy everything within reach that could be made useful for [the] continuance of the Rebellion."[15]

Wilson carried out his plan with ruthless efficiency. Local troops were easily brushed aside by the Union veterans. By 17 April, the

Confederate arsenal, the naval works, quartermaster depot, 15 locomotives, 250 freight cars, 2 powder magazines, and 3 foundries were all in flames. The Columbus paper mill and the city's ten flour and textile mills were also put to the torch. As Wilson's men headed north toward Macon, local mobs took over and finished what the Yankees had begun. A Union soldier recorded the scene for posterity: " 'It is a strange scene, and it is interesting to watch the free play of human nature. Soldiers are going for substantials, women for apparel and the niggers for anything red. There is evident demoralization among the females. They frantically join . . . in the chaos, and seem crazy for plunder.' "[16]

Georgia militia and home guard units harassed but could not stall Federal forces. In the spring of 1865, Georgians from Columbus to Augusta knew that the end was at hand, and that realization led to demoralization, local riots, and general lawlessness. The end finally did come when word reached the state in May that General Robert E. Lee had surrendered his Army of Northern Virginia to General Ulysses S. Grant in Virginia and General Joseph E. Johnston had capitulated to Sherman in North Carolina. President Davis and his cabinet disregarded the Confederate military's actions. Although on the run, Davis urged Southerners to continue to resist the invaders. Such entreaties were of no avail. Exhausted physically and economically, Georgians had had enough. It was time to accept defeat, to tally the losses, and to assess the wreckage four years of total war had wrought.

War had been cruel to Georgia. Lush farmland had been turned into battlefields; banking capital was wiped out; over one-quarter of the state's 1,420 miles of railroad was destroyed. Factories and mills were reduced to rubble or severely damaged. Cities were wastelands, and $272 million in property had been lost by the emancipation of the slaves alone. The state's comptroller general, who had the thankless task of assessing the disaster, concluded that "almost four-fifths of the entire wealth of Georgia had been either destroyed or rendered unproductive."[17] The most desolate sections of the state were the areas that lay in the path taken by General Sherman. He had cut a swath of destruction three hundred miles long and forty miles wide from Atlanta to Savannah. Crops and livestock that could not be consumed had been randomly destroyed. Houses, mills, and plantations had been put to the torch, and railroads were torn up, heated, and twisted into "Sherman's hairpins" (see Map 2).[18]

To the weary soldiers and refugees who tramped home, and to the

Map 2. Georgia Campaigns, 1864

inhabitants who had lived through the whirlwind of Sherman, the despoliation must have appeared ubiquitous. A Georgia woman recorded in her diary that "the desolation was more complete than anything we had . . . seen." She went on to note: "The props that held society up are broken. Everything is in a state of disorganization and tumult. We have no currency, no law save the primitive code that might makes right. We are in a transition from war to subjugation, and it is far worse than was the transition from peace to war."[19] An Augustan wrote to his Savannah relatives that "we are all . . . as poor as poverty can make us." Savannah, too, was changed. As one resident noted: "Externally the city is the same; but the iron has entered its soul, its whole social organization has been subverted. . . . Its rich have become poor, and new aspirants for wealth and honor rise upon the ruins of its ancient inhabitants."[20]

Elsewhere, personal ruin was matched by physical ruin. Atlanta, according to one resident, "beggars description . . . the angel of destruction seemed still to hover over the apparently hopeless wreck, making it . . . a fit habitation only for bats and owls." The ruin everywhere must have seemed irreparable. One Georgian, assessing conditions in the summer of 1865, summed up the sentiments of most when he wrote: "At present, I see no future for the South; all is dark, and Hope itself seems to have abandoned my unhappy section."[21]

That Georgians wanted to be left alone to heal their wounds was understandable but impossible. To ensure that the former rebels accepted their defeat with obedience, if not humility, U.S. troops remained in the state and region. The army of occupation was not, however, an unwelcome millstone. Federal troops represented a needed source of revenue to desolate towns. More important, Federal authorities helped to rebuild some sections of the state's railroads and aided the recovery of scattered rolling stock.[22] Still, Georgians knew that the full restoration of the state's railroad network depended upon home initiative. Only by reestablishing trade links and by rebuilding the roads that served Georgia's commercial and industrial centers could any semblance of prosperity and normality return. Hence Georgia's railroad managers, who had tendered their services to the Confederacy, reemerged to restore the state's rail network.

In the wake of the devastation, men such as John P. King of the Georgia Railroad, William M. Wadley, who took over management of the Central of Georgia, and Campbell Wallace, who supervised the Western & Atlantic, assumed the burden of reconstructing the industry with the same intensity they had demonstrated in creating it in the 1840s. They faced a daunting challenge, for Sherman's "bummers" had done their job well. Tracks had been torn up and iron heated and twisted into grotesque shapes. Depots, roundhouses, bridges, cars, engines, and rolling mills had been blown up or burned to render them useless. The state-owned Western & Atlantic was destroyed from Fairburn, near Atlanta, to Madison. The Georgia Railroad was torn up for eighty miles, from Atlanta to the Oconee River, and virtually all of its depots in that region were ruined. The Macon & Western fared a little better in that only twenty-one miles of its track were destroyed. The Savannah-based Central of Georgia suffered the most from the invaders. The entire road from Gordon to Savannah, a distance of over one hundred miles, was torn up, and other damage had been done on the Central's spurs to Eatonton and Millen.[23]

Mutilation of the tracks was not the only disaster that hit the Georgia railroad system. The rail carriers had also lost precious rolling stock. The Western & Atlantic's master of transportation reported in October 1865 that 250 boxcars were "in bad condition and pretty well run down." Only 2 of the 47 engines were considered in "good order." The Macon & Western listed 18 cars and 3 engines lost. The Georgia Railroad had 378 "utterly worthless cars," and 22 of 51 engines serviceable. Overall, an estimated 300 cars were lost or destroyed. The Georgia Railroad's antebellum rival, the Central, reported that "all the Cars belonging to the Road were scattered from Thomasville, Georgia, to Wilmington, North Carolina and without exception, [are] in a most dilapidated condition." To underscore its losses, the Central noted that before the war, it possessed 729 cars; in 1865, the number stood at 537.[24]

John P. King of the Georgia Railroad must have been struck by the similarities between his position in the spring of 1865 and that in 1841, when he became president of the road. Both periods were characterized by tight money, expensive materials, and high labor costs. In 1841, King had used his personal fortune to complete the projected Georgia Railroad. King thus probably had an even greater interest in the rebuilding of the road: not only was he the Georgia Railroad's chief manager, he was also its part-owner. This personal stake in a railroad was the exception rather than the rule in railroad management circles: virtually no railroad presidents held ownership in the company they managed. King's vested interest, coupled with his presidency of the company, undoubtedly played a key role in his rebuilding strategies. His personal success and the success of the Georgia Railroad were inextricably linked. Hence King's perceptions of opportunities would be predicated on his own financial interests and those of his company.[25]

King's greatest task was to reassemble the Georgia Railroad's scattered rolling stock and to assess how many cars and engines were needed to operate at prewar levels. While the cars were being rounded up, the road's machine shop in Atlanta was rebuilt and portions of the destroyed roadbed were relaid. The Georgia Railroad was operational by May 1865, and by the beginning of 1866 traffic on the line started to return to normal. King reported in late March 1866 that the road had earned, in gross receipts, $1,155,397. Expenses amounted to $640,478, leaving the company a net profit of over $500,000. King continued to push the Georgia road to regain its hefty antebellum business through the late 1860s. The first two years of peace witnessed an increase of net earnings at a rate of 12.5 percent per annum. In those same two years, the number of rolling stock increased from 70 to 399 cars and engines from 12 to 28. The company built nine new depots and laid 283,900 new cross ties. All improvements were financed from the road's profits—earned at the expense of shippers, who discovered that the Georgia Railroad's rates were significantly above prewar and wartime standards. Stockholders, however, approved of the road's new rate structure: not only did it pay for the line's reconstruction, it also paid them yearly dividends ranging from 4 to 6 percent. Credit reporters noted as early as December 1865 how rapidly the Georgia Railroad was recovering. In that month, the company's stock was valued at "75[c] on the $1 . . . wor[th] 74c."[26]

As repairs progressed and business returned to normal, the Georgia Railroad continued to make money for its stockholders. By the spring of 1869, the road was operating 47 engines and 498 cars. Expenses remained high—the company spent three-quarters of a million dollars for fiscal 1868–69 for new engines and buildings alone—but net profits averaged $500,000, and sizable dividends continued to be paid.[27]

King moved to consolidate his company's position by continuing to operate the Atlanta & West Point and the Macon & Augusta railroads. Those subsidiary corporations were also refurbished and rebuilt, and they, too, proved to be profitable investments for stockholders. By the early 1870s, King presided over a company that compared favorably with its antebellum status. Physical and financial devastation was only a memory. The Georgia Railroad was "one of the strongest corporations in the State. . . . Its assets am[oun]t to 7 mill[ion]," and its credit stood at "A No. 1."[28] The almost astonishingly rapid recovery of the Georgia Railroad demonstrated that the managerial spirit, the drive to link markets and hence stimulate growth and prosperity, had not been crushed by war or defeat.

The Central of Georgia Railroad underwent a similar transformation. This rival of the Georgia Railroad, however, entered the Reconstruction era with an added handicap. The Central's able president, Richard R. Cuyler, had died in April 1865, leading some officials of the company to believe that "his health was undermined and his death precipitated through his great solicitude for and efforts to secure the safety" of his road. Superintendent George Adams reported to the acting president, John W. Anderson, that of 292 miles of road, only 151 were in use. Bridges, depots, and rolling stock were masses of rubble. Adams did note, however, that the Central's Savannah car shop was intact and ready for reassembly and that repairs begun by Lemuel P. Grant in November 1864 were progressing smoothly. Contracts for new rails and for relaying 139 miles of track Sherman had destroyed had been consummated, but delays had blocked the completion of repairs. Shortages of labor and raw materials, the twin bugaboos that had haunted all Southern railroads during the war, continued to plague the Central in the immediate postwar period.[29]

Conditions on the Central took a dramatic turn for the better late in 1865. Problems of reconstruction remained, but the company had at its helm a new and dynamic manager: William M. Wadley. Wadley was no stranger to company stockholders, having served as superintendent of the road during the late antebellum era. Wadley's skills had been recognized by the Confederate government in 1862, when he was made military superintendent of all Southern railroads. His brief tenure as railroad czar was marked by tireless efforts to bring order out of the chaos that had characterized the Confederate transportation system. His dismissal had resulted from too much efficiency rather than negligence. Wadley had seen how localistic management policies hamstrung Confederate supply efforts and had determined that railroads could function properly only if managed on a systemwide basis. Such sentiments ran counter to those of Confederate politicians and bureaucrats and the railroad managers who remained wedded to localism.[30] Wadley's ouster from Confederate service and his return to Savannah after the war, however, benefited the Central Railroad. Using strategies of consolidation and coordination he had advocated during the war—strategies that epitomized a broader managerial mind-set—Wadley restored the Central to its position of dominance in the state.

Wadley worked quickly and diligently to restore the company's fortunes. In December 1866, he reported that although some further work was needed, "the Road has been so far reconstructed as to enable it to meet all reasonable demands by the public for transportation . . . and that, to some extent, its former business has been resuscitated." The Central had earned over $1.6 million and had netted

$712,799 during 1866. Repairs were proceeding, and the company's car shops were refurbished and reopened. Forty-two engines and 537 cars were in operation purveying the Central's business. Like the Georgia Railroad, the Central was almost back to its lofty antebellum status by 1867. In that year, the road's capital stock was reportedly worth $4,661,800; the Central earned $2.2 million and netted over $900,000. That year the Central paid out 12 percent dividends to stockholders.[31]

Despite these accomplishments, Wadley was not content to rest on his laurels. Feeling the competition of the Georgia Railroad in the form of diminished profits, Wadley moved to expand the company's interests—and investments. In 1869, he obtained the lease of the Southwestern Railroad and thereby gained an outlet to the rich cotton regions of southwestern Georgia. He also invested in the Montgomery & West Point, the Western Railroad of Alabama, and the Mobile & Girard Railroad. By 1871, Wadley had won control of the Macon & Western as well, again through leasing arrangements, and he was preparing to expand the Central's steamship business. As the 1870s opened, the Central had regained its solid reputation and its domination of rail transportation in the state. Its stock was ranked highest in Georgia, and credit agents considered the company "the most solvent of this character in the South."[32]

The state-owned Western & Atlantic Railroad suffered twin blows during the war. Hood had failed to remove all of the road's rolling stock during his evacuation of Atlanta in September 1864, and, determined not to leave anything behind for Sherman, he ordered that the cars and engines that remained be destroyed. Then, when Sherman abandoned the city the following November, he ordered that the Western & Atlantic's machine shops and rolling mill be destroyed as well. This destruction at the hands of friend and enemy alike was particularly devastating because both of Georgia's major independent railroads depended on the Western & Atlantic for their trade with the West. Despite the efforts of King and Wadley, the lucrative markets of Tennessee and the Mississippi River Valley would remain inaccessible until the Western & Atlantic was restored.[33]

U.S. military authorities returned the Western & Atlantic to state authorities in September 1865. Upon receipt of the road, Provisional Governor James Johnson appointed five directors to oversee the restoration of the Western & Atlantic. These men, Richard Peters, Robert M. Goodman, J. R. Parrot, Robert Batey, and William B. Whitman, named Robert Baugh superintendent and Lemuel P. Grant chief engineer. The newly constituted board of directors also resolved to buy the necessary iron, cars, and engines from the United States government and instructed Baugh to establish rate schedules and to see to the rebuilding of the road's Atlanta machine shops.[34]

Charles Jenkins, who succeeded Johnson as governor in 1866, reported to the General Assembly that the Western & Atlantic had been returned to Georgia "in a dilapidated condition." The state road's "track and bridges [were] hastily and insufficiently repaired for temporary use; many of the buildings . . . [were] destroyed and the rolling stock reduced far below the exigencies of the service." Jenkins noted that the state had been required to pay U.S. military authorities over $400,000 for supplies and cars and that the Federal government wanted Georgia to endorse a claim against the United States for the use of the railroad during the Federal occupation of Atlanta. Jenkins concluded that the conflicting claims would not be settled at any time soon. He implied that it would be up to the state authorities to restore the Western & Atlantic.[35]

After Baugh resigned in late 1865, the task of reconstructing the Western & Atlantic fell to Campbell Wallace, who proved to be an excellent manager. He supervised the erection of temporary bridges and the restoration of rolling stock. Under his leadership, the Western & Atlantic took in $1.6 million from April to September of 1866 with expenses of only $700,000. A year later Wallace reported a gross income of $1,273,191.35 and a net profit of $131,115.82. Roadmaster Martin Dooly concluded that "the whole track is in better condition than it was at any previous time." By 1867, the Western & Atlantic had begun to approach its antebellum status.[36]

The grand progress of the Western & Atlantic stopped dead in 1868. Beginning in that year, one of Georgia's greatest financial assets became a source of boodle and corruption. The Western & Atlantic's decline coincided with the end of military Reconstruction and the start of radical rule. Federal military authorities closely supervised the elections for constitutional convention delegates and gubernatorial and state House seats. These elections resulted in the dismissal of Charles Jenkins and the inauguration of Augusta Republican Rufus B. Bullock. Bullock immediately replaced Wallace as superintendent with fellow radical Ed Hulbert. Another radical, Foster Blodgett, became treasurer. These men had been political cronies in Augusta, and the appointments of Hulbert and Blodgett were designed to pay off some of Bullock's political debts. [37]

To his credit, Hulbert continued to make repairs on the state road, and the line continued to make money—$300,000 in 1868–69 alone. Hulbert was convinced that areas traversed by the Western & Atlantic promised great things for Georgia's economic development: north Georgia contained rich iron and coal deposits that could be tapped for manufacturing enterprises. Through the medium of Western & Atlantic reports, Hulbert urged Governor Bullock to push for the development of the coal beds, as the combination of cheap, available coal and proximity to regular transportation would ensure the state's prosperity.[38]

Unfortunately for Georgia, Bullock ignored these recommendations, even though they were fully in keeping with the Republican party's commitment to economic growth and development. Actually, he ignored most of Hulbert's advice. A split between the two resulted in Hulbert's dismissal late in 1869. In January 1870, Foster Blodgett succeeded Hulbert as superintendent of the Western & Atlantic. Like Bullock, Blodgett had resided in Augusta. Before the war, he operated a shoe store, but he virtually abandoned his business after he was elected mayor of Augusta in 1859. Local credit reporters accorded Blodgett a low rating because the bulk of his assets were tied up in politics. The credit agents also remarked on Blodgett's character, noting that he was "immoral . . . he does not stand well as a man."[39]

Blodgett's personal flaws became public knowledge when he succeeded Hulbert as superintendent. The Western & Atlantic became a veritable patronage mill, used to curry favor with national Republicans and to consolidate the party's control in Georgia, which by 1869 was by no means secure. Bullock and Blodgett used appointments to the Western & Atlantic to pay off political debts and to pay for various state programs. With the General Assembly dominated by conservatives of both parties, Bullock could squeeze little money out of the legislators. Hence the Western & Atlantic was treated as a sort of subtreasury. The end result was mismanagement and corruption. Instead of buying iron and rolling stock, purchasing agents paid for the transportation of state legislators and freedmen to the polls. The Western & Atlantic, which had once paid over $400,000 a year into the state treasury, became a financial burden and an embarrassment. Public outcry against graft and fraud was silenced momentarily by a state senate investigating committee, but over time, such political whitewashings grew thin.[40]

Bullock and his cronies became convinced in 1870 that they could no longer cover up such blatant mismanagement: popular opinion demanded that the Western & Atlantic either be sold or leased. The Georgia General Assembly subsequently passed a bill to allow the leasing of the state road. According to this act, which was passed on 24 October 1870, the Western & Atlantic was to be leased for twenty years at a monthly rent of $25,000. The lessees had to guarantee an $8 million bond, and local freight rates had to be in line with those charged by the Georgia Railroad, the Central, and the Macon & Western. To guard against further political misuse, the legislature also stipulated that the majority of potential lessees had to have been Georgia residents for at least five years.[41]

Although the Western & Atlantic lease was designed initially to remove the road from carpetbagger politics, it had the effect of making the road even more of a political football. Indeed, Bullock dreamed up the lease idea not only to be rid of bad press but to be able to retain some control over Georgia politics. Bullock and the Republicans had lost in the state elections of 1870, and the Democrats were in firm control of the legislature that was scheduled to convene in November 1871. Bullock hoped to lease the state road to a consortium of prominent Republicans and Democrats. With these individuals indebted to him for the lease, Bullock felt his control of elements of state policy would remain secure.

The first bid for the Western & Atlantic came from a group of capitalists headed, ironically, by former governor Joseph E. Brown. Included in Brown's company were John P. King, president of the Georgia Railroad, and Bullock's friend Hannibal I. Kimball. This group was exactly what Bullock desired, for they had ties both to other railroad companies in Georgia and to the Republican party. King's presence on a board of potential lessees, however, made Macon railroad interests suspicious. Those railroad magnates feared King would come to dominate the Western & Atlantic and use it to further the interests of the Georgia Railroad at the expense of the Central and the Macon & Western. To guard against such an occurrence, a rival company, composed of representatives of the Central, the Southwestern, and the Macon & Western, was formed, and this group scored a coup when it secured the support of prominent national Republicans Simon Cameron, John S. Delano, and Thomas A. Scott. The presence of such formidable competitors induced the Brown group to compromise. When the Western & Atlantic lease was finally perfected, the lease company contained twenty-three directors, representing both the Brown and the Macon-based interests. Further, it symbolized, according to one scholar of Georgia's Reconstruction, "the kind of economic and political alliance which would characterize the New South of the latter 1870's and 1880's."[42]

Though Georgians insisted that an investigative committee be appointed to inquire into the nature of the lease and the previous management of the road, most were relieved when the Western & Atlantic was removed from the sphere of politics. Moreover, fears that Bullock's cohorts, who were represented in the new corporation, would continue their machinations were put to rest when Brown replaced Blodgett as superintendent and the radical governor fled the state to avoid impeachment.

The lease company found that the Western & Atlantic had suffered at the hands of the radicals. President Joseph E. Brown reported that when he received the road, the track and rolling stock were "nearly rundown as it probably could have been to remain in working order." Up to January 1872, the lease company had expended $1,678,765.11 in repairs but had earned only $1,397,742.60, leaving a deficit of over $280,000. Brown concluded that much work and many more cars and engines were needed to bring the Western & Atlantic back to normal conditions.[43]

The lease company, however, proved equal to the task of rebuilding and refurbishing the much-abused Western & Atlantic. Surprisingly, Brown proved to be an able manager, and he must be credited with the restoration of the state road. While serving as governor, Brown had overseen the glory days of the road in the 1850s, when, for the first time in its history, the road became one of the state's greatest sources of revenue. Brown continued to monitor the Western & Atlantic during the Civil War, but his attention to maintenance and management frequently brought him into conflict with Confederate authorities.[44] Brown's wartime policies mirrored the provincial actions of the Confederacy's other railroad managers: he had refused to operate the Western & Atlantic with a view of its relation to the Confederate railroad network. Whether Brown's war experiences affected his postwar management of the Western & Atlantic is uncertain, but policies he pursued indicated that he may have altered his notion of the road's function in Georgia.

As president of the lease company, Brown worked diligently to extend the scope of the state road's operations. He succeeded in expanding the Western & Atlantic's routes and secured new markets in St. Louis, Louisville, and Cincinnati. He also moved to develop the mining and manufacturing region of north Georgia. By 1873, the Western & Atlantic's fortunes had turned around. Despite some "embarrassment" during the financial panic of that year, the road recorded a profit. Five years later, credit reporters were characterizing the road as the "most profitable line in the State. . . . The road & appurtenances are valued at 8 million dollars . . . & stands high not only in respect to credit but in the estimation of the citizens."[45]

Although the Georgia railway system continued to be dominated by the big three—the Western & Atlantic, the Georgia, and the Central of Georgia lines—boosters revived other projects and proposed new ones. Indeed, like their counterparts throughout the South, Georgians came to believe that only railroads could restore the state to its lofty antebellum standing as the Empire State of the South. To be sure, capital was glaringly absent, and the first Reconstruction governments proved chary of overextending themselves. But boosters remained active, and with the advent of the Bullock administration in 1868, state aid again flowed to railroad projects.

Bullock was generous—too generous, as would become apparent—in extending state aid and endorsing bonds for proposed railroads. Fully subscribing to the Republican "gospel of prosperity," Bullock promised more than $5.75 million to prospective companies that sought to build lines in southern and western Georgia. Bullock, however, was not the only advocate of such plans. Indeed, Georgians in general in the postwar period saw the railroad as the panacea to all their economic woes. Hence Bullock enjoyed bipartisan support in the state legislature for most of his schemes, proving that even some "unreconstructed" Democrats advocated economic development. State aid under Bullock closely approximated policies enacted during the antebellum period: it consisted of outright grants, tax exemptions, and state endorsement of railroad bonds.[46] Unfortunately for Bullock, more than half of the state's bonds went to companies headed by his close friend Hannibal I. Kimball. Although Kimball and others let contracts for grading and construction, few of the proposed projects were completed, and those that were built were poorly constructed. By the end of 1871, charges of corruption, mounting state debts, and the bankruptcy of most state-aided companies gave Georgia Democrats potent ammunition for their campaign to "redeem" Georgia. Nevertheless, state aid did allow capitalists to build over 740 miles of new lines by 1872. Moreover, Georgia's Redeemers remained committed to economic development, especially via railroads, and continued to pursue the economic policies of the hated radicals. As C. Vann Woodward has noted, Reconstruction and Redemption were not discontinuous in policy formulations. Unfortunately for Georgia's Redeemers, not everyone in the state fully embraced their vision. Indeed, a hostile upcountry yeomanry and a conservative General Assembly would stymie their efforts to achieve a full realization of a diversified state developed along Northern lines. Revulsion to Republican largess resulted in the repudiation of most of Bullock's bonded debt. Perhaps most significant, the reaction resulted in the call for and ratification of a new state constitution in 1877. This constitution forbade tax exemptions, state aid, and state loans to any companies or corporations.[47]

The response of Georgia's chief railroad managers to postwar rebuilding indicates that their wartime experiences played an important role in their rebuilding strategies. The war years proved that adherence to antebellum managerial notions, which had emphasized what one scholar has characterized as "the localization of traffic at the principal terminus," were ill-suited to the Confederacy's requirements.[48] A new orientation was needed, one that viewed the railroads within the context of the nation they served.

John P. King's management of the Georgia Railroad in the postbellum era indicates that he learned little from his wartime service. To be sure, the Georgia Railroad resumed its status as one of the South's most solid and profitable concerns. But King's adherence to conservative management policies, necessary in the early days of rebuilding, proved detrimental in the long run. The Georgia Railroad's president remained wedded to a localistic outlook that rarely transcended Augusta's city limits: King made all management decisions with Augusta uppermost in his mind. Such a choice was logical, at least from King's standpoint. In addition to the money he had invested in the Georgia Railroad, King had a sizable financial stake in many of Augusta's manufacturing enterprises. Hence self-interest and a desire to bolster further Augusta's economic base led King to follow the policies he did. The Georgia Railroad's board of directors also had extensive investments in other Augusta companies so they, initially at least, followed King's direction. Postwar changes in commercial patterns, however, steadily reduced Augusta's role as a major interior market, especially for cotton. King's ongoing resistance to change ultimately produced serious company infighting which led to his removal as president in the 1870s. Changes in Georgia Railroad policies thereafter came too late: King's company was leased to his more aggressive rival on the Central in 1881.[49]

William M. Wadley of the Central of Georgia Railroad demonstrated most convincingly how his war service influenced his postwar direction of the Central. More than any other manager in the state, Wadley perceived of railroads in the largest sense. This perception was undoubtedly a by-product of his wartime tenure as Confederate railroad chief. Wadley became acutely aware of the need to coordinate and systematize the functions of all railroads, and he viewed the individual lines as part of a national network. Wadley's investments in and lease of other roads and his rebuilding of the Central's steamship business symbolized his awareness of the importance of inter- and intraregional trade and transportation. Because of his vision, the Central had no peer in postwar Georgia. Its domination of the state's transportation system stood as testimony to Wadley's aggressiveness, foresight, and expertise.[50]

Joseph E. Brown of the Western & Atlantic lease company also demonstrated that war experiences altered his notions concerning railroad management. As governor, Brown had made the state road a profitable and essential component of Georgia's economy. He had watched the Western & Atlantic become a political football, which had hindered its service to the state. Brown used the administrative qualities refined during his governorship to resuscitate the much abused Western & Atlantic. In resuming management, however, Brown transcended the parochialism that had marked his wartime service. With peace, Brown saw the Western & Atlantic as an essential component in the state's recovery. He firmly believed that railroads, not to mention an alliance with the moderate wing of the Republican party, held the key to Georgia's future. For that reason, he embraced Republican economic policies, called for a New South in Georgia, and used the Western & Atlantic as his instrument to achieve those goals. Brown's new awareness and appreciation of the Western & Atlantic's function led him, like Wadley, to embrace an intraregional management strategy. As Brown knew, "the railroad manager who has not an eye for new business openings and enterprises near and remote, in his state and beyond . . . is soon displaced for one who can see and act."[51] Brown's statement testifies to his awareness of the importance of anticipating and responding to opportunities. In short, he epitomized the manager as entrepreneur.

The response of Georgia's railroad managers to postwar conditions indicates that the war years left a mixed legacy. Brown and Wadley used wartime failures to institute changes in management strategies and decision making. King did not. Although devotion to old ideas and the emergence of a new orientation were to have important ramifications for the general pattern of Georgia's railroad development at the close of the nineteenth century, such consequences did not appear so ominous in the early 1870s.[52]

The men who built Georgia's railroads before the war combined entrepreneurial interest with managerial skills: they saw economic opportunities in the expanding trade and constructed their lines accordingly. Then, having built the roads, these men assumed a managerial function, delegating authority and making decisions designed to enrich their stockholders and the cities they served. This managerial function continued into the war years but was found wanting because it did not adjust to the needs of the Confederate war machine. With peace, those who rebuilt the railroads saw that if they were to stay competitive, parochialism had to be abandoned. Those who learned from war experiences and who adapted—men such as William Wadley and Joseph Brown—succeeded in producing a more comprehensive network that transcended local and even regional interests. Their achievements made possible Georgia's overall economic resurrection in the postbellum period.

6 The Reconstruction of Urban Georgia

At one point in David O. Selznick's classic production of *Gone With the Wind*, Scarlett O'Hara finds herself after the war with insufficient funds to pay the taxes on her beloved Tara, and she takes herself to Atlanta in an effort to coax the money out of Rhett Butler. What she finds in Atlanta is a boom town. Stores are reopening, burned-out shells are being rebuilt, and entrepreneurs and charlatans of every stripe are working the sidewalks and streets. Though she fails to get the money from Rhett, Scarlett does marry Frank Kennedy, an entrepreneur himself, who owns and runs a hardware and lumber store in the midst of this boom. The number of clichés in this scene cannot be counted. But there is one great truth in it, too: Atlanta, like many of Georgia's other urban centers, was a boom town after the Civil War.

Though the seeds of this revival were planted in the antebellum years, the Civil War accelerated the pace of change, which was especially evident in Atlanta. Unlike most other Southern commercial centers, Atlanta had never been totally dependent on either the cotton market or the seacoast trade for its economic livelihood. Moreover, it retained certain characteristics of the frontier, including a "society independent of a money aristocracy."[1] But the crisis of civil war changed Atlanta and its residents forever. From a modest commercial town of nine thousand inhabitants, Atlanta metamorphosed into the single most important distribution center in the Deep South. Its commercial economy was forced to adapt to the changed conditions, and its economic leaders were compelled to diversify and innovate to meet the new demands.

Atlanta's war record was the product of local initiative. The city's entrepreneurs found the crucible of war to be an inviting opportunity to experiment. They became convinced that industry was a necessary component to the local—and Southern—economy. Those individuals functioned well, in spite of shortages in materials and labor. When their labors were destroyed, they returned to rebuild and extend their vision of an industrial city.[2] Postbellum Atlanta became a symbol of what war-forged opportunities could promote. Catalyzed by war, Atlanta and her people would mature in peace.

Physically, Atlanta had suffered greatly at the hands of both her defenders and the invaders. Months of siege and Union shelling, Confederate evacuation and negligence, and Yankee destruction had combined to lay waste to almost three-quarters of the city's businesses and residences. Visitors and returning residents could not help but be struck by the devastation. As newspaper correspondent Sidney Andrews reported, "The entire business portion, excepting the Masonic Hall building and one block of six stores and a hotel was laid in ruins." Andrews went on to note: "The marks of the conflict are everywhere strikingly apparent. The ruin is not so massive and impressive as that of Columbia and Charleston; but so far as it extends it is more complete." Gutted buildings and debris offered mute testimony to Atlanta's importance as a Confederate military center.[3]

Atlanta's merchants were among the first to return to the war-scarred city. If they were dismayed by the desolation that greeted them, they did not show it. Wholesalers and retailers, unaccustomed to manual labor, joined other residents in clearing the rubble and salvaging materials "preparatory to rebuilding." Eager to get back to business, they erected flimsy shanties, tents, indeed, "anything with a roof and four sides," and stocked their makeshift shelves with the few goods they had hauled off to safety before the capture of the city. By the end of 1865, no fewer than 338 mercantile firms had been licensed by the City Council and over 150 stores were back in business.[4]

Despite the general poverty of the population, which rebounded to almost eight thousand by the end of 1865, sales boomed. Merchants could barely keep their stocks of food, clothing, and other necessities replenished as Atlantans, starved for goods of all sorts after four years of privation, bought anything and everything offered. Margaret Mitchell's fictional Frank Kennedy was not the only retail merchant who prospered in these years. Storekeepers estimated that sales were running 30 percent higher than during the most profitable antebellum years, and by the end of 1866 they exceeded $4.5 million. As the trade boom continued, more permanent edifices replaced temporary store structures, and the population stream approached flood levels as other former residents, Southerners, and a sprinkling of former Yankee soldiers inundated the Gate City, hoping to share in the general prosperity.[5]

Few in Atlanta—or elsewhere—could remain unimpressed by the rapidity of the city's reconstruction and revival. All were struck by the "new city" that was emerging from what seemed total "ruin and devastation." Sidney Andrews noted that: "The narrow and irregular . . . streets are alive from morning till night with drays and carts . . . with a never-ending throng of pushing and crowding and scrambling and eager and excited and enterprising men, all bent on building and trading and swift fortune-making. Chicago, in her busiest days[,] could scarcely show such a sight."[6] Local editors, publicists, and city boosters relished retelling stories of Atlanta's destruction to underscore her miraculous renaissance. Such tales usually concluded with the call, "Look at her now! . . . From her ruins she has sprung, as if by some magical influence, into a city again, commerce flourishing in her midst, and the 'busy hum of industry' animating her people." Observers were hard-pressed to dispute Atlanta's drive to "build up a great city at all hazards," nor did they doubt one resident's boast that "in five years at the farthest, Atlanta will be to the South what St. Louis is to the mighty West."[7]

Atlanta's resurrection did attract some mixed—and hostile—reviews from envious urban rivals. A correspondent for Augusta's *Southern Field and Fireside* found the Gate City "a devil of a place. . . . The men rush about like mad people and keep up such bustle, worry and chatter that it runs me crazy. . . . Everybody looks as if nearly worked to death." In a similar vein, the *Milledgeville Federal Union* reported that Atlanta was "a fast place in every sense of the word and our friends in Atlanta are a fast people. They live fast and die fast. They make money fast and they spend it fast. . . . To a stranger, the whole city seems to be running on wheels."[8] Proud Atlanta boosters did not take such assessments in good humor. Most attributed Atlanta's resurgence to the "progressive men" who dominated the city's trade and commerce. Such individuals did not "still themselves on their dignity and wait for trade to flow upon them"; rather, they "endeavor[ed] to make it flow." Some retorts were more caustic. Implicitly attacking critics in Georgia who "reviled" Atlanta's growth, the *Daily New Era* announced: "Hang the old customs! . . . Take a good running start and catch up with the times! Pile old customs as a monumental heap over the remains of an honored ancestry. . . . Old things, old opinions, old customs . . . we have no use for you!"[9]

Atlanta's business leaders during this postwar boom were the same men who had led the city's wartime mobilization effort. Though they had suffered significant losses in Atlanta's dark winter of 1864–65, their vision of a city restored to its wartime importance as a major Confederate manufacturing and distribution center was stimulated anew in the postbellum period. Many of them had advocated industrial development as a necessary complement to commerce throughout the late antebellum era, and to them the war appeared to be the medium through which industrialization could be achieved.

Peace and the reestablishment of Atlanta's rail connections spurred those individuals to action again. Those who rebuilt the Gate City shared common experiences and assumptions. Each entrepreneur had settled in Atlanta when it was little more than a hamlet. They had built their stores and trade and had worked energetically to expand and diversify the city's economic base. With war, they had responded to new challenges, always with an eye to how wartime mobilization could further enhance Atlanta's position, and the citizens—and Confederate government—accorded them hero status for their efforts. These hardy entrepreneurs faced peacetime reconstruction with little but experience. Yet that experience, coupled with ambition, produced remarkable results. John C. Peck, builder of the Atlanta Arsenal and manufacturer of "Joe Brown" pikes, put his skills to work as a local contractor and aided the physical reconstruction of the city. In time, Peck branched out and opened a dry goods firm and planing mill.[10] Joseph Winship and his sons rebuilt their ironworks and cast hardware and agricultural implements instead of ordnance, proving again that swords could be transformed into plowshares.[11] Yet another example of a successful conversion of wartime to peacetime activities is furnished by the firm of McNaught, Ormond & Company. The wartime manufacture of "novelty goods" provided the foundation for the peacetime manufacture of agricultural implements. Success encouraged the firm to diversify still further: in 1870, it established the Atlanta Paper Mill.[12] Men like Peck, the Winships, and McNaught and Ormond were not exceptional in Atlanta. Rather, they epitomized the "Atlanta Spirit," the drive to recoup and rebuild. They represent just a few of the many who responded to Reconstruction with the same energy and inventiveness as they had responded to wartime mobilization.

City boosters and political leaders used statistical advances—the 1870 census reported that Atlanta's seventy-four manufacturing establishments produced goods worth $2 million—to urge locals to even greater exertions.[13] The *Atlanta Daily New Era* pledged its support for all plans to establish factories in Atlanta—and Georgia—and urged that the city endeavor to become self-sufficient in every line of goods. In a similar manner, the *Constitution* exalted manufacturing pursuits and warned that unless Atlanta became a "manufacturing community . . . we shall continue to be mere hewers and drawers—the menials and slaves of those who run the machinery and pocket the profits." The press also boosted plans for the formation of immigrant companies. Such associations, designed to encourage European immigrants to settle in Atlanta, were hailed as providing the city with more honest and industrious factory workers who would be needed for factories being contemplated. The Atlanta City Council added to the drive for manufacturing by extending inducements to local capitalists in the form of ten-year tax exemptions on capital invested in industry. Business associations such as the Atlanta Board of Trade in 1866 and its reorganized successor, the Chamber of Commerce, used their meetings to discuss ways to broaden the manufacturing and commercial base of the city. The Chamber appointed special committees to collect and distribute pertinent information to interested industrialists in and outside of the city. The 1870s also witnessed the formation of manufacturing associations, which were organized with a view to promoting local industrial development.[14]

But despite all this enthusiastic boosterism, manufacturing in Atlanta failed to attain the levels hoped for by the city's proponents of industrialization. Obstacles that had hampered industrial development during the war returned to stymie Atlanta's postbellum champions of manufacturing. Chief among the impediments to Atlanta's drive for industrialization was the city's location. Ironically, the railroads that had sparked the city's rise as the southeastern commercial entrepôt discouraged manufacturing. Because of the lack of a system of water routes that could have provided competition for rail lines, freight rates on coal to the city were inordinately high. Plans to tap Georgia's iron and coal fields and those in neighboring Alabama with the Atlantic & Great Western Canal and the Georgia Western Railroad were scotched by the Panic of 1873 and the depression that followed. Some local leaders tried to garner private contributions to push those projects to completion, but tight money markets discouraged most Atlantans from tendering their support. Still, entrepreneurs remained hopeful, and with economic recovery in the late 1870s, Atlantans resumed their quest to build a city where commerce complemented industry.

Atlanta's stunning rebirth in the Reconstruction era was unequaled in Georgia. Nonetheless, Columbus also demonstrated remarkable recuperative powers. In many ways, Columbus's resurrection represented a mirror image of events in Atlanta. Columbus, too, had blossomed during the war. Military mobilization had encouraged manufacturing on an even greater scale and led to the creation and expansion of numerous factories. Flush times and high morale had waned and eventually evaporated as the Yankees approached. The town's status as a manufacturing center attracted the invaders and assured its destruction. When Northern troops finally left Columbus late in the spring of 1865, the once prosperous city lay in smoldering ruins. Indeed, Columbus's devastation surpassed that of Atlanta: not one factory, machine shop, or mill was left standing, and all rail connections to northern Georgia and Alabama were destroyed. Residents and visitors alike were stunned by the universal desolation, and credit reporters, who returned to the city in 1866, could report nothing but "burnt out" or "destroyed during Wilson's raid."[15]

Residents of Columbus proved hardy. By December 1865, Northern news correspondents noted that the town's commerce was rebounding. As rail links were reestablished and obstructions placed in the Chattahoochee by the contending navies were removed, cotton and produce again flowed into the town's markets. Former residents slowly returned to the area, and rebuilding proceeded. Although Columbus's commercial recovery never matched Atlanta's in either volume or pace, it was steady and consistent. Approximately one and a half years after the city had been destroyed, the volume of trade reached the antebellum standard.[16]

Columbus may have lagged behind Atlanta in commerce, but in manufacturing it proved an example worthy of emulation. As local merchants struggled to recoup lost fortunes and to reestablish trade connections, Columbus's industrialists were rebuilding their factories. William H. Young, who had figured prominently in the creation of the Eagle Manufacturing Company, contacted his partners and undertook the factory's reestablishment. In February 1866, he made plans to rebuild the cotton factory on a new site and to commence operations in the fall of that year. Young and his associates met their deadline and reopened one mill late in 1866. To commemorate its "miraculous" rebirth, the company was renamed the Eagle & Phoenix Manufacturing Company, "as it had literally sprung from the ashes."[17]

The initial success of the Eagle & Phoenix Manufacturing Company allowed the company to expand. Another mill was added in 1869 and the capital stock increased to $450,000. Credit agents considered the mill "g[oo]d in every way" and accorded the company the highest possible rating. By 1870, the Eagle & Phoenix Company's capital stock exceeded $1 million, and the company had unlimited credit. The mill continued to expand, adding, in due course, a woolen mill, dyehouse, and extra storerooms and dry rooms. Assets, in the form of real estate, plant machinery, and the reserve fund, burgeoned to over $2.5 million; annual dividends during the period from 1870 to 1880 averaged between 6 and 10 percent per year. By 1879, more than a thousand operatives were working the company's 44,000 spindles and 1,600 looms, and their total wages came to $400,000 per annum. Eagle & Phoenix put out 150 varieties of textile goods, including finished products. These goods were sold all over the state and the nation, and Georgians considered them to be of "unsurpassed" quality. Locals and other Georgians took especial pride in the achievements of the Eagle & Phoenix mills. The *Atlanta Constitution* argued that the firm's example of "Southern enterprise . . . show[s] what is in the future for the South by a utilization of our capacities and resources." In a similar vein, the *Columbus Sun* credited the city's rebirth to companies such as the Eagle & Phoenix. "Columbus has grown," the *Sun* proclaimed, "because of the energy of Southern men, not of others' capital." Prejudiced residents and unbiased observers alike were amazed that not even the serious depression of the mid-1870s checked the company's progress. Though New England and European mills were seriously affected by the economic downturn, the Eagle & Phoenix Company maintained full employment and full production. Its products continued to be of "an unusually good quality," and the concern was "conducted with good judgment and strict economy."[18]

The Eagle & Phoenix Company's local rival, the Columbus Factory, had also been "burnt out" in the last days of the war. In 1866, the Columbus Factory, too, began rebuilding. Those who had directed the mill from its incorporation in 1849 resumed their management of the concern in the postwar period. By 1869, the factory had reopened with 4,000 spindles and 116 looms, manufacturing brown sheetings and shirtings, cotton yarn, batting, and wool rolls. Credit reporters declared the Columbus Factory "well-managed" and "one of the safest concerns in Columbus." Its officers enjoyed a solid reputation, and those credit reporters considered them good for any amount of credit. Although the Columbus Factory (renamed the Columbus Manufacturing Company in 1873) never approached the Eagle & Phoenix mills in production and capital investment, it was yet another example of what local money, talent, and enterprise could achieve under trying conditions.[19]

Not every textile firm in Columbus could boast such a dramatic recovery. The factory of Daniel and John J. Grant, destroyed during the war, never fully recovered. Even in its demise, however, the history of this firm demonstrated Columbus's powers of recovery. At the end of the war, the Grants had fully intended to rebuild their factory and continue their business. In February 1866, however, Daniel Grant died, and John went into business with George P. Swift, a native of Massachusetts, who had owned and operated several textile mills in Upson County, Georgia, that had also been destroyed during the war. Pooling their financial resources, Grant and Swift formed J. J. Grant & Company in 1867, and soon thereafter, Grant sold out to Swift, who changed the name of the firm to the Muscogee Manufacturing Company. Built on the site of the old Coweta Manufacturing Company, the new firm was a family-run enterprise: Swift's sons served as the general officers and members of the board of directors. Capitalized at $150,000, the concern grew steadily until by 1880 it was valued at a quarter of a million dollars.[20]

Residents of Columbus had just cause to view with satisfaction the status of textile manufacturing in their town in the late 1860s and 1870s. A Macon correspondent to the *Atlanta Daily New Era* called attention to the travails the "Lowell of the South" had faced in 1865: "War's cruel hand rested heavily upon you . . . leaving the people without capital . . . but not without energy." Through hard work and faith, local entrepreneurs had rebuilt the mills that had made Columbus such an important manufacturing city before the war. Those men—the Swifts, William Young, J. R. Clapp, and others—were "*heroes* in the ranks of energetic, persevering and industrious businessmen." The *New Orleans Picayune* argued that Columbus's textile rebirth proved unequivocally that "here, in the South, where the climate is salubrious, where waterpower is plenty, where the material is at our door, and the market open . . . is par excellence the place to manufacture cotton and woolens." The *Picayune* went on to predict that in time more capitalists would see in Columbus and other Southern cities opportunities for lucrative investments that would "be more potent towards establishing Southern independence than the sword."[21]

Although Columbus's textile establishments were accorded the lion's share of the press's praise and coverage, several other factories important to the city's antebellum and wartime economy were also rebuilt. The Palace Mills, Columbus's largest grain mills, virtually controlled the city's flour and grain meal production and trade and had produced extensively for the Confederate Quartermaster Department. Owned by wealthy stage owner Randolph Mott, the Palace Mills were rebuilt and reopened in the late 1860s. Mott, considered to be of "unexceptional char[acter] as a bus[iness] man," nevertheless used his personal fortune and profits from the Palace Mills to branch out. He bought an interest in an Alabama grain mill and became president of the Columbus Gas Works and vice-president of the Mobile & Girard Railroad Company. In 1872, disaster struck the Palace Mills: a devastating fire virtually destroyed it and cost Mott $100,000. Undaunted, Mott bought into the Palace's old competitor, the City Mills, and continued to manufacture flour and meal. He continued to operate the City Mills, with varying success, through the 1870s.[22]

Two of Columbus's three ironworks resumed operation immediately after peace was restored. The Columbus Iron Works, which had produced army ordnance until leased to the Confederate navy in 1862, was rebuilt and operating almost immediately. This firm, owned by William R. Brown, had regained its high credit rating by 1867. By the spring of 1868, however, business was "dull," and the company's prospects were uncertain owing to Brown's ill health. Brown's recovery coincided with the ironworks' revival. In 1869, the firm's capital stock was worth $60,000, and it was deemed a "good & strong conc[ern] wor[th] all the cr[edit] they may ask." By the 1870s the ironworks' stock had increased to $100,000 and the firm was conducting a large business and had earned an "A No. 1" credit rating. Likewise, the record of the Muscogee Railroad's ironworks demonstrated remarkable powers of recovery. By February 1866, the Muscogee Foundry was repairing rolling stock and manufacturing railroad iron. In August of that year, credit agents reported that the firm's solid antebellum standing as a responsible and well-managed concern had been reestablished.[23]

The postwar record of Columbus's smaller manufacturing firms was less impressive. In particular, those firms that had converted to war-related production were adversely affected by the invading Yankees, and they did not evince the willingness to rebuild their concerns that the larger factories did. Their failure to adapt to changed circumstances and to transfer war-honed skills into peacetime endeavors demonstrates that war mobilization had an uneven effect on Columbus's economy.

Examples of war-induced activity and peacetime failures abound. For instance, Julius Brands and William Korner, music store owners who turned to manufacturing India rubber cloth, dissolved their partnership after the war. Brands left Columbus for Europe, while Korner struggled to salvage the old business. In 1870, Korner established himself as a grocer and general merchant, eventually branching out into trunk manufacturing. By 1873, however, Korner's luck and reputation had soured. His general store and trunk manufactory failed, and he was accused of swindling creditors. He left Columbus—and his debts—and went to Alabama to manage his new mother-in-law's farm. Alabama also attracted Columbus jeweler A. H. DeWitt. DeWitt had enjoyed a solid reputation locally and had conducted a profitable business. He had failed early in the war as a sword manufacturer and did not resume his original vocation. In 1866, DeWitt was in Montgomery, conducting his trade in jewelry. Similarly, though Simon Rothchild and his brother Frank had found wartime demands profitable, when the war ended, the Rothchilds took what remained of their fortune and moved to New York, where they entered trade in shoes.[24]

Of all Columbus's small military manufacturers, only the Haiman brothers were able to convert their war experiences into useful—and successful—peacetime pursuits. Their rise from petty tinners to major Confederate arms manufacturers was as swift as the demolition of the brothers' Columbus Fire Arms Manufacturing Company was total. Immediately after the war, Louis and Elias Haiman turned to farming, but they worked the land for only one year. In 1867, the brothers, who were "said to have made $ during the war and are now possessed of [property]," began operating as grain and produce dealers. Two years later, they used skills attained during the war to manufacture plows. Haiman & Brother continued dealing in foodstuffs and manufacturing plows until Louis's death in 1872. Elias stayed on in Columbus until 1877, when he opened an office of his Southern Agricultural Works in Atlanta. The company retained its home office in Columbus.[25]

Several factors may account for the failure of small war-related manufacturing concerns to adapt to peacetime conditions. Smaller firms simply did not have the resources to rebuild after the war. Local capital and credit were glaringly absent in the city until 1870, when several banks reopened their doors. When money was available, the older factories with established reputations and a heritage of achievement received those funds. Moreover, Columbus lacked extensive rail connections that could have stimulated greater commercial activity and hence more available capital for industrial rebuilding. Although the Southwestern Railroad was reopened in 1866, that line was controlled by the Savannah-based Central of Georgia. Management decisions tended to favor policies that enriched the port at the expense of the Chattahoochee River town. Not until the mid-1870s were other rail connections with interior points in Georgia and Alabama established.[26]

Local merchants had been the city's most active and vocal boosters, but apparently they relinquished their leadership after the war. The Columbus Board of Trade, established in 1850 to promote local manufacturing, lapsed during the war. Letters from "merchants" in the *Columbus Daily Sun* encouraged businessmen to regroup and charter a chamber of commerce. Such an organization, those individuals argued, would protect local interests and encourage new industrial enterprises to replace those lost in the war. Appeals to be "energetic" because ambitious rivals in Atlanta, Macon, and Montgomery were forging ahead fell on deaf ears, and the idea died quietly.[27]

Some perceptive residents had difficulty reconciling the city's slow recovery in manufacturing with its wartime performance. The *Daily Sun* pointed up the disparity to city residents: "Our capacity for success in . . . industrial pursuits was settled beyond question or dispute during the war. . . . Under the most disadvantageous circumstances that could result from a want of material and a lack of skilled labor, we manufactured at this point almost everything for . . . an army. . . . If such results could be accomplished, what might we not expect with cheap and abundant supplies of iron and coal . . . at our very doorstep?"[28]

The failure to build immediately upon and expand the warspawned industrial superstructure may have discouraged but it did not destroy local efforts to realize a "new" Columbus. Although most of Columbus's war-forged manufacturers could not adjust to the peacetime economy, the city's prewar industrial leaders could—and did. George Schley, Randolph Mott, William R. Brown, and others who had launched Columbus's industrial development in the antebellum era and contributed to war mobilization propelled Columbus's industrial resurgence in the 1870s. The revival of the Columbus Iron Works, the Eagle & Phoenix Manufacturing Company, and other industrial establishments indicates that the war did not destroy the hopes of all the city's industrialists. By 1870, Columbus boasted 108 manufacturing establishments, which represented a capital investment of $1,889,770. That showing was impressive, considering that Wilson's raid had cost the city $57 million. The reestablishment of Columbus's industrial base in textiles encouraged others to resume manufacturing, and throughout the 1870s, more foundries, cotton mills, two furniture factories, and a railroad machine shop were added to Columbus's manufacturing sector. Visitors began to comment on Columbus's "energy" and "activity." Though the town had struggled through hard times, its progress was assured.[29]

Unlike either Atlanta or Columbus, Augusta had been spared widespread devastation. Indeed, a visitor to Augusta in 1865 remarked that the Savannah River city appeared to be "an oasis . . . in the midst of scenes made desolate by the acts of war—for, from the commencement of the great struggle up to its termination . . . no Federal bayonet ever glistened in the streets of Augusta, and the sad pictures and turmoil of the late civil war are, in a great measure, unknown in its history."[30] Augusta had been menaced by Sherman's March to the Sea and had been victimized by a general lawlessness in the aftermath of Lee's surrender, but the city's homes, stores, and factories were left unscathed. Indeed, except for the presence of Major General John Pope's occupation troops and the stream of former Confederate soldiers who passed through en route to their homes, Augusta seemed little different in 1865 than in 1860.

Yet Augusta had changed. Visitors might comment on its pastoral location on the banks of the Savannah and on its fine residences, but Augusta in 1865 stood as one of Georgia's—and the South's—few intact industrial centers. The city's rail connections to other urban areas, though partially destroyed, were rebuilt rapidly. The city's antebellum textile leader, the Augusta Factory, had expanded during the war. Other firms had been created to meet the Quartermaster Department's demand for uniforms and camp supplies. Confederate General George Washington Rains had introduced heavy industry when he established the Augusta Arsenal and Powder Works. Civilians had augmented the arsenal's production by converting local businesses to armament manufacturing. The success of privately owned and government-sponsored manufacturing had convinced many uninterested Augustans that industrial pursuits were not only necessary but profitable. Conditions in Augusta in 1865 were unsettled. Substantial capital was lacking (only the Georgia Railroad's bank had survived the war), and tools and materials were in short supply. Nevertheless, Augusta possessed all the ingredients necessary to resume its stand as one of Georgia's greatest cities.[31]

But Augusta did not immediately regain her wartime eminence. Commerce recovered first as the Georgia Railroad was repaired. Goods of all sorts streamed into the city, and local merchants quickly took advantage of consumer demand. Residents noted as early as September 1865 that stores, damaged during the looting, were being repaired and were "laden with the choicest goods." The streets were "thronged with men." To admittedly biased observers, Augusta seemed to resound with "the flutter of wheels . . . the lumbering of heavily laden drays . . . and the sharp clip of the adz." The local press encouraged such activity and urged Augustans to embrace the "new era" that was unfolding. The *Augusta Chronicle and Sentinel* exhorted Augustans in particular and Georgians and Southerners in general to return to their wartime industrial pursuits. If the "enthusiasm and energy" that had been "applied to the persecution [sic] of the war" were "turned to industrial pursuits," the editors argued, the South would have no peer. In a similar though more restrained fashion, the *Chronicle and Sentinel* urged that "men of enterprise and energy . . . [move to] make Augusta equal to Lowell or Newark."[32]

Only a few answered the *Chronicle and Sentinel*'s call, and most of those were individuals connected with the Augusta Factory. The Augusta Factory entered the postbellum era in an enviable condition. Its president, William E. Jackson, and its directors had been—and remained—some of Augusta's wealthiest and most influential citizens. The factory had prospered greatly during the dark days of 1861–65, as the Confederacy's insatiable demand for uniforms and blankets had kept the mill's 15,000 spindles and 462 looms operating incessantly. Military contracts had facilitated (demanded might be a better word) the factory's expansion and had pushed daily production to 20,000 yards. Such demands had naturally resulted in much mechanical wear, but new machinery installed just before the outbreak of hostilities rendered the Augusta Factory better able than others to withstand such abuse. That the Augusta mill was a solid and profitable concern was amply demonstrated by its stock, which, even during the most desperate period of the war, was quoted at $100 in gold. With peace, the company's stock was valued at $125 in gold.[33]

After the war, Jackson and the mill's other directors were not content to rest on their laurels. They dispatched mill superintendent
Francis Cogin to obtain new and better machinery for the factory and
entrusted him with making improvements in the mill's design that
would increase production. Within one year of Appomattox, the Augusta Factory's capital stock had increased to $600,000 and profits had
grown so enormously—they were in excess of $100,000—that 20 per-
cent annual dividends were paid to stockholders. In due course, more
looms were added and the mill's work force expanded to 500 operatives who manned the spindles and looms that produced 25,000
yards of cloth a day. By 1871, the firm had compiled an unbroken
record of success. The Augusta Factory was worth an estimated $1
million in that year, and credit reporters described it as "a prosperous
business & in undoubted stand[in]g & cr[edit] . . . [the] best paying
factory in the country."[34]

As in Columbus, however, the Augusta Factory's success after the
war was widely hailed but not imitated by the smaller firms that had
gone into business solely to meet wartime needs. J. K. Hora, for
example, had converted a storeroom in his clothing shop into a ready-
made clothing factory which produced several thousand uniforms for
the Confederate Quartermaster Department and the Georgia militia.
He resumed his general clothing business in 1865, but in 1868 he
closed his store and never reopened. S. S. Jones & Company's experience was similar. Considered a responsible and profitable hardware
firm, Jones & Company had branched out into the manufacture of
camp equipment. With peace, however, the firm went out of business.[35]

Other wartime manufacturers returned to their peacetime pursuits.
W. C. Jessup returned to his prewar occupation of making saddles and
harnesses, conducted a profitable business in that line, and by 1866,
he had opened a store in New York. Jessup's business continued to
flourish and he enjoyed a solid reputation and credit rating until his
death in 1875. Jesse Ansley, too, returned to his antebellum job as a
wholesale and commission merchant. Partnered with his disabled
Confederate veteran brother, Ansley struggled to reestablish his local
business, but failed in the attempt. In 1868, the partnership was dissolved, and one year later, Ansley left Augusta for Atlanta. There,
Ansley opened a commission house with his son, and despite having
"little ready capital," he was considered a strong and reliable businessman of high integrity.[36]

The failure of Augusta's smaller manufacturing establishments after the war seems somewhat paradoxical, given the general enthusiasm for industrial development. Several factors, however, shed light on this gap between theory and practice. For obvious reasons, gun manufacturers and equipage suppliers were not in great demand in postbellum Augusta. Yet their knowledge of and expertise in manufacturing pursuits might have been transferred into peacetime industrial enterprises such as agricultural implement production. Instead, it was channeled into trade, usually trade in cotton, and there it was lost. Small merchants and entrepreneurs who had risked their fortunes on war production tended to try to recoup their losses in the cotton trade. Since Augusta had been one of Georgia's preeminent cotton markets, such a choice seemed not only logical but profitable. Unfortunately for many moderate-sized firms, the fall in the price of cotton in 1868 and 1870–71 spelled disaster. Small capitalists in particular were adversely affected by low cotton prices. Similarly, smaller concerns had neither the collateral nor the extensive ties to Northern financial houses to carry them through rough periods.[37]

Augusta's continued reliance on King Cotton in the postbellum period naturally made the local economy subject to the vagaries of the cotton market. Yet the city's monopoly of the region's cotton trade was by no means assured after the war. Changes in patterns of commerce were, in part, a consequence of the war. The reestablishment of rail lines to the interior of the state coincided with and indeed precipitated Atlanta's rise as Georgia's major interior cotton mart. Cotton flowed into and through Augusta via the Western & Atlantic, the Atlanta & West Point, and the Central of Georgia railroads. Savannah had long competed with Augusta for the cotton trade of Georgia and had bristled while the Augusta-based Georgia Railroad enriched its rival port, Charleston. Augusta was not totally stripped of its share of the cotton market, but Augustans were aware that trade in the staple was not a dependable source of income: local merchants were displaced by more aggressive competitors inland.[38]

Altered trade channels alone do not explain Augusta's failure to build on the expanded industrial base of the war years. By the late 1860s, the city's chief manufacturing power source, the Augusta Canal, could no longer meet the demands of large factories. Local advocates of industrial expansion recognized the problem and urged that the canal be expanded. Those boosters pointed out that the reorganized Langley Manufacturing Company had decided to establish its works in South Carolina because the Augusta Factory had extracted a promise from the city fathers that no mills would be built until the canal was expanded.[39]

The loss of a factory that could have enhanced the city's economic base prompted Mayor J. V. H. Allen to announce in 1869 that canal enlargement would receive top priority during his administration. While the City Council and citizens' committees discussed financing, other committees were at work obtaining estimates for expansion. After this initial flurry of activity, however, work slowed. Mayor Allen's call for "mature reflections" and the avoidance of "hasty action" that might embarrass city finances put a brake on canal expansion. Such statements seemed inconsistent with earlier declarations of the tremendous benefits of a larger canal. Yet the project was expensive, and only by passing a city bond issue could the enlargement be financed. Money was still tight in Augusta, and residents were wary of all extraordinary expenditures. Moreover, possible litigation over property rights and canal land threatened to delay the project indefinitely. All those factors came together in 1869 to stall the plan that some believed "contain[ed] the germ of future greatness" for Augusta.[40]

Persistent lobbying and the promise that chartered companies would establish their plants in the city if proper facilities were provided finally convinced Augustans to finance the canal's enlargement. The city passed a bond issue in 1871 and began construction the next year. In 1875, the enlarged Augusta Canal opened at a cost three times higher than the original estimate of $325,000.[41]

Augusta immediately felt the effect of the new canal. Indeed, as soon as the citizens approved the bond issue, city boosters went to work. In 1871, Augusta merchants and manufacturers formed the Cotton Exchange, and one of its purposes was the promotion of the canal and more factories. Shortly thereafter, the City Council offered to pay a 3 percent bonus to any cotton mill that located on the Augusta Canal. That inducement enhanced a Georgia statute which exempted new capital investments in cotton mills from taxation for ten years.[42]

Despite such offers, dreams of an industrial Augusta that would rival the city's wartime achievements were deferred again by the depression of the mid-1870s. Business concerns that were chartered and planned in the years 1873 to 1875 were doomed until the national economy began an upswing in 1877. In that year, and continuing into the 1880s, a mill-building mania seized Augusta. The Enterprise Manufacturing Company, the C. W. Simmons Mill, the John Pendleton King Mill, and others were put into operation. They produced cotton goods worth in excess of $3 million annually and were valued, in the aggregate, at $4 million.[43]

Those Augustans who had lived during the war and who had witnessed the expansion of the city's manufacturing base must have been gratified by Augusta's industrial "takeoff" after 1877. They had seen how manufacturing had enhanced the local economy during the war, and the defeat of the Confederacy merely affirmed their belief in the efficacy and necessity of industry. Physical and financial obstacles had postponed the realization of Augusta's potential in the immediate postwar years, but those elements did not discourage the city's first industrialists. The persistence of business leaders such as William E. Jackson, William D'Antignac, John P. King, and others in promoting local industry demonstrates that some war-spawned advances had benefited the city. Those entrepreneurs, with their established mills and factories, had spearheaded Augusta's antebellum industrial revolution and war mobilization. They were also responsible for the city's new industrial spurt in the 1870s.[44]

A little more than a hundred miles south of Augusta was another city that was left physically untouched by the war but was nevertheless scarred by it. Savannah was spared undoubtedly because of its almost cordial welcome of General Sherman's army in December 1864.[45] The absence of gutted buildings and factories, however, did not imply a city unscathed by war. Rather, Savannah had been one of Georgia's first casualties, for the Union blockade and the fall of Fort Pulaski in 1862 had effectively removed the Forest City from active participation in the war. Moreover, it had inaugurated an economic decline that seemed to have no end. A Union soldier of occupation noted that Savannah was "in a most dilapidated condition. It is really mournful for a man from the prosperous, determined and . . . *glorious North*, to walk along the streets of Savannah. . . . Business is almost entirely suspended, and nearly every store is closed . . . fences are broken down, sidewalks and wharves are going to ruin, and Sherman's dead horses are laying about the streets by the dozen."[46] For three years, commercial paralysis had rendered the city a shadow of its former self, when it had stood as Georgia's largest and most important trade entrepôt.

The Yankees, who established quarters in the city, were not a particularly onerous burden. Indeed, Federal occupation benefited the city, for goods and money circulated freely. Moreover, Savannah's stockpile of cotton, a legacy of the effectiveness of the Union blockade, was snatched up by eager Northern merchants who made their way to the port as quickly as possible. Savannah benefited, too, in the early days of the occupation, from the food, supplies, and money sent by concerned and sympathetic New Yorkers and Bostonians. All those elements worked together to bring the city out of its economic doldrums.[47]

For most residents, however, Savannah's recovery did not come soon enough. The local press bemoaned the pall that continued to hang over the city and alternately pleaded with residents to forget the past and castigated them for not moving forward. The economic base was there, the *Savannah Republican* argued; it needed only to be put to work. Money and the reestablishment of the Central of Georgia Railroad to Savannah's market centers were needed to restore Savannah to its rank as the "commercial emporium of Georgia." The paper challenged the "monied men of Savannah . . . [to] rally to [your] own interests, and throwing off [your] supineness, seek to enrich our city." The *Republican* further urged that Northern capital, enterprise, and "vim" be enticed to the city.[48]

The resumption of the cotton trade finally stimulated Savannah's revival in late 1865. Sidney Andrews, who visited the city in December 1865, noted, "Everybody seems to have a passion for keeping store. . . . Business in the city has been very brisk all fall and many a merchant has had all he could do who moaned last spring for the 'good old days.' " The Northern correspondent was especially struck by Savannah's "faith in the recuperative energies of the people." Though some businessmen feared a "dull season" in 1866, most believed that "when the railroads connecting with Augusta, Macon and Thomasville are repaired, the trade of the city will be fifty percent greater than ever."[49]

The completion of repairs on the Central of Georgia Railroad in late 1866 stimulated business activity anew. Savannah's merchants opened banking facilities in the city and began to reestablish steamship lines. As prosperity proceeded, city fathers drew up plans to build a new market house to provide local businessmen with better facilities. Factors and merchants chartered new companies to carry Savannah's commerce to the Northeast and Britain. Sawmilling and grain milling, two cornerstones of the antebellum economy, were revived as capital became more accessible and abundant. Shipbuilding, too, received new life, and municipal authorities considered plans to increase Savannah's waterfront facilities. The City Council contracted with a dredging company to remove the obstructions placed in the Savannah River during the war so as further to increase the shipping business. Optimism and prosperity pervaded the venerable old seaport, and most residents would have agreed with Mayor John Screven that "our citizens have reason to congratulate themselves on the marked progress made during the past year[s]. Every interest has shared in the general prosperity and a general spirit of enterprise seems to animate the community. The future of Savannah is assured, and nothing stands in the way of her becoming, in a very short time, the most important point in the South."[50]

As Savannah entered the 1870s, her status as Georgia's chief seaport was secure. Visitors and locals all spoke with unabashed enthusiasm about the city's growth. Merchants and businessmen used the city's railroads to the utmost advantage; numerous steamers plied Savannah's cotton and timber to coastal cities and to Europe; local firms advertised widely in and outside of the state; real estate values were high; and the city's population had grown to over twenty-eight thousand—an increase of almost 28 percent over 1860. Savannah, the *Atlanta Constitution* proclaimed, had "risen into great prominence" and had become "the second city of the South in regard to the amount of exports and of its business generally." Unable to refrain from gloating, the paper noted that Savannah's antebellum rival, Charleston, "seems to have sunk into a kind of sullen stupor and inactivity. Mobile likewise is dead and New Orleans declining." A local and even more biased observer chronicled Savannah's resurgence and concluded that the "Savannah of today is almost a stranger to the city before the war."[51]

This statement was not really true. Savannah's continued reliance on the cotton market mirrored the city's antebellum experience. Its formidable array of steamers continued to return to port in ballast because of the disparity between imports and exports. Savannah's business leaders and city government continued to be controlled by commission merchants and cotton factors. The city was determined to become the preeminent cotton port, and during the Reconstruction era it was well on its way to achieving that rank. Dependence on that fleecy staple in the postwar world was, however, fraught with difficulty. As one observer remarked, "If cotton were taken from the town there would be little vivacity left."[52]

Savannah's adherence to prewar business activities was a result of the port's war experience. Because the city was sealed off early by the Union blockade, residents never had the opportunity to mobilize the local economy for war needs. The Confederate government did establish a few ordnance plants and facilities for shipbuilding, but Federal advances down the Atlantic coast necessitated their removal to safer interior cities. Once the city was surrounded, economic activity virtually ceased. Potential military suppliers and blockade runners left, and the once mighty port languished. Whereas Confederate military demands had catalyzed diversification, innovation, and industrialization in Atlanta, Columbus, and Augusta, the absence of those same demands yielded economic paralysis in Savannah. With peace, however, Savannah was in an enviable position. Pent-up demands for cotton and lumber reinvigorated the city's business sector. Merchants moved aggressively to reopen trade channels and to take advantage of Savannah's location. By 1870, Savannah was second only to New Orleans in cotton exports. Ironically, constricted business activity during the war enhanced Savannah's position afterward. The city's businessmen had lost money, but their services were now in demand, and this boosted still further economic recovery. The lack of the artificial stimulus of war prompted Savannah's business community to make up for lost time and to compete with old rivals in Augusta and Charleston who had apparently benefited from wartime service. In addition to the thriving commercial sector, by 1870 the city boasted numerous steam presses and gristmills that had been either newly created or reestablished. The city's lucrative trade and strong manufacturing sector boded well for future prosperity.[53]

Georgians would have been justified if they indulged in some self-congratulation in 1870. In five years they had accomplished a great deal. Though parts of the state remained ravaged, most evidence of the war had vanished. Urban populations had increased 1.3 percent over 1860 totals; but more important, the number of manufacturing establishments had grown from 1,890 to 3,836, and capital investment in manufacturing had increased $3 million from 1860 totals. Perhaps the most notable increase occurred in the value of manufactured products: the 1870 total of $31,196,115 represented almost a 100 percent increase over 1860 figures.[54]

Naturally, boosters used such evidence to support their assertion that Georgia was realizing in defeat the economic independence it had hoped to attain in victory. Though a trifle exaggerated, such boasting was not too far off the mark. War and Reconstruction had allowed established industrialists to pursue, relatively unhindered, the dream of diversification and development. Reconstruction policies and plans furthered this growth and innovation and even prompted some of Georgia's urban entrepreneurs to give more than lip service to Republican economic policies. Thus Georgia's urban entrepreneurs of the war mobilization proved hardy enough to play a leading role in rebuilding the state's economy. Even those who had abandoned the quest for self-sufficiency after the war did not oppose the resumed drive for industrialization and diversification.

The persistence of Georgia's urban businessmen naturally raises questions about their role in local and state politics and their relations with other social classes in Georgia. In Atlanta, the men who had led the war effort resumed a leading place in the city's municipal government. As James Michael Russell has shown so effectively, Atlantans were more than willing to make peace with any and all parties— Radical Republican or Conservative Democrat—so long as the business interests of the city were well served.[55] Though in Savannah the old elite of commission merchants and factors resumed control of city politics, their domination did not handicap ambitious entrepreneurs as it did in other old Southern seaports such as Charleston and Mobile.[56] Even before the war, Savannah's business community had been alive to opportunities to enhance the economic base of the city. Reconstruction merely allowed the economic and political leaders to extend those policies.

Augusta and Columbus are exceptions to the pattern established by Atlanta and Savannah. There, it was the lack of banking capital and changes in railroad routes, not a hostile or "hegemonic" planter elite, that stymied ambitious businessmen from extending wartime gains into postwar successes. But even in these cities, those who were successful never missed an opportunity to encourage others to imitate their example and thus aid in the realization of a New South. Indeed, one scholar of the Augusta region argues that the New South boosters of the immediate postwar period "liberated men from a dead past" and allowed the new worldview to percolate throughout Georgia.[57]

Georgia's urban entrepreneurs of the war and postwar periods constituted a new elite. Though many had been prominent before the war and had enjoyed solid reputations within their communities, others were what C. Vann Woodward deemed individuals "with but a nominal connection with the old planter regime."[58] They had served the mobilization well and continued to render noteworthy service during the Reconstruction period. Because of their contribution to the Lost Cause, they continued to be accepted within their communities. They were not always considered heretics because they accepted defeat and worked to rebuild; if anything, they were hailed as Southern heroes who had put the past behind them and were endeavoring to create a more just liberal capitalist order. In this respect, they were the direct antecedents of the New South boosters usually associated with the 1880s.

Still, Georgia's urban businessmen did not enjoy unchecked successes in the postbellum period. Many were acutely aware that there were weaknesses in the state's economy which did not bode well for the future. The agricultural sector remained in difficulty, for farm values were half what they had been before the war. The number of farms had increased, but improved acreage and the average size of Georgia's farms still lagged behind antebellum levels. More ominous still, the amount of acreage devoted to cotton was increasing. Ironically, Georgia was becoming more dependent on cotton than at any time in its history.[59] Calls for more diversified and scientific farming were bandied about, but few efforts were made to attain a New South in agriculture.

These soft spots in the state's economy would not go away. Instead, they worsened and were accompanied by another calamity: the financial panic of 1873. Historians have not accorded this depression the attention it deserves in Southern history. The contraction on Wall Street was nearly as disastrous to Southerners, and especially Georgians, as General Sherman had been. Businesses closed down, bank capital dried up, factories suspended operations, and railroads went into receivership. It must have seemed to many as if eight years of hard work and sacrifice had been wiped out overnight. Like their counterparts elsewhere in the South, Georgians had to struggle through another period of lean times. Not until the late 1870s and even into the 1880s were they able to resume their quest for a New South economy grounded on prewar and war-honed foundations.[60] Even then they would face obstacles. But Georgia's entrepreneurs would endure; they would continue to press forward in their quest for a diversified and balanced state economy.

Conclusion

Building a New South in Urban Georgia

Scholars of urban history have long argued that cities are crucibles of change. The diverse activities of urban centers, the presence of residents from different classes, of different social and economic status and even racial groups—these factors and others made urban centers a unique milieu for change. Modernization in trade, manufacturing, or transportation more often than not originated in the urban center and percolated to the hinterland.

That Georgia's cities were crucibles of change is borne out by examining the antebellum, wartime, and postwar periods. Cities like Augusta and Columbus witnessed the first steps toward diversification and industrialization in the American South. In cities like Atlanta and Savannah, ambitious entrepreneurs first envisioned the role and importance of railroads to economic growth. In all four Georgia cities, ambitious men responded to opportunities to expand and diversify the local and regional urban-industrial economy. In this way, Georgia's urban entrepreneurs created the infrastructure of a diversified economy, distinguished by textile and rolling mills and an extensive railroad network.

Georgia's entrepreneurial revolution of the antebellum years was catalyzed anew by the demands of Civil War mobilization. The Confederate war machine's insatiable appetite for military hardware, uniforms, and accoutrements, and for effective communication and transportation, accelerated trends that had been afoot for nearly twenty years when the first shots were fired. Established leaders used the war mobilization to expand their activities—and their profits. For Georgia's urban entrepreneurs, war created nothing but opportunity: a chance to continue their quest for a balanced urban-industrial order. Far from opposing the emergence of an ambitious entrepreneurial cohort, the Confederate government actively encouraged business endeavor by extending capital advances and by detailing workers from the ranks. Georgia's aggressive entrepreneurs partook of these opportunities and aided the effort. For many Georgians, these businessmen were patriots, selflessly serving the Confederate cause; others saw them as patriots with a profit motive, eagerly capitalizing on conditions in a society made fluid by war. But even those who recognized the role of the profit motive did not necessarily condemn it. Indeed, though speculators and, often, manufacturers bore the brunt of the invective of Southern newspapers, in general and for most of the war, the public manifested an approving attitude toward entrepreneurial endeavor. This public approbation of business enterprise helped chip away at any lingering doubts as to the efficacy or desirability of Southern industrialization.

With peace, most of Georgia's urban entrepreneurs found their enterprises in physical or financial ruin. Many who had climbed aboard the mobilization bandwagon found peacetime too unsettled to continue risky and innovative endeavors. Rebuilding cities and railroads seemed to sap whatever inventiveness—and capital—those entrepreneurs may have possessed during wartime. Others, however, were undaunted by such tasks. Indeed, the rapid revival of cities like Atlanta and Savannah testifies to the persistence of the entrepreneurial ethos. Prewar foundations, especially in Atlanta, had been augmented by the demands of mobilization. After the war, Atlanta business leaders were determined that the wartime advances would not be wasted. Implicitly, defeat acted as yet another catalyst: it prompted a psychological need to "out-Yankee the Yankees," to prove that the wartime gains, achieved under tremendous handicaps, were not a fluke but the product of careful planning and execution.

Georgia's urban entrepreneurs would persist. After exerting the "last full measure" in war, nothing seemed impossible. With peace, these men adapted to the new realities. They rebuilt and expanded the textile factories, rolling mills, and sawmills and the Georgia railroad system. They used the opportunities of defeat and Reconstruction to resume the drive for a diversified economy. In essence, Georgia's entrepreneurs matured with war mobilization. They continued to exhibit foresight and inventiveness after hostilities ended, but they also assumed a more advanced role: that of manager. After recreating the diverse urban-industrial economy of the prewar and wartime periods, they worked to conserve and extend it. In so doing, they acted as role models for the new generation of innovators: the entrepreneurs who emerged in the 1880s to extend the promise of war-induced manufacturing into the industrial resurgence of the New South. The persistence of these entrepreneurs demonstrates that economic change in antebellum and wartime Georgia was neither illusory nor evanescent; nor was the aggressive entrepreneurial spirit that launched the antebellum and wartime industrial revolutions extinguished in the holocaust of 1861–65.

Notes

Preface

1. Barrington Moore, *Social Origins of Dictatorship and Democracy: Lord and Peasant in the Making of the Modern World* (New York: Beacon Press, 1966), pp. 111–55; Eugene Genovese, *The Political Economy of Slavery: Studies in the Economy and Society of the Slave South* (New York: Pantheon Books, 1965), pp. 180–208; Genovese and Elizabeth Fox-Genovese, *Fruits of Merchant Capital: Slavery and Bourgeois Property in the Rise and Expansion of Capitalism* (New York: Oxford University Press, 1983), pp. 148–49, 167.

2. Jonathan Wiener, *Social Origins of the New South: Alabama, 1860–1885* (Baton Rouge: Louisiana State University Press, 1978), and Wiener, "Class Structure and Economic Development in the American South, 1865–1955," *American Historical Review* 84 (October 1979): 970–92; Dwight B. Billings, Jr., *Planters and the Making of the "New South": Class, Politics, and Development in North Carolina, 1865–1900,* (Chapel Hill: University of North Carolina Press, 1979).

3. David R. Goldfield, *Urban Growth in an Age of Sectionalism: Virginia, 1847–1861* (Baton Rouge: Louisiana State University Press, 1977); J. Mills Thornton III, *Politics and Power in a Slave Society, Alabama, 1800–1860* (Baton Rouge: Louisiana State University Press, 1978).

4. See, for example, Raimondo Luraghi, *The Rise and Fall of the Plantation South* (New York: Franklin Watts, 1978), and Luraghi, "The Civil War and the Modernization of American Society: Social Structure and Industrial Revolution before and during the War," *Civil War History* 18 (September 1972): 230–50.

5. Emory M. Thomas, *The Confederate Nation, 1861–1865* (New York: Harper Torchbooks, 1979), pp. 212–14.

6. Joseph A. Schumpeter, "The Creative Response in Economic History," *Journal of Economic History* 7 (1949): 149–59. See also Burton W. Folsom, *Urban Capitalists: Economic Leadership and Growth in the Lehigh and Lackawanna Regions of Pennsylvania, 1800–1920* (Baltimore: Johns Hopkins University Press, 1981).

Chapter 1

1. Robert Sobel, *Panic on Wall Street: A History of America's Financial Disasters* (London: Macmillan, 1968), p. 72. See also Bray Hammond, *Banks and Politics in America from the Revolution to the Civil War* (Princeton: Princeton University Press, 1957), pp. 451–57, 542–48; and Peter Temin, *The Jacksonian Economy* (New York: Norton, 1969), pp. 113–47.

2. Charles S. Sydnor, *The Development of Southern Sectionalism, 1819–1848*

(Baton Rouge: Louisiana State University Press, 1948), p. 263; J. G. Johnson, "Notes on Manufacturing in Antebellum Georgia," *Georgia Historical Quarterly* 16 (March 1932): 219–20; Richard H. Shryock, *Georgia and the Union in 1850* (Durham: Duke University Press, 1926), pp. 21–22; Milton Sydney Heath, *Constructive Liberalism: The Role of the State in Economic Development in Georgia to 1860* (Cambridge: Harvard University Press, 1954), p. 205.

3. Philip G. Davidson, "Industrialism in the Antebellum South," *South Atlantic Quarterly* 27 (October 1928): 414; Richard H. Shryock, "The Early Industrial Revolution in the Empire State," *Georgia Historical Quarterly* 11 (June 1927): 110–13.

4. Shryock, *Georgia and the Union,* pp. 222–23; Shryock, "The Early Industrial Revolution in the Empire State," pp. 110–13.

5. W. K. Wood, "A Note on Pro-Urbanism and Urbanization in the Antebellum South: Augusta, Georgia, 1820–1860," *Richmond County History* 6 (Winter 1974): 25.

6. Richard W. Griffen, "The Augusta (Georgia) Manufacturing Company in Peace, War, and Reconstruction, 1847–1877," *Business History Review* 32 (Spring 1958): 60–61; Salem Dutcher and Charles C. Jones, Jr., *Memorial History of Augusta, Georgia, from Its Settlement in 1735 to the Close of the Eighteenth Century* (Syracuse, N.Y.: D. Mason, 1890), p. 401. This consortium consisted of Nicholas DeLaigle, James Fraser, John P. King, Andrew J. Miller, and Henry C. Cumming.

7. Georgia, vol. 1b, p. 126, R. G. Dun & Co. Collection, Baker Library, Harvard University Graduate School of Business Administration, Cambridge, Mass.

8. Ibid., pp. 60, 51, 53, 13, 145, 126; Wood, "A Note on Pro-Urbanism," pp. 25–26; Dutcher and Jones, *Memorial History of Augusta,* pp. 428–29. The businessmen in this group included Lambeth Hopkins, William E. Jackson, R. H. Gardner, George Schley, Henry C. Cumming, William D'Antignac, and John P. King.

9. Griffen, "Augusta (Georgia) Manufacturing Company," pp. 62–63; Wood, "A Note on Pro-Urbanism," p. 26.

10. Diffee W. Standard, *Columbus, Georgia, in the Confederacy: The Social and Industrial Life of the Chattahoochee River Port* (New York: William Frederick Press, 1954), p. 27.

11. Georgia, vol. 23, pp. 32, 24, 43, R. G. Dun & Co. Collection; Standard, *Columbus, Georgia, in the Confederacy,* p. 28. The Howard and Coweta manufacturing companies were merged with the Grant Factory and the Eagle Factory in the late 1850s. See Georgia, vol. 23, pp. 110, 156, 125, R. G. Dun & Co. Collection.

12. Georgia, vol. 23, p. 14, R. G. Dun & Co. Collection; Standard, *Columbus, Georgia, in the Confederacy,* p. 29.

13. Georgia, vol. 23, pp. 60, 61, 63, R. G. Dun & Co. Collection; Standard, *Columbus, Georgia, in the Confederacy,* p. 30.

14. Richard W. Griffen, "The Origins of the Industrial Revolution in Georgia: Cotton Textiles, 1810–1865," *Georgia Historical Quarterly* 42 (1958): 371. Perhaps the best example of a Columbus planter turned industrialist is Colo-

nel Farish Carter. Renowned as the largest landowner and slaveholder in the state, Carter owned and invested in several mills in the Columbus area. His extensive business dealings are chronicled in the Farish Carter Papers, Southern Historical Collection, University of North Carolina, Chapel Hill.

15. Standard, *Columbus, Georgia, in the Confederacy*, p. 28.

16. *DeBow's Review* 9 (October 1850): 430.

17. Griffen, "Origins of the Industrial Revolution in Georgia," p. 371. In 1850, Columbus had a population of 5,942; in 1860, the figure stood at 9,621. See U.S. Census Office, *Compendium of the Seventh Census* (Washington, D.C.: Beverly Tucker, Senate Printer, 1854), p. 366, and *Eighth Census of the United States: Population* (Washington, D.C.: U.S. Government Printing Office, 1864).

18. Supt. of the United States Census, *Seventh Census of the United States, 1850, Embracing Statistical View of Each of the States and Territories* (Washington, D.C.: Beverly Tucker, Printer, 1854), p. 180; see also Treasury Department returns, as cited in Shryock, *Georgia and the Union*, p. 25.

19. *Columbus Times*, 29 December 1850.

20. Griffen, "Origins of the Industrial Revolution in Georgia," pp. 366, 368.

21. *DeBow's Review* 7 (1849): 177.

22. U.S. Census Office, *Manufactures of the United States in 1860: Compiled from the Original Returns of the Eighth Census* (Washington, D.C.: U.S. Government Printing Office, 1865), pp. 715–18, 60–64; see also McWhorter S. Cooley, "Manufacturing in Georgia during the Civil War Period" (M.S. thesis, University of Georgia, 1929), pp. 16–17.

23. Ulrich B. Phillips, *A History of Transportation in the Eastern Cotton Belt to 1860* (New York: Columbia University Press, 1908), p. 252; Heath, *Constructive Liberalism*, p. 256.

24. Heath, *Constructive Liberalism*, p. 258.

25. "Minutes and Resolutions," *American Railroad Journal*, 10 December 1836, as cited in ibid., p. 268.

26. Mary G. Cumming, *Georgia Railroad and Banking Company, 1833–1945* (Augusta: Walton Printing House, 1945), p. 26. A bank charter was added to the Georgia Railroad Charter in 1836. See Heath, *Constructive Liberalism*, p. 263.

27. Heath, *Constructive Liberalism*, pp. 272, 276–77; Phillips, *History of Transportation*, pp. 240–43; W. J. Northen, ed., *Men of Mark in Georgia*, 7 vols. (Atlanta: A. B. Caldwell, 1910), 3:424–31. The Georgia Railroad's original terminus was Decatur, but residents of that town protested that the "noise" of road traffic would frighten farm animals and lower local land values. Company officials were thus forced to push the line farther west to Marthasville, which was renamed Atlanta in 1847. See *Atlanta Journal*, as quoted in Cumming, *Georgia Railroad and Banking Company*, p. 67.

28. The presidency of the Central passed to Gordon's son-in-law Richard R. Cuyler upon Gordon's death in 1842. See Charles C. Jones, Jr., *History of Savannah, Georgia, from Its Settlement to the Close of the Eighteenth Century* (Syracuse, N.Y.: D. Mason, 1890), pp. 480–81. Heath discusses the back-

ground of the Central of Georgia Railroad's bank charter in *Constructive Liberalism*, pp. 262–63; see also Phillips, *History of Transportation*, pp. 252, 263, 294. Additional information on the founding of the Central may be found in the company's *Annual Reports*, Georgia Historical Society, Savannah and Georgia State Library, Atlanta.

29. Contemporaries clearly recognized the developmental impact of the railroads. Indeed, all projects contemplated in Georgia and elsewhere were designed to expand the local economies and surrounding areas or hinterlands. See Allan R. Pred, *The Spatial Dynamics of U.S. Urban-Industrial Growth, 1800–1914: Interpretive and Theoretical Essays* (Cambridge: MIT Press, 1966), pp. 163–67; see also David R. Goldfield, *Urban Growth in an Age of Sectionalism: Virginia, 1847–1861* (Baton Rouge: Louisiana State University Press, 1977), p. 250; and J. Mills Thornton III, *Politics and Power in a Slave Society: Alabama, 1800–1860* (Baton Rouge: Louisiana State University Press, 1978), pp. 280–81.

30. Heath, *Constructive Liberalism*, provides an excellent analysis of Georgia's role as railroad entrepreneur; see pp. 258–60, 269–70. For the legislative and financial history of the Western & Atlantic, see James H. Johnston, *The Western and Atlantic Railroad of the State of Georgia* (Atlanta: Stein Printing, 1932).

31. Johnston, *Western & Atlantic*, pp. 106–7. See also Western & Atlantic Cash Journals of the Treasurer, 1856–66, vol. 6, and *Reports of the Superintendent and Treasurer of the Western & Atlantic Railroad for 1859–60*, Georgia Department of Archives and History, Atlanta. The *Annual Report of the Comptroller General of the State of Georgia Made to the Governor* (October 1857), University of Georgia Library, Athens, also contains pertinent information, as does the *Report of the State Finance Committee, 1851*, pp. 2–12. Actually, the state approved of plans to sell the Western & Atlantic to private interests, but there were no buyers. See Heath, *Constructive Liberalism*, p. 271.

32. W. K. Wood, "The Georgia Railroad and Banking Company," *Georgia Historical Quarterly* 57 (Winter 1973): 551–52; Phillips, *History of Transportation*, p. 247.

33. Superintendent's Report, *Georgia Railroad and Banking Company Annual Report for 1859*, p. 20, Georgia State Library, Atlanta.

34. Ibid., pp. 20–21; also Cumming, *Georgia Railroad and Banking Company*, p. 74; Wood, "Georgia Railroad and Banking Company," pp. 548, 552–53. The company did build two steamers that were docked at Charleston to launch the road's coastal steamship operations. The onset of sectional hostilities, however, forced the Georgia Railroad to suspend those operations. All these developments underscore the reality that as Georgia cities diversified (largely through the effects of the railroads), they grew more connected with and dependent on the national market, headquartered in New York. See Robert G. Albion's classic *Rise of New York Port, 1815–1860* (New York: Scribner's and Sons, 1939), esp. chap. 7, "The Cotton Triangle," pp. 95–122; also Goldfield, *Urban Growth*, pp. 235–51, who explores this phenomenon in the context of Virginia's cities.

35. Central Railroad and Banking Company, *Reports of the Presidents and Su-*

*perintendents of the Central Railroad and Banking Company of Georgia, No. 20 to
32, Inclusive, and the Amended Charter of the Company* (Savannah: G. N.
Nichols, Printer, 1868), 1857, p. 75; 1858, pp. 101–3; see also Jones, *History of
Savannah*, pp. 480–81; Phillips, *History of Transportation*, pp. 252, 263, 294;
and Richard H. Haunton, "Savannah in the 1850s" (Ph.D. dissertation,
Emory University, 1968), pp. 159–60.

36. Central Railroad and Banking Company, *Reports*, President's Report,
1856, pp. 52–54; 1857, pp. 74–75; 1859, pp. 126–27. Ironically, the Central's
steamship line increased the road's dependence on Northern services. See
Haunton, "Savannah in the 1850s," p. 177.

37. Henry V. Poor, *Manual of the Railroads of the United States, 1869–70* (New
York: L. G. Wemyss, Binder, 1869), pp. xxvi–xxvii.

38. Georgia's roads were of a uniform five-foot gauge—the approximate
"standard" gauge in most of the South. A perfect example of a lack of
through city connections existed in Augusta. The Augusta City Council refused until after the Civil War began to allow the different railroads to meet
at a common terminal; hence freight destined for Savannah on the Georgia
Railroad had to be unloaded and hauled across town to the Augusta & Savannah. See Georgia Railroad and Banking Company, *Annual Reports*, 1860;
also Cumming, *Georgia Railroad and Banking Company*, p. 74. For breakdowns
of state, local, and private investment in Georgia's railroads, see Heath, *Constructive Liberalism*, Tables 15 and 16, pp. 287–89.

39. Maury Klein explores the "provincial" mind-set of the South's antebellum railroad managers in "The Strategy of Southern Railroads," *American
Historical Review* 73 (April 1968): 1054. This view and the notion that railroads
in Georgia benefited the state and the communities they served deviates
from the line once developed by Ulrich B. Phillips, who argued that "the cotton belt railroads did not greatly increase the local productive resources; nor
did they vastly increase commerce." But I attempt to show in this chapter,
and other scholars such as Milton Heath and Maury Klein have demonstrated, that the railroads in this part of the cotton belt, in Georgia, did in
fact boost the local economies and stimulate trade. See Phillips, *History of
Transportation*, p. 390.

40. Heath, *Constructive Liberalism*, p. 277.

41. Heath provides an interesting analysis of the interplay between public
and private sources of aid in ibid., pp. 286–92. For observations on the nature of Southern railroad development overall, and public and private
sources of funding, see Heath, "Public Railroad Construction and the Development of Private Enterprise in the South before 1861," *Journal of Economic
History* 10, Supplement (1950): 40–53.

42. Lester J. Cappon, "Trend of the Southern Iron Industry under the
Plantation System," *Journal of Economic and Business History* 2 (1930): 364–65,
374–75.

43. Georgia, vol. 1b, p. 61, R. G. Dun & Co. Collection; Wood, "Georgia
Railroad and Banking Company," p. 551.

44. Central Railroad, *Annual Report*, 1852, n.p. See also Haunton, "Savannah in the 1850s," p. 135.

45. Georgia, vol. 13, pp. 162, 164, R. G. Dun & Co. Collection. The Northern owners were Colonel William Markham and Lewis Scofield, natives of Connecticut who had settled in Atlanta when it was just a railroad terminus.

46. Ibid., vol. 23, pp. 90, 102–3.

47. U.S. Census Office, *Statistical View of the United States, Being a Compendium of the Seventh Census* (Washington, D.C.: Beverly Tucker, 1854), p. 179.

48. U.S. Census Office, *Manufactures of the United States in 1860*, p. 82.

49. Albert W. Niemi, Jr., has traced the convergence of manufacturing in the United States in his *State and Regional Patterns in American Manufacturing, 1860–1900* (Westport, Conn.: Greenwood Press, 1974), pp. 102–3. Comparing Georgia's industrial production to that of a Northern manufacturing state such as Massachusetts is instructive but misleading. For example, in 1836, Lowell contained 20 mills which operated 130,000 spindles and 4,200 looms. The firm's assets stood at $6.1 million. Fourteen years later, Lowell boasted 40 mills, 320,000 spindles, 9,900 looms, and assets of $12 million. The town's population grew from 6,000 to 33,000, to become Massachusetts's second largest city. In contrast, Georgia's two textile leaders, Columbus and Augusta, contained approximately 60,000 spindles. Yet when viewed in isolation, Georgia's total growth in textile manufacturing was impressive: the industry increased 58.8 percent from 1850 to 1860. It may well be, as Stephen Goldfarb has persuasively argued, that lags in Southern—and Georgian—textile manufacturing were more the result of geographic constraints than planter hostility. See Stephen J. Goldfarb, "A Note on Limits to the Growth of the Cotton Textile Industry in the Old South," *Journal of Southern History* 48 (November 1982): 545–58; also Thomas Dublin, *Women at Work: The Transformation of Work and Community in Lowell, Massachusetts, 1826–1860* (New York: Columbia University Press, 1979), p. 133; and Philip Scranton, *Proprietary Capitalism: The Textile Manufacture at Philadelphia, 1800–1885* (New York: Cambridge University Press, 1983), p. 19, Table 2.1.

50. Cooley, "Manufacturing in Georgia during the Civil War Period," p. 11.

51. *Milledgeville Southern Recorder*, in *DeBow's Review* 13 (January 1850): 39.

52. *DeBow's Review* 25 (December 1858): 725.

53. *Annual Report of the Comptroller General . . . 1857*, p. 19.

54. Representative examples of the various theories advanced may be found in Eugene Genovese, *The Political Economy of Slavery: Studies in the Economy and Society of the Slave South* (New York: Pantheon Books, 1965); Robert Fogel and Stanley Engermann, *Time on the Cross: The Economics of American Negro Slavery* (Boston: Little, Brown, 1974); and Gavin Wright, *The Political Economy of the Cotton South: Households, Markets and Wealth in the Nineteenth Century* (New York: Norton, 1978).

55. D. R. Hundley, *Social Relations in Our Southern States* (1860; rpt. Ann Arbor: University Microfilms, 1973), pp. 104, 131, 157.

56. Frederick Law Olmsted, *A Journey in the Seaboard Slave States* (New York: Dix and Edwards, 1856), pp. 523, 529–30.

57. "A Charleston Gentleman," *Incidents of a Journey from Abbeville, South Carolina to Ocala, Florida* (1852), as quoted in Shryock, *Georgia and the Union*, p. 83. For examples of urban rivalries, see *Milledgeville Southern Recorder*, 9

July 1850, 10 February 1852, 25 October 1853, 11 April 1854, 3 April 1855; *Augusta Chronicle and Sentinel*, 7 March, 12 September, 11 November 1860; and *Atlanta Daily Intelligencer*, 17 December 1862.

58. The 1860 census shows that the vast majority of the state's populace were born-and-bred Georgians. Of a total free population of 583,417, approximately 81 percent were natives. Other Southerners (defined here as future Confederate South) represented 18.5 percent of Georgia's population. In sum, close to 99 percent of the state's population was born and reared south of the Mason and Dixon line. This factor makes the existence of a Yankee ethos all the more interesting. Next to Georgians, population rankings of inhabitants by their state of birth are as follows: South Carolina, 50,112; North Carolina, 29,213; Tennessee, 7,705; Virginia, 5,275; Alabama, 4,628; New York, 2,125; Florida, 1,659; and Pennsylvania, 981. There were also 11,671 foreign-born residents of the state. This element (about 2 percent) hailed primarily from Ireland, Germany, and England. See U.S. Census Office, *Seventh Census*, p. 366, and *Eighth Census, Population*, p. 76.

59. Joseph A. Schumpeter, "The Creative Response in Economic History," *Journal of Economic History* 7 (November 1947): 150; see also Arthur H. Cole, *Business Enterprise in Its Social Setting* (Cambridge: Harvard University Press, 1959), p. 77.

60. Arthur H. Cole has analyzed the role of the state in encouraging entrepreneurship in "primitive conditions" using ideas advanced by William T. Easterbrook. See Cole, *Business Enterprise*, pp. 158–59. For Easterbrook's ideas, see "The Climate of Enterprise," in Hugh G. J. Aitken, ed., *Explorations in Enterprise* (Cambridge: Harvard University Press, 1965), pp. 70–75.

61. Heath, *Constructive Liberalism*, pp. 323, 334. Although a Whig party did not, in name, exist in Georgia, its forerunner, the Troup and States Rights parties, championed policies later identified with Whiggery. See Shryock, *Georgia and the Union*, and Kenneth Coleman, ed., *A History of Georgia* (Athens: University of Georgia Press, 1977), pp. 130–34.

62. The Southern Whig Industrial Gospel emerged in the early 1850s in response to political developments that arose in the aftermath of the Compromise of 1850. Southerners of both parties urged that economic dependence on the North be ended by developing home manufacture and diversifying agriculture. For a complete analysis of this movement and the role of the Southern Whigs in general, see Arthur C. Cole, *The Whig Party in the South* (Washington, D.C.: American Historical Association, 1913), pp. 206–8.

63. The 1843 and 1847 acts required that prospective firms had only to file statements on the nature and purpose of their organization and the amount of capital subscribed. See Georgia *Laws* (1843), pp. 108–9, and Georgia *Laws* (1847), pp. 219–21, as cited in Heath, *Constructive Liberalism*, pp. 312, 322. Georgia's move toward more liberal incorporation statutes paralleled Southern trends. See Goldfarb, "A Note on Limits to the Growth of the Cotton Textile Industry in the Old South," pp. 546–47. Heath's analysis, as well as my own, supports theories Cole and Easterbrook advanced about the role of the state in fostering an entrepreneurial class in the early stages of economic development. See Cole, *Business Enterprise*, pp. 158–59, and Easterbrook, "Cli-

mate of Enterprise," pp. 70–77. For the "creative response" thesis, see Schumpeter, "Creative Response," p. 150; see also Burton W. Folsom, Jr., *Urban Capitalists: Economic Leadership and Growth in the Lehigh and Lackawanna Regions of Pennsylvania, 1800–1920* (Baltimore: Johns Hopkins University Press, 1981), p. 147.

64. Steven Hahn explores this issue in his thoughtful book *The Roots of Southern Populism: Yeoman Farmers and the Transformation of the Georgia Upcountry, 1850–1890* (New York: Oxford University Press, 1983), pp. 103–4. Thornton finds similar developments in Alabama. See *Politics and Power*, pp. 305–6.

65. See Brown's inaugural address on the banking issue in *Augusta Constitutionalist*, 5 November 1858; see also Joseph H. Parks, *Joseph E. Brown of Georgia* (Baton Rouge: Louisiana State University Press, 1977), p. 69.

66. *Senate Journal*, 1857, as quoted in Parks, *Joseph E. Brown*, p. 48.

67. Brown to James H. Bethune, 25 March 1860, as cited in ibid., p. 123.

68. Heath, *Constructive Liberalism*, p. 335. Heath provides excellent tables and charts documenting this phenomenon. See ibid., Chart II, p. 307, Table 21, p. 306. Special acts of incorporation rebounded significantly in 1859 but fell again in 1860, undoubtedly because of the general economic uncertainty that mirrored the deteriorating political situation.

A similar experience in corporation baiting has been documented for Virginia by David Goldfield and for Alabama by Mills Thornton. See Goldfield, *Urban Growth*, p. 179, and Thornton, *Politics and Power*, pp. 290–91, 304, 310, 328.

69. The idea that planters' political hegemony stymied greater industrial growth and development is explored in Genovese, *Political Economy of Slavery*, p. 246, and Genovese and Elizabeth Fox-Genovese, *Fruits of Merchant Capital: Slavery and Bourgeois Property in the Rise and Expansion of Capitalism* (New York: Oxford University Press, 1983), pp. 148–49, 167.

70. Here, Easterbrook's notion of "minimum security" is particularly salient. As Easterbrook notes, it is imperative for the people of a society to feel that "entrepreneurial health" is synonymous with "the welfare of society." Changes in perception will change such feelings and hence could lead to a withdrawal of popular—and state—sanction. See Easterbrook, "Climate of Enterprise," p. 73.

71. Coleman, ed., *History of Georgia*, pp. 172–73.

72. Thornton found similar conditions and attitudes in antebellum Alabama. See *Politics and Power*, pp. 281–82, 291–93, 297–300.

73. Two studies in particular have informed my thinking and illuminate such trends: Goldfield's *Urban Growth* and Thornton's *Politics and Power*.

74. Don H. Dodd and Wynelle Dodd, *Historical Statistics of the South, 1790–1970* (University, Ala.: University of Alabama Press, 1975), pp. 18–20.

75. See George Fitzhugh, *Sociology of the South, or the Failure of Free Society* (1854; rpt. New York: Burt Franklin, 1965), p. 15; *Knoxville Register* in *Augusta Chronicle and Sentinel*, 20 September 1849; Lewis E. Atherton, *The Southern Country Store, 1800–1860* (Baton Rouge: Louisiana State University Press, 1949), pp. 203–4; and Clement M. Eaton, *The Growth of Southern Civilization, 1790–1860* (New York: Harper and Brothers, 1961), pp. 222–23.

Chapter 2

1. See Table 1, above; also Robert C. Black III, "The Railroads of Georgia in the Confederate War Effort," *Journal of Southern History* 13 (November 1947): 516; and *Annual Report of the Comptroller General of the State of Georgia, 1863* (Milledgeville: Boughton, Nisbet & Barnes, 1863), p. 3.

2. Savannah's Chamber of Commerce was founded in 1841 to "introduce into the management and transaction of the varied and extended operations of merchants . . . order and regularity." The founders justified the organization on the grounds of necessity for collective action to advance local interests. Savannah's leading commercial and industrial leaders were members, and they used the Chamber as a forum for their interests throughout the antebellum era. Unfortunately, the minutes of the Chamber for the antebellum period were destroyed just after the war. Scattered accounts indicate, however, that the Chamber enjoyed the respect of all Savannahians. See Constitution and By-Laws of the Savannah Chamber of Commerce, Georgia Historical Society, Savannah. Richard Haunton presents a detailed analysis of the socioeconomic composition of the Savannah elite in his "Savannah in the 1850s" (Ph.D. dissertation, Emory University, 1968), esp. pp. 34–36, 100.

According to the 1860 census, Savannah accounted for 8.3 percent of capital investment in manufacturing in Georgia and 11.3 percent of manufacturing output. The chief industries were in agricultural processing. See U.S. Census Office, *Eighth Census of the United States: Manufactures* (Washington, D.C.: Beverly Tucker, 1863), p. 64; also Haunton, "Savannah in the 1850s," pp. 129–31. For contemporary accounts of Savannah's business activity, see J. S. Buckingham, *The Slave States of America*, 2 vols. (1842; rpt. New York: Negro Universities Press, 1968), 1:123. Savannah's population in 1860 was composed of 13,875 whites and 8,417 slaves and free blacks.

3. Richard W. Griffen, "The Origins of the Industrial Revolution in Georgia: Cotton Textiles, 1810–1865," *Georgia Historical Quarterly* 42 (1958): 371–72; David R. Goldfield, "Pursuing the American Urban Dream: Cities in the Old South," in David R. Goldfield and Blaine A. Brownell, eds., *The City in Southern History* (Port Washington, N.Y.: Kennikat Press, 1977), pp. 56–58; *Columbus Enquirer*, 24 October 1854; *DeBow's Review* 9 (October 1850): 430; U.S. Census Office, *Eighth Census, Manufactures*, p. 70.

4. See Chapter 1 for Augusta statistics.

5. Grigsby H. Wotton, Jr., "New City of the South: Atlanta, 1843–1873" (Ph.D. dissertation, Johns Hopkins University, 1973), pp. 39–40, 65, 88; James Michael Russell, "Atlanta, Gate City of the South, 1847 to 1885" (Ph.D. dissertation, Princeton University, 1972), pp. 55–57; E. Merton Coulter, *Georgia: A Short History* (Chapel Hill: University of North Carolina Press, 1947), p. 260. For an overview of the differences between Southern cities and the countryside—specifically the "Northern values" evident in antebellum Southern cities, see Clement M. Eaton, *The Growth of Southern Civilization, 1790–1860* (New York: Harper & Brothers, 1961), p. 270.

6. See, for example, *Milledgeville Southern Recorder*, 8 March, 1, 8 November 1859, and 10 January 1860, on the need and ability of Georgia to manufacture, the resources available for manufacturing, and the successful estab-

lishment of manufacturing concerns such as the Atlanta Rolling Mill.

7. For a complete analysis of the South's drive for direct trade, see Herbert Wender, *Southern Commercial Conventions, 1837–1859* (Baltimore: Johns Hopkins University Press, 1930).

8. *Augusta Chronicle and Sentinel*, 26 January 1860. See also ibid., 29 January, 1, 5 February, and 1 March 1860.

9. In Georgia, the election of 1860 prompted a record turnout. Extreme Southern Rights candidate John C. Breckinridge received 51,893 votes. John Bell and the Constitutional Union ticket tallied 42,886 votes, while the Democrats' Stephen A. Douglas garnered 11,580. See Kenneth Coleman, ed., *A History of Georgia* (Athens: University of Georgia Press, 1977), p. 149.

10. Allen D. Candler, ed., *The Confederate Records of the State of Georgia*, 6 vols. (Atlanta: Charles P. Byrd, 1909–12), 1:54–57, 2:109, 365, 3:90; *Report of the Comptroller General of the State of Georgia for 1862* (Milledgeville: Boughton, Nisbet & Barnes, 1862), pp. 135–36.

11. Brown to John P. Floyd, 26 November 1860, in Governor's Letterbooks, Georgia Department of Archives and History, Atlanta. After secession and the outbreak of hostilities, Floyd, a Virginian and later a Confederate general, was accused of stockpiling arms in Federal arsenals in the South—arsenals that were ultimately seized by the Confederates. An investigation later exonerated Floyd. See E. Merton Coulter, *The Confederate States of America, 1861–1865* (Baton Rouge: Louisiana State University Press, 1950), p. 199.

12. Candler, ed., *Confederate Records*, 2:13–16.

13. Coleman, ed., *History of Georgia*, p. 151. See also Donald Arthur DeBats, "Elites and Masses: Political Structure, Communication and Behavior in Antebellum Georgia" (Ph.D. dissertation, University of Wisconsin, 1973), p. 407; Michael P. Johnson, *Toward a Patriarchal Republic: The Secession of Georgia* (Baton Rouge: Louisiana State University Press, 1977), pp. 33–34, 46, 119–20, 201; Johnson, "A New Look at the Popular Vote for Delegates to the Georgia Secession Convention," *Georgia Historical Quarterly* 66 (1972): 259–75. For contemporary reactions to the secession of the state and the celebrations that ensued, see the *Savannah Republican*, 20 January 1861, *Augusta Chronicle and Sentinel*, week of 20 January 1861, and *Atlanta Southern Confederacy*, week of 20 January 1861. See also T. Conn Bryan, *Confederate Georgia* (Athens: University of Georgia Press, 1953), pp. 10–11, 14.

14. Brown to General Assembly, in Candler, ed., *Confederate Records*, 2:108–9. Brown had, in fact, called for that gunsmiths' convention of 6 November 1861. See *Atlanta Southern Confederacy*, 31 August 1861, with the governor's call for that meeting.

15. Mary Elizabeth Massey, *Ersatz in the Confederacy* (Columbia: University of South Carolina Press, 1952), pp. 159–60. For an account of the Confederacy's deficiencies, see Judah P. Benjamin to Jefferson Davis, February 1862, in U.S. War Department, *The War of Rebellion: A Compilation of the Official Records of the Union and Confederate Armies*, Ser. 4, 4 vols. (Washington, D.C.: U.S. Government Printing Office, 1902), 1:955–56; John W. Mallett, "Work of the Ordnance Bureau of the War Department of the Confederate States, 1861–1865," *Southern Historical Society Papers* (Richmond: Southern Historical

Society, 1909), 37:1–2; Charles W. Ramsdell, *Behind the Lines in the Southern Confederacy* (Baton Rouge: Louisiana State University Press, 1944), p. 100; Claud E. Fuller and Richard D. Steuart, *Firearms of the Confederacy* (Huntington, W.Va.: Standard Publications, 1944), p. 114.

16. *Charleston Mercury,* as quoted in *Augusta Chronicle and Sentinel,* 20 July 1861.

17. *Atlanta Southern Confederacy,* 6 September 1861.

18. *Atlanta Daily Intelligencer,* 8 December 1861.

19. Coulter, *Confederate States of America,* pp. 212–13. See also Milton Sydney Heath, *Constructive Liberalism: The Role of the State in Economic Development in Georgia to 1860* (Cambridge: Harvard University Press, 1954), p. 335.

20. *Official Records,* Ser. 4, vol. 1, p. 532. See also Charles B. Dew, *Ironmaker to the Confederacy: Joseph R. Anderson and the Tredegar Iron Works* (New Haven: Yale University Press, 1966), p. 86.

21. Massey, *Ersatz in the Confederacy,* pp. 160–61.

22. Mallett, "Work of the Ordnance Bureau," pp. 5–6. See also Massey, *Ersatz in the Confederacy,* p. 161, and Coulter, *Confederate States of America,* p. 202.

23. Davis to Congress, 18 November 1861, in *Official Records,* Ser. 4, vol. 1, p. 733.

24. Benjamin to Davis, February 1862 [n.d.], ibid., p. 955.

25. Benjamin to Davis, 12 March 1862, ibid., pp. 987–88.

26. "An Act to Organize the Bureau of Artillery and Ordnance," 12 March 1861, ibid., pp. 990–91.

27. Victor S. Clark, in his *History of Manufactures in the United States,* 2d ed., 3 vols. (New York: McGraw-Hill for Carnegie Institution of Washington, 1929), argues that through the organization of the Niter and Mining Bureau and the Ordnance Bureau, the Confederacy anticipated by fifty years the organization and functioning of the War Industries Board (2:42–43).

28. Special Orders No. 86, Adj. and Insp. Genl. Office, 15 April 1862, in *Official Records,* Ser. 4, vol. 1, pp. 1059–60.

29. 17 April 1862, ibid., p. 1070. A supplemental act of 19 April 1862 authorized Davis to extend similar contracts to iron and steel producers (ibid., p. 1074).

The Confederate government's actions demonstrated that even states'-rights advocates were not averse to extending government aid to potential manufacturers and army suppliers. Indeed, the Confederacy's early program of incentives, which was to be augmented and continued throughout the war, provides evidence that the state actively encouraged business endeavor. In providing cash advances and contracts for manufacturing, the government established a climate that encouraged the business community to diversify and innovate so as to aid the mobilization effort. In short, the Confederacy reduced many of the risks associated with entrepreneurial endeavor. See William T. Easterbrook's analysis of the state and its role in fostering enterprise in "The Climate of Enterprise," in Hugh G. J. Aitken, ed., *Explorations in Enterprise* (Cambridge: Harvard University Press, 1965), p. 77.

30. Fuller and Steuart, *Firearms of the Confederacy*, p. 126.

31. George Washington Rains Papers, Southern Historical Collection, University of North Carolina, Chapel Hill.

32. George Washington Rains, *History of the Confederate Powder Works* (Augusta: Chronicle & Constitutionalist, 1882), pp. 10–11. See also Florence Fleming Corley, *Confederate City: Augusta, Georgia, 1860–1865* (Columbia: University of South Carolina Press, 1960), p. 53.

33. Rains, *History of the Confederate Powder Works*, p. 11; see also Corley, *Confederate City*, pp. 53–56, and Frank E. Vandiver, *Ploughshares into Swords: Josiah Gorgas and Confederate Ordnance* (Austin: University of Texas Press, 1952), pp. 76–77; Rains Papers; Records of Government Stores Received and Issued at (Augusta) Powder Factory, 1862–65, Microfilm copy, University of Georgia Library, Athens.

34. Vandiver, *Ploughshares into Swords*, p. 148.

35. Rains, *History of the Confederate Powder Works*, Appendix.

36. John Screven to Mary Screven, 28 April 1862, Arnold-Screven Papers, Southern Historical Collection; *Augusta Chronicle and Sentinel*, 18 January 1861; Corley, *Confederate City*, pp. 46, 76.

37. Beverley M. DuBose III, "The Manufacture of Confederate Ordnance in Georgia," *Atlanta Historical Bulletin* 12 (December 1967): 11–12.

38. Georgia, vol. 1b, p. 57, R. G. Dun & Co. Collection, Baker Library, Harvard University Graduate School of Business Administration, Cambridge, Mass.; DuBose, "Manufacture of Confederate Ordnance in Georgia," pp. 11–12; Rains, *History of the Confederate Powder Works*, Appendix; *Augusta Chronicle and Sentinel*, 11 May 1862; Georgia, vol. 1b, pp. 85, 90, R. G. Dun & Co. Collection. Small manufacturing firms flourished and enjoyed local favor because of their activities on behalf of the Southern cause. The creation of large, privately owned facilities, however, did produce a division of opinion among many Augustans. The press, acting as a local spokesman, voiced uncertainty and opposition to major industrial works throughout 1860 and 1861. This hostility played a key role in delaying Augusta's mobilization drive in the area of quartermaster supply. See Chapter 3, below.

39. Fuller and Steuart, *Firearms of the Confederacy*, pp. 268–71; Corley, *Confederate City*, pp. 47–48; William A. Albaugh III and Edward N. Simmons, *Confederate Arms* (New York: Bonanza Books, 1967), pp. 12–14. Information on C. R. Keen and A. J. Smythe is scanty, but Jesse Ansley was a former Wells Fargo clerk who had bought out the Augusta Wells Fargo office to establish himself as a grocer and wholesale commission merchant. See Georgia, vol. 1b, pp. 11, 97, R. G. Dun & Co. Collection.

40. Fuller and Steuart, *Firearms of the Confederacy*, pp. 269–71; DuBose, "Manufacture of Confederate Ordnance," p. 12. Local accounts of Rigdon's activities may have ended because of the Federal invasion of Georgia. As General William T. Sherman began his March to the Sea, Confederate authorities feared he would strike at Augusta's extensive war production facilities. Most local manufacturing concerns were dismantled and moved, and the city press printed faulty accounts so as to deceive the advancing Federals. It is believed that Rigdon moved his concern to Macon, though confirmation has never been found.

41. James M. Merrill, ed., " 'Personne' Goes to Georgia: Five Civil War Letters," *Georgia Historical Quarterly* 43 (June 1959): 204–5.

42. Arthur J. L. Fremantle, *Three Months in the Southern States, April–June, 1863* (Edinburgh: William Blackwood & Sons, 1863), p. 178.

43. *Augusta Chronicle and Sentinel*, 30 March 1862; see also ibid., 3 February 1864.

44. Bryan, *Confederate Georgia*, p. 102.

45. DuBose, "Manufacture of Confederate Ordnance," pp. 16 17. Columbus was linked to Pensacola, Florida, by 1861 by the Montgomery & West Point and Alabama & Florida railroads. J. Mills Thornton III provides an excellent map of these railroad connections in his *Politics and Power in a Slave Society: Alabama, 1800–1860* (Baton Rouge: Louisiana State University Press, 1978), p. 270.

46. Diffee W. Standard, *Columbus, Georgia, in the Confederacy: The Social and Industrial Life of the Chattahoochee River Port* (New York: William Frederick Press, 1954), pp. 40–43; DuBose, "Manufacture of Confederate Ordnance," pp. 16–17.

47. Ordnance Memo, November 1862, from personal files, Adjutant General's Office, in Vandiver, *Ploughshares into Swords*, p. 148.

48. Georgia, vol. 23, pp. 3, 61, R. G. Dun & Co. Collection; Standard, *Columbus, Georgia, in the Confederacy*, p. 30; *DeBow's Review* 33 (May–August 1862): 77.

49. Georgia, vol. 23, p. 101, R. G. Dun & Co. Collection; Standard, *Columbus, Georgia, in the Confederacy*, p. 30; Fuller and Steuart, *Firearms of the Confederacy*, p. 282; *DeBow's Review* 33 (May–August 1862): 77. DeBow reported that the Haimans operated out of the second floor of the Columbus Arsenal, but Standard places their establishment in the Carter Factory.

50. Fuller and Steuart, *Firearms of the Confederacy*, pp. 282–83; Georgia, vol. 23, p. 101, R. G. Dun & Co. Collection. For a local account of the firm's activities during the war, see *Columbus Daily Sun*, 18 August 1862.

51. Georgia, vol. 23, pp. 39, 293, R. G. Dun & Co. Collection.

52. Albaugh and Simmons, *Confederate Arms*, pp. 224–25.

53. *Columbus Daily Sun*, 12 June 1863.

54. Ralph Benjamin Singer, "Confederate Atlanta" (Ph.D. dissertation, University of Georgia, 1973), pp. 158–59; Wotton, "New City of the South," pp. 93–94.

55. Russell, "Atlanta, Gate City of the South," pp. 132–34, 143.

56. Pioneer Citizens' Society of Atlanta, *Pioneer Citizens' History of Atlanta, 1833–1902* (Atlanta: Byrd Printing Co., 1902), pp. 279–80; Records of the Ordnance Establishments at Dalton, Savannah, Augusta, and Atlanta, Georgia, and Nashville, Tennessee, March, 1862, War Department Collection of Confederate Records, Record Group 109, reel 6, vol. 78, pp. 62–71, Microfilm copy, University of Georgia Library, Athens.

57. Nelson and Asa Tift to Stephen Mallory, 27 November, 6 December 1861, 10 January, 26 August 1862, in U.S. Navy Department, *Official Records of the Union and Confederate Navies in the War of Rebellion*, Ser. 2 (Washington, D.C.: U.S. Government Printing Office, 1922), 1:581, 583, 585, 599; *Atlanta Daily Intelligencer*, 31 July 1857, 20 November 1859, 25 February 1860; Geor-

gia, vol. 13, p. 164, R. G. Dun & Co. Collection.

58. Elizabeth Bowlby, "The Role of Atlanta during the War between the States," *Atlanta Historical Bulletin* 5 (July 1940): 187; Franklin M. Garrett, *Atlanta and Environs: A Chronicle of Its People and Events,* 2 vols. (Athens: University of Georgia Press, 1954), 1:629; Pioneer Citizens' Society of Atlanta, *Pioneer Citizens' History of Atlanta,* pp. 313–15. Contemporaries commented on Scofield and Markham's dubious allegiance to the Confederacy. Although the two men remained in Atlanta, locals noticed their impatience to flee after Sherman left the city in November 1864. The *Atlanta Daily Intelligencer,* forced to publish from Macon after the Confederate evacuation, reported on 17 November 1864 that "all the sympathizers who affiliated with U.S. troops have taken flight northward—Dunning, Scofield, Markham . . . and all the rest of the mongrel curs took their departure early last week. The curse of their traitorous presence will no longer disgrace Atlanta . . . for which we should be devoutly thankful." See the *Intelligencer,* as reprinted in the *Augusta Chronicle and Sentinel,* 17 November 1864. See also James Ormond to William McNaught, 31 October 1864, William McNaught Papers, Folder 1, Atlanta Historical Society.

59. Georgia, vol. 13, p. 162, R. G. Dun & Co. Collection; Stephens Mitchell, "Atlanta: The Industrial Heart of the Confederacy," *Atlanta Historical Bulletin* 1 (May 1930): 22; Garrett, *Atlanta and Environs,* 1:350; Russell, "Atlanta, Gate City of the South," p. 129.

60. Mitchell, "Atlanta," p. 22; Contract of Hammond Marshall & Co., 22 May 1862, War Department Collection of Confederate Records, chap. 10, vol. 78, Record Group 109, Microfilm copy, University of Georgia Library, Athens. For a breakdown on the nativity of the Atlanta population, see Ruth Blair, "Federal Census of Atlanta, DeKalb County," *Atlanta Historical Bulletin* 3 (January 1942): 16–82. See also William McNaught Papers, Folder 7; Garrett, *Atlanta and Environs,* 1:532.

61. Singer, "Confederate Atlanta," p. 161.

62. Records of Ordnance Establishments, 78:73–151; Singer, "Confederate Atlanta," p. 161.

63. For local complaints about slow business, see *Atlanta Southern Confederacy,* 21 June, 26 July 1861, and *Atlanta Daily Intelligencer* 17 December 1862, 25 January 1863.

64. *South Carolinian,* 26 March 1863, as reported in *Atlanta Southern Confederacy* 7 April 1863; *Atlanta Southern Confederacy,* 23 May 1863; *Charleston Courier,* 7 March 1863, as reprinted in *Atlanta Southern Confederacy,* 24 March 1863.

65. *Atlanta Southern Confederacy,* 10 September 1861, 4 February 1862, 11 March, 18 April 1863. See also *Augusta Chronicle and Sentinel,* 19 January 1864, and *Atlanta Daily Intelligencer,* 6 June 1862.

66. *Savannah Republican,* 7 February 1861; *Official Records of the Union and Confederate Navies,* Ser. 2, vol. 1, pp. 329, 331–32, 362, 401; George Anderson Mercer Diary, 13 September 1861, Southern Historical Collection.

67. Mercer Diary, 10 November 1861; Alexander A. Lawrence, *A Present for Mr. Lincoln: The Story of Savannah from Secession to Sherman* (Macon: Ardvian Press, 1961), p. 83; J. L. Locke to Laura, 3 March 1862, Bulloch Family Pa-

pers, Southern Historical Collection; Memo of Chief Engineer John McCrady, 18 August 1863, Arnold-Screven Family Papers, ibid.

68. Lawrence, *A Present for Mr. Lincoln*, p. 51.

69. Mercer Diary, 14 April 1862; Charles H. Olmstead, "Fort Pulaski," *Georgia Historical Quarterly* 1 (June 1917): 100–104; Lawrence, *A Present for Mr. Lincoln*, p. 59. For a listing of the total losses sustained from the fall of the fort, see *Savannah Republican*, as reprinted in *Augusta Chronicle and Sentinel*, 26 April 1862. Although General David Hunter was in command of the Union forces before Fort Pulaski, Union engineer officer General Quincy A. Gillmore was in charge of the attack. See U.S. War Department, *The War of Rebellion: A Compilation of the Official Records of the Union and Confederate Armies*, Ser. 1, 53 vols. (Washington, D.C.: U.S. Government Printing Office, 1880–1902), 6:133–69.

70. One Savannahian continued active in blockade-running activities. Gazaway Bugg Lamar, a Savannah banker, formed the Import and Export Company of Georgia and contracted with the Confederate government to run cotton through the blockade in exchange for war materials. Lamar bought and equipped three steamers, with the aid of London bankers, and carried on a brisk trade that netted the Confederacy badly needed supplies— and, not incidentally, made him a wealthy man. By 1864 Lamar had five ships in operation running from Bermuda and the Bahamas. Although he based his company in Savannah, Lamar's chief ports of entry were Wilmington and Charleston; hence Savannah received little aid for his daring. See *Official Records*, Ser. 4, vol. 1, p. 557, and Thomas R. Hay, "Gazaway Bugg Lamar, Confederate Banker and Businessman," *Georgia Historical Quarterly* 37 (June 1953): 89–124; Chief Constructor John L. Parker to Stephen Mallory, 1 November 1864, in *Official Records of the Union and Confederate Navies*, Ser. 2, vol. 2, p. 755. See also Henry Frederick Willink, Jr., Papers, Georgia Historical Society, Savannah; Frank Vizetelly, as cited in Lawrence, *A Present for Mr. Lincoln*, p. 88; John L. G. Wood to Father, 25 February 1862, as cited in ibid.

71. J. L. Locke to Laura, 22 October 1862, 12 September 1863, Bulloch Family Papers.

72. Mercer Diary, 4, 21 November 1862, 23 April, 31 May, 18 September 1863, 5 January 1864; J. L. Locke to Laura, 14 June 1863, Bulloch Family Papers.

73. Emory Thomas coins this term to characterize the military-industrial revolution that took place in the Confederate South. See *The Confederate Nation, 1861–1865* (New York: Harper Torchbooks, 1979), pp. 210–12.

74. Frank E. Vandiver, ed., *The Civil War Diary of General Josiah Gorgas* (University, Ala.: University of Alabama Press, 1947), pp. 90–91; see also James Seddon to Jefferson Davis, 3 January 1863, 3 November 1864, in *Official Records*, Ser. 4, vol. 2, pp. 279–90, 759.

75. David R. Goldfield, *Cotton Fields and Skyscrapers: Southern City and Region, 1607–1980* (Baton Rouge: Louisiana State University Press, 1982), p. 82.

76. Blaine A. Brownell, "Urbanization in the South: A Unique Experience?" *Mississippi Quarterly* 26 (Spring 1973): 111. See also Heath, *Constructive Liberalism*, p. 335.

77. Mallett, "Work of the Ordnance Bureau," pp. 10–11; I. M. St. John to

G. W. Randolph, 31 July 1862, in *Official Records*, Ser. 4, vol. 2, pp. 26–28.

78. *Milledgeville Southern Recorder*, 11 November 1862; Reports of Georgia House Resolutions to Foster Development of State Iron Resources, 18 November 1862, ibid. See also Special Orders No. 36, Adj. and Insp. Genl. Office, Government Confiscation of Iron, 12 February 1863, in *Official Records*, Ser. 4, vol. 2, p. 393; and Dew, *Ironmaker to the Confederacy*, pp. 176–78.

79. U.S. War Department, *Journal of the Congress of the Confederate States of America*, 7 vols. (Washington, D.C.: U.S. Government Printing Office, 1904–5), 1:286, 7:441, 471, 472, 516, 618, 691; Candler, ed., *Confederate Records*, 2:56–57; Mallett, "Work of the Ordnance Bureau," p. 11. Clarence Mohr exhaustively investigates the use of slave labor in Georgia war industries in *On the Threshold of Freedom: Masters and Slaves in Civil War Georgia* (Athens: University of Georgia Press, 1986), pp. 128, 137, 143, 149, 150. See also editorials urging exemptions of skilled workers and criticizing the government for "overmobilizing" in *Augusta Chronicle and Sentinel*, 14 January, 30 April 1864, *Talladega Watchman*, as reprinted in ibid., 7 June 1864.

80. Herman Hattaway and Archer Jones, *How the North Won: A Military History of the Civil War* (Urbana: University of Illinois Press, 1983), p. 86; Seddon to Davis, 3 January 1863, in *Official Records*, Ser. 4, vol. 2, p. 291. See also Richard D. Goff, *Confederate Supply* (Durham: Duke University Press, 1969), p. 157, and Dew, *Ironmaker to the Confederacy*, pp. 175–76.

81. Russell, "Atlanta, Gate City of the South," pp. 109–10.

82. Thomas, *Confederate Nation*, p. 212. But Thomas's caveat on the nature of Confederate industrialization seems off the mark. Thomas argues that though "briefly successful," the South's military-industrial revolution was "pre-eminently Southern" because it was directed by "traditional intellectuals" and the government. He neglects to mention the notable contribution made by private firms, which obtained government contracts and operated in conjunction with Confederate ordnance centers. This omission is curious because elsewhere in *The Confederate Nation* Thomas discusses the great contributions independent businesses made to the war effort. Further, Thomas's contention that government controls made the "profit motive . . . less a factor" can be viewed in another way: government regulations on profit and raw materials and workers were designed to ensure that private firms holding government contracts remained faithful to those contracts. Georgia's urban mobilizers in particular manifested few of those quintessential Southern qualities Thomas alleges existed. Moreover, as later chapters detail, these same men worked after the war in decidedly unstereotypical Southern fashion in boosting—and acting upon—the "industrial gospel."

83. Dew, *Ironmaker to the Confederacy*, pp. 177–78; see also Hattaway and Jones, *How the North Won*, pp. 186–87. Dew correctly criticizes scholars who have placed undue emphasis on the weakness of Southern manufacturing as a cause of Confederate defeat. "This emphasis on the Confederacy's overall industrial impotence," Dew writes, "has largely ignored the disparity between the potential of the manufacturing plant and the ability of the raw materials sector to feed it" (p. 177). For a different interpretation, one which stresses the decline of morale, see Richard E. Beringer, Herman Hattaway,

Archer Jones, and William N. Still, Jr., *Why the South Lost the Civil War* (Athens: University of Georgia Press, 1986), pp. 424–42.

84. Coleman, ed., *History of Georgia*, p. 191; McWhorter S. Cooley, "Manufacturing in Georgia during the Civil War Period" (M.S. thesis, University of Georgia, 1929), p. 40; *Annual Report of the Comptroller General*, 1861, pp. 58–62; 1864, pp. 12–16.

85. See, for example, Raimondo Luraghi, "The Civil War and the Modernization of American Society: Social Structure and Industrial Revolution in the Old South before and during the War," *Civil War History* 18 (September 1972): 230–50; Luraghi, *The Rise and Fall of the Plantation South* (New York: Franklin Watts, 1978), pp. 106–7; Thomas, *Confederate Nation*, pp. 212–14; Charles W. Ramsdell, "The Control of Manufacturing by the Confederate Government," *Mississippi Valley Historical Review* 8 (December 1921): 231–49.

86. In many ways, this analysis both corroborates and revises C. Vann Woodward's view of the class composition of the South after the Civil War. In his monumental *Origins of the New South, 1877–1913* (Baton Rouge: Louisiana State University Press, 1951), Woodward argues that the Civil War destroyed the old planter ruling class and that "new men" with "nominal connections" to the old elite took their places. These new men were professionals—merchants, lawyers, and the like—who championed economic development and progress of a Whig/Yankee variety. Those members of the old guard who persisted willingly embraced the capitalistic developmental schemes of the new leadership.

In Georgia's cities, established industrialists and urban boosters from before the war led the mobilization effort. They were joined by newcomers, men who innovated and responded to war-forged opportunities and hence acted like classic entrepreneurs. Both the established elite and the "new men" enjoyed the support of planters but were by no means subordinate to them. After the war, as later chapters will illuminate, many of these same individuals led in Georgia's rebuilding. Ultimately, they were joined by those "new men" Woodward identified in *Origins*, chap. 1.

Chapter 3

1. U.S. War Department, *The War of Rebellion: A Compilation of the Official Records of the Union and Confederate Armies*, Ser. 4, 3 vols. (Washington, D.C.: U.S. Government Printing Office, 1880–1902), 1:884.

2. Ibid., p. 188.

3. Jon L. Wakelyn, ed., *Biographical Dictionary of the Confederacy* (Westport, Conn.: Greenwood Press, 1977), pp. 328–29; Richard D. Goff, *Confederate Supply* (Durham: Duke University Press, 1969), pp. 8–9; Frank E. Vandiver, *Their Tattered Flags: The Epic of the Confederacy* (New York: Harpers Magazine Press Book, 1970), p. 54. The North's quartermaster general, Montgomery C. Meigs, possessed similar attributes. According to Meigs's biographer, Russell Weigley, Meigs epitomized the "materialistic, mechanically and scientifically inclined American" of the mid-nineteenth century, but his professional

military training at West Point also created in Meigs "an occasional myopia which suggests the limitations of a mind trained under a rigid code and considerable isolation from the main currents of American life" (*Quartermaster General of the Union Army: A Biography of M. C. Meigs* [New York: Columbia University Press, 1959], pp. 7–8).

4. Myers to Walker, 18 April 1861, Quartermaster Department, Communications with the Secretary of War, p. 8, as cited in Goff, *Confederate Supply*, pp. 15–16.

5. "An Act Concerning the Transportation of Soldiers and Allowance for Clothing of Volunteers," 21 May 1861, in James M. Matthews, ed., *The Statutes at Large of the Provisional Government of the Confederate States of America, from the Institution of the Government, February 8, 1861, to Its Termination, February 18, 1862* (Richmond: R. M. Smith, 1864), p. 126.

6. Goff, *Confederate Supply*, p. 16; Charles W. Ramsdell, "The Control of Manufacturing by the Confederate Government," *Mississippi Valley Historical Review* 8 (December 1921): 231–34.

7. See, for example, *Augusta Chronicle and Sentinel*, 7 June 1861.

8. Diffee W. Standard, *Columbus, Georgia, in the Confederacy: The Social and Industrial Life of the Chattahoochee River Port* (New York: William Frederick Press, 1954), pp. 33–34. For the firm's status in 1860, see Georgia, vol. 23, p. 110, R. G. Dun & Co. Collection, Baker Library, Harvard University Graduate School of Business Administration, Cambridge, Mass. See also *DeBow's Review* 33 (May–August 1862): 77–78.

9. Standard, *Columbus, Georgia, in the Confederacy*, p. 28. Evidently, only aggregate statistics of the Columbus Factory's output exist.

10. Georgia, vol. 23, p. 109, R. G. Dun & Co. Collection. There exists some confusion as to names. Diffee Standard refers to S. M. Sappington, but the Dun ledgers contain listings only for James W. Since both men operated grocery stores and are the only Sappingtons listed, it is assumed that they are one and the same. See Standard, *Columbus, Georgia, in the Confederacy*, p. 32, and *DeBow's Review* 33 (May–August 1862): 77.

11. Georgia, vol. 23, p. 52, R. G. Dun & Co. Collection.

12. Ibid., p. 32; *DeBow's Review* 33 (May–August 1862): 77.

13. T. Conn Bryan, *Confederate Georgia* (Athens: University of Georgia Press, 1953), p. 102; Standard, *Columbus, Georgia, in the Confederacy*, pp. 30–31, 36–37. For background on Dillard's antebellum commercial activities, see Georgia, vol. 23, p. 51, R. G. Dun & Co. Collection.

14. Goff, *Confederate Supply*, p. 70; Ramsdell, "Control of Manufacturing," pp. 245–46; Standard, *Columbus, Georgia, in the Confederacy*, pp. 36–37.

15. Florence Fleming Corley, *Confederate City: Augusta, Georgia, 1860–1865* (Columbia: University of South Carolina Press, 1960), pp. 41, 45.

16. *Augusta Chronicle and Sentinel*, 7 June 1861.

17. *Savannah Republican*, in *Augusta Chronicle and Sentinel*, 14 February 1861. See also *Chronicle and Sentinel*, 8 February, 14 August, 12 September 1860.

18. *Augusta Chronicle and Sentinel*, 6 June, 12 August 1861; Corley, *Confederate City*, p. 46.

19. *Augusta Chronicle and Sentinel*, 12 May 1861.

20. Corley, *Confederate City*, p. 45. A change in ownership of the *Augusta Chronicle and Sentinel* also helped make the climate more amenable to industrial pursuits. Dr. Will Jones sold his interest to fellow Augustan Thomas Chichester and Charleston's Wellington Stevenson in April 1862. The new publishers hired former Connecticut journalist-Copperhead Nathan Morse as editor. Morse used the columns of the *Chronicle* to champion the Southern cause and to encourage economic diversification. Morse's honeymoon with the Confederacy ended, however, in 1865, when he stopped supporting the Confederate government and championed a peace campaign. See Earl L. Bell and Kenneth C. Crabbe, *The Augusta Chronicle: Indomitable Voice of Dixie, 1785–1960* (Athens: University of Georgia Press, 1960).

21. Corley, *Confederate City*, pp. 48–49.

22. Salem Dutcher and Charles C. Jones, Jr., *Memorial History of Augusta, Georgia, from Its Settlement in 1735 to the Close of the Eighteenth Century* (Syracuse, N.Y.: D. Mason, 1890), p. 397.

23. *Augusta Chronicle and Sentinel*, 25 February 1862. See also *Atlanta Southern Confederacy*, 26 February 1862. Oilcloth had been added to the Belleville's line of products to enable the company to furnish tents to the Confederacy.

24. *Official Records*, Ser. 4, vol. 1, pp. 314–15, 688.

25. Ibid., pp. 883–84.

26. War Department Collection of Confederate Records, chap. 5, Quartermaster Department, Letters and Telegrams Sent, December 1861–August 1862, roll 8, vol. 15, p. 480, 21 March 1862, Center for Research Libraries, Chicago, Ill.

27. Matthews, ed., *Statutes at Large*, pp. 29, 77–79.

28. *Official Records*, Ser. 4, vol. 2, pp. 160–62.

29. Ibid., 1:1127. See also War Department Collection of Confederate Records, chap. 5, Quartermaster Department, Letters and Telegrams Sent, vol. 16, pp. 234–35, 462.

30. *Official Records*, Ser. 4, vol. 2, pp. 160–62.

31. *Atlanta Southern Confederacy*, 9 November 1861, reports on such legislation in Tennessee and Alabama. The *Atlanta Daily Intelligencer* reported on the Georgia law in its 25 December 1861 issue.

32. *Atlanta Southern Confederacy*, 12 October, 11 September 1861. See also Albert B. Moore, *Conscription and Conflict in the Confederacy* (New York: Macmillan, 1924), pp. 63–64.

33. Allen D. Candler, ed., *Confederate Records of the State of Georgia*, 6 vols. (Atlanta: Charles P. Byrd, 1909–12), 2:332–33; *Atlanta Southern Confederacy*, 8 November 1862. The resolutions passed without Governor Brown's signature. Though Brown did seize all establishments in accordance with the act, he initially protested its passage because of its nature: Brown believed the act impractical, felt the governor should determine compensation to owners for seized properties, and maintained that too many factories and manufactured articles were omitted from the final piece of legislation. See Brown to the Georgia Senate, in Candler, ed., *Confederate Records*, 2:354–55, 332–33.

34. *Atlanta Southern Confederacy*, 8 January 1863; McWhorter S. Cooley, "Manufacturing in Georgia during the Civil War Period" (M.S. thesis, Uni-

versity of Georgia, 1929), pp. 25–26. Georgia was not alone in taking over factories. Until almost the end of the war, North Carolina factories produced for North Carolina soldiers and civilians alone—no articles went outside the state's borders. By 1864, the state of Virginia considered taking over the Petersburg Manufacturing Company.

35. *Atlanta Southern Confederacy*, 22 November 1862.

36. *Milledgeville Southern Recorder*, 9 December 1862.

37. *Official Records*, Ser. 4, vol. 1, pp. 111, 204, vol. 2, p. 109.

38. Goff, *Confederate Supply*, pp. 75–76; *Official Records*, Ser. 4, vol. 2, pp. 435–36. Tennessee and Kentucky, and Missouri and Arkansas, as pairs, constituted separate purchasing districts. For an example of the "average" state-level quartermaster hierarchy, see Goff, *Confederate Supply*, pp. 130–31.

39. *Official Records*, Ser. 4, vol. 2, p. 697. See also Goff, *Confederate Supply*, p. 141, for additional background on the reasons for Myers's ouster.

40. Wakelyn, ed., *Biographical Dictionary of the Confederacy*, p. 278.

41. *Official Records*, Ser. 4, vol. 2, pp. 895–97; Goff, *Confederate Supply*, pp. 144–46. Secretary of War Seddon's report of 23 November 1863 provides a more encouraging view of the extent of domestic resources, supplies, and manufacturing. See *Official Records*, Ser. 4, vol. 2, pp. 1007–8.

42. See, for example, Edward Younger, ed., *Inside the Confederate Government: The Diary of Robert Garlick Kean, Head of the Bureau of War* (New York: Oxford University Press, 1957), pp. 114–15; see also U.S. War Department, *The War of Rebellion: A Compilation of the Official Records of the Union and Confederate Armies*, Ser. 1, 53 vols. (Washington, D.C.: U.S. Government Printing Office, 1880–1902), vol. 30, pt. 4, p. 686; vol. 29, pt. 2, pp. 784–85.

43. Goff, *Confederate Supply*, p. 147.

44. Ibid., pp. 147–48.

45. Lawton to Cunningham, 9 April 1864, War Department Collection of Confederate Records, chap. 5, Quartermaster Department, Letters and Telegrams Sent, February 1864–January 1865, vol. 19, p. 186.

46. Myers to Dillard, 17 January 1862, ibid., vol. 15, p. 145; Myers to Dillard, 11 June 1862, ibid., p. 290; Larkin Smith to Dillard, 18 July 1862, ibid., p. 400; W. B. B. Cross to T. C. Johnston, 8 February 1862, ibid., vol. 19, p. 9; Lawton to Dillard, 19 September 1864, ibid., vol. 20, p. 130.

47. *Milledgeville Southern Recorder*, 9 December 1862; Goff, *Confederate Supply*, p. 70.

48. *Columbus Daily Sun*, 13 October 1862, as reported in *Atlanta Southern Confederacy*, 17 October 1862; *Augusta Chronicle and Sentinel*, 7 January, 3 April 1864; Standard, *Columbus, Georgia, in the Confederacy*, p. 54.

49. *Columbus Daily Sun*, 12 June 1863; Standard, *Columbus, Georgia, in the Confederacy*, p. 53.

50. Standard, *Columbus, Georgia, in the Confederacy*, pp. 54–58; Goff, *Confederate Supply*, p. 70.

51. Goff, *Confederate Supply*, p. 70.

52. Robert Manson Myers, ed., *The Children of Pride: A True Story of Georgia and the Civil War* (New Haven: Yale University Press, 1972), p. 952.

53. *Augusta Chronicle and Sentinel*, 14 April 1864. See also Richard Griffen,

"The Origins of the Industrial Revolution in Georgia: Cotton Textiles, 1810–1865," *Georgia Historical Quarterly* 42 (1958): 374–75. A comparison with Philadelphia, the leading Northern textile manufacturing city during the Civil War, presents some interesting parallels. Philadelphia textile men had long enjoyed quartermaster contracts with the U.S. Army; indeed, they supplied the Schuylkill Arsenal throughout the late antebellum period. During the war, the mill owners went to work to garner government contracts. For example, Benjamin Bullock's Sons eventually obtained ten contracts with quartermaster agents to produce over 2 million yards of uniform kersey. In 1862 alone, the firm manufactured 400,000 yards of broadcloth. In general, Philadelphia manufacturers reaped handsome gains and expanded the city's textile base significantly, largely because of lucrative government contracts. Georgia's mill output compares favorably with these figures, even surpasses them, when one takes into account that Georgia's mill cities did not have the long-standing tradition of government contracts.

Another contrast can be made with Lowell, Massachusetts, the antebellum American king of textile manufacture. Lowell suffered a major decline when the supply of cotton from the Southern states was cut off. Many factories were forced to shut down, and some that converted to war-related production were, according to one authority, "stung with losses." During the 1870s, Lowell recouped its losses, but the 1880s would prove disastrous once again. See Philip Scranton, *Proprietary Capitalism: The Textile Manufacture at Philadelphia, 1800–1885* (New York: Cambridge University Press, 1983), pp. 273, 276–78, 287, 310–13.

54. *Augusta Chronicle and Sentinel*, 14 April 1864.

55. Arthur J. L. Fremantle, *Three Months in the Southern States, April–June 1863* (Edinburgh: William Blackwood & Sons, 1863), p. 176; *Milledgeville Southern Recorder*, 24 February 1863. For background on J. K. Hora & Company, see Georgia, vol. 1b, pp. 113, 139, R. G. Dun & Co. Collection; and Corley, *Confederate City*, p. 70.

56. Rowland Diary, 10 November 1863, as quoted in Corley, *Confederate City*, pp. 78, 73, 75.

57. Candler, ed., *Confederate Records*, 2:395. See also Brown to Zebulon Vance, 4 February 1863, Governor's Letterbooks, 1861–65, pp 417–18, Georgia Department of Archives and History, Atlanta.

58. Candler, ed., *Confederate Records*, 2:450–51.

59. Ibid., pp. 408–11; Quartermaster General's Annual Report, 15 October 1863, pp. 36–38, Adjutant General's Reports, 1861–64, Georgia Department of Archives and History.

60. *Official Records*, Ser. 4, vol. 2, pp. 64–65; Quartermaster General's Annual Report, 15 October 1864, p. 15. Interestingly, the contracts with Georgia mills did not include establishments in Augusta and Columbus. This underscores Foster's previous objection to the magnitude of government operations in the state.

61. *Official Records*, Ser. 4, vol. 2, pp. 514–24, vol. 3, pp. 967–68; Frank E. Vandiver, *Rebel Brass: The Confederate Command System* (1956; rpt. Westport, Conn.: Greenwood Press, 1969), p. 94; *Augusta Chronicle and Sentinel*, 4 Janu-

ary, 30 April 1864; W. B. B. Cross to G. W. Cunningham, chap. 5, Quartermaster Department, Letters and Telegrams Sent, February 1864–January 1865, vol. 20, p. 181. The Union blockade slowly but effectively shut down Port Royal, New Orleans, Roanoke Island, and Fort Pulaski in 1862; 1863 saw Galveston fall; Mobile succumbed to Admiral David Farragut in August 1864. Only Charleston and Wilmington held out against Federal incursions until the very end.

62. Lawton to Hardee, 12 January 1865, chap. 5, Quartermaster Department, Letters and Telegrams Sent, February 1864–January 1865, vol. 20, p. 422; Lawton to Beauregard, 12 January 1865, Alexander R. Lawton Papers, Southern Historical Collection, University of North Carolina, Chapel Hill.

63. Lawton to Cunningham, 7 April 1864, chap. 5, Quartermaster Department, Letters and Telegrams Sent, February 1864–January 1865, vol. 19, p. 150; Lawton to R. B. Winder, 25 August 1864, ibid., vol. 20, p. 16; Lawton to Winder, 13 July 1864, ibid., vol. 19, p. 347.

64. *Official Records*, Ser. 4, vol. 3, pp. 1090, 1040. See also ibid., Ser. 1, vol. 45, pt. 2, p. 704.

65. Goff, *Confederate Supply*, pp. 250–51.

66. Ibid., pp. 125, 245–46.

67. E. Merton Coulter, *The Confederate States of America, 1861–1865* (Baton Rouge: Louisiana State University Press, 1950), pp. 229–30; see also Bryan, *Confederate Georgia*, p. 108.

68. *Augusta Chronicle and Sentinel*, 26 May 1864.

69. Emory M. Thomas, *The Confederate Nation, 1861–1865* (New York: Harper Torchbooks, 1979), p. 207.

70. Ibid., p. 212.

71. See *Augusta Chronicle and Sentinel*, 12 May 1861.

72. Here, again, the Georgia experience supports C. Vann Woodward. The individuals who came forward to experiment, innovate, and aid the mobilization effort were "new men" to manufacturing endeavors. They manifested an aggressive, acquisitive spirit that stands in stark contrast to the stereotypical Southerner of lore. Though many failed to convert wartime success to peacetime success, enough did to lend credence to the New South dream of the late 1870s and 1880s. See below, Chapter 6.

Chapter 4

1. Alfred D. Chandler, Jr., *The Visible Hand: The Managerial Revolution in American Business* (Cambridge: Belknap Press of Harvard University Press, 1977), pp. 87, 109; see also Thomas C. Cochran, *Railroad Leaders, 1845–1890: The Business Mind in Action* (Cambridge: Harvard University Press, 1953), pp. 9, 11, 14.

2. *DeBow's Review* 30 (May 1860): 593–94; R. S. Cotterill, "Southern Railroads and Western Trade, 1840–1850," *Mississippi Valley Historical Review* 3 (March 1917): 436.

3. *American Railroad Journal*, 5 January 1861, as quoted in Robert C. Black

III, *Railroads of the Confederacy* (Chapel Hill: University of North Carolina Press, 1952), pp. 3–4, 8–10, 22–23; George Rogers Taylor and Irene D. Neu, *The American Railroad Network, 1861–1890* (Cambridge: Harvard University Press, 1956), pp. 51–52.

4. James A. Ward, "A New Look at Antebellum Southern Railroad Development," *Journal of Southern History* 39 (August 1973): 412–13, 419; Black, *Railroads of the Confederacy*, pp. 26–28.

5. Ulrich B. Phillips, *A History of Transportation in the Eastern Cotton Belt to 1860* (New York: Columbia University Press, 1908), pp. 222, 238; W. J. Northen, ed., *Men of Mark in Georgia*, 7 vols. (Atlanta: A. B. Caldwell, 1910), 3:424–31.

6. Northen, ed., *Men of Mark*, 3:424–31.

7. Salem Dutcher and Charles C. Jones, Jr., *Memorial History of Augusta, Georgia, from Its Settlement in 1735 to the Close of the Eighteenth Century* (Syracuse, N.Y.: D. Mason, 1890), pp. 401–10; Florence Fleming Corley, *Confederate City: Augusta, Georgia, 1860–1865* (Columbia: University of South Carolina Press, 1960), pp. 7–8.

8. Black, *Railroads of the Confederacy*, p. 27; Charles C. Jones, Jr., *History of Savannah, Georgia, from Its Settlement to the Close of the Eighteenth Century* (Syracuse, N.Y.: D. Mason, 1890), p. 480.

9. Jon L. Wakelyn, ed., *Biographical Dictionary of the Confederacy* (Westport, Conn.: Greenwood Press, 1977), pp. 422–23; Northen, ed., *Men of Mark*, 3:100–101.

10. Clement A. Evans, ed., *Confederate Military History*, 12 vols. (Atlanta: Confederate Publishing Co., 1899), 6:683–86. For Grant's activities on behalf of the Georgia Western, see his correspondence, Lemuel P. Grant Papers, Box No. 2, Atlanta Historical Society.

11. Black, *Railroads of the Confederacy*, pp. 26–27. A caveat is in order, however. R. R. Cuyler was active in politics in Savannah, first as a Whig and then as a Constitutional Unionist. Indeed, Cuyler helped frame the Constitutional Union platform in the city in 1860. See Richard H. Haunton, "Savannah in the 1850s" (Ph.D. dissertation, Emory University, 1968); also Cotterill, "Southern Railroads and Western Trade," pp. 436–37.

12. U.S. War Department, *The War of Rebellion: A Compilation of the Official Records of the Union and Confederate Armies*, Ser. 4, 4 vols. (Washington, D.C.: U.S. Government Printing Office, 1902), 1:269; see also Black, *Railroads of the Confederacy*, pp. 52–53.

13. *Montgomery Daily Mail*, 29 April 1861, as cited by Black, *Railroads of the Confederacy*, p. 54. In the summer of 1861 several other meetings were called by the central committee. Convocations in Chattanooga and Richmond attracted the major Southern carriers, but the agenda of business was slightly different. Of chief concern at those gatherings was the disruption of business that secession had produced. Though nonmilitary concerns dominated the proceedings, the delegates assembled at those meetings generally reaffirmed the rate schedules established at the April Montgomery convention. See *Report of the Railroad Convention*, Chattanooga, Tennessee, 4–5 June 1861, Georgia State Library, Atlanta.

14. Black, *Railroads of the Confederacy*, pp. 25, 59–60; Central Railroad and Banking Company, *Reports of the Presidents and Superintendents of the Central Railroad and Banking Company of Georgia, No. 20 to 32, Inclusive, and the Amended Charter of the Company* (Savannah: G. N. Nichols, Printer, 1868), pp. 189–92.

15. Black examines the key role the railroads played at Manassas in *Railroads of the Confederacy*, pp. 60–62.

16. "Resolution on Legislation to facilitate Railroad transport," 1 August 1861, U.S. War Department, *Journal of the Congress of the Confederate States of America, 1861–1865*, 7 vols. (Washington, D.C.: U.S. Government Printing Office, 1904–5), 1:305–6.

17. Davis to Congress, 17 December 1861, ibid., p. 586.

18. Black, *Railroads of the Confederacy*, pp. 78–81; Charles B. Dew, *Ironmaker to the Confederacy: Joseph R. Anderson and the Tredegar Iron Works* (New Haven: Yale University Press, 1966), pp. 140–42.

19. Goodman to Jefferson Davis, 25 January 1862, in *Official Records*, Ser. 4, vol. 1, pp. 880–81; see also Neill S. Brown to Judah Benjamin, 12 January 1862, ibid., p. 839, and Thomas C. Perrin to Benjamin, 14 January 1862, ibid., pp. 842–43.

20. Report of T. N. Waul of Special Committee to examine the Quartermaster, Commissary, and Medical Departments, 29 January 1862, ibid., pp. 884–85. Waul's report is also printed in U.S. War Department, *Journal of the Congress*, 1:721.

21. *Atlanta Southern Confederacy*, 16 February 1862; A. C. Myers to Davis, 31 January 1862, in *Official Records*, Ser. 4, vol. 1, pp. 896–97, and War Department Collection of Confederate Records, chap. 5, Quartermaster Department, Letters and Telegrams Sent, 1862, vol. 15, p. 206, Center for Research Libraries, Chicago, Ill.; U.S. War Department, *Journal of the Confederate Congress*, 1:781–82; *Official Records*, Ser. 4, vol. 2, pp. 505–7.

22. U.S. War Department, *Journal of the Confederate Congress*, 5:122, 251–54. For protests against the bill, see ibid., p. 269; also Black, *Railroads of the Confederacy*, pp. 98–99.

23. Randolph to Davis, 12 August 1864, in *Official Records*, Ser. 4, vol. 2, pp. 48–49; Davis to Congress, 18 August 1862, ibid., p. 54.

24. *Atlanta Southern Confederacy*, 16 September 1862, reports the convention's proceedings.

25. Dutcher and Jones, *Memorial History of Augusta*, p. 493; Georgia Railroad and Banking Company Annual Statement, 16 July 1861, in *Augusta Chronicle and Sentinel*, 17 August 1861; Phillips, *History of Transportation*, p. 245.

26. Central Railroad and Banking Company, *Reports*, p. 193. The *Savannah Republican*, 13 December 1862 and 14 August 1861, also contains the Central's annual reports; President's Report, Southwestern Railroad Company, in *Savannah Republican*, 14 August 1861; and Phillips, *History of Transportation*, p. 279.

27. *Reports of the Superintendent and Treasurer of the Western & Atlantic Railroad*, 30 September 1861 (Atlanta: Intelligencer Book & Job Office, 1861),

Georgia Department of Archives and History, Atlanta. See also James H. Johnston, *The Western and Atlantic Railroad of the State of Georgia* (Atlanta: Stein Printing, 1932), p. 107.

28. Benjamin to Myers, 24 September 1861, in *Official Records*, Ser. 4, vol. 1, p. 617.

29. Benjamin to Brown, 30 September 1861, and Brown to Benjamin, 2 October 1861, in Allen D. Candler, ed., *The Confederate Records of the State of Georgia*, 6 vols. (Atlanta: Charles P. Byrd, 1909–12), 3:132–33.

30. Brown to Schlatter, 7 October 1861, with Executive Order, Governor's Letterbooks, 1861–65, Georgia Department of Archives and History.

31. Brown's Annual Message, 6 November 1862, in Candler, ed., *Confederate Records*, 2:283–308; Brown to R. R. Cuyler, 8 June 1861, Governor's Letterbooks; G. D. Phillips to Brown, 18 December 1861, Incoming Correspondence to the Governor, 1861–65, Georgia Department of Archives and History; *Reports of the Superintendent and Treasurer of the Western & Atlantic Railroad*, 1 October 1862, ibid. Rowland replaced John W. Lewis as superintendent of the Western & Atlantic on 14 October 1861. See *Savannah Republican*, 14 October 1861.

32. Houston to Walker, 14 September 1861, in *Official Records*, Ser. 4, vol. 1, pp. 612–13.

33. "An Act to enable the President . . . to provide means of military transportation . . . between Blue Mountain . . . and Rome . . . ," 2 October 1862, U.S. War Department, *Journal of the Confederate Congress*, 5:480, 485; see also *Official Records*, Ser. 4, vol. 2, pp. 200–201; and J. F. Gilmer to L. P. Grant, 22 October 1862, ibid., p. 139.

34. For accounts of the meetings, see *Atlanta Daily Intelligencer*, 20 December 1862, and *Atlanta Southern Confederacy*, 23 December 1862.

35. See *Atlanta Southern Confederacy*, 23 December 1862, and *Atlanta Daily Intelligencer*, 20 December 1862, for opinions favoring such projects and the motivations of the promoters.

36. Shorter to Davis, 25 October 1862, in *Official Records*, Ser. 4, vol. 2, pp. 144–45; Black, *Railroads of the Confederacy*, pp. 148–58, 213.

37. *Augusta Chronicle and Sentinel*, 16 December 1862. See also *Charleston Mercury*, as reprinted in *Atlanta Southern Confederacy*, 15 November 1862.

38. *Official Records*, Ser. 4, vol. 2, p. 225; General Orders No. 98, 3 December 1862, ibid.; *Savannah Republican*, 6 December 1862.

39. Myers to Seddon, 9 December 1862, 8, 26 January 1863, in *Official Records*, Ser. 4, vol. 2, pp. 231–32, 304–5, 372–73. See also Myers to W. P. Chilton, 3 October 1862, on Myers's opposition to government control or takeover of railroads, ibid., p. 108.

40. Wadley to Cooper, 31 December 1862, with enclosures, *Official Records*, Ser. 4, vol. 2, pp. 270–77.

41. Wadley to Cooper, 31 December 1862, ibid., pp. 270–72.

42. Wadley to Cooper, 31 December 1862, ibid., pp. 295–96; Davis to Congress, 12 January 1863, ibid., p. 348.

43. Seddon to Wadley, 25 March 1863, ibid., p. 457.

44. Wadley to Seddon, 14 April 1863, ibid., pp. 483–86.

45. R. R. Cuyler to Seddon, 22 April 1863, with enclosure, ibid., pp. 508–10; P. V. Daniel to Seddon, 22 April 1863, ibid., pp. 499–500.

46. "Bill to facilitate transportation," 27 April 1863, U.S. War Department, *Journal of the Confederate Congress*, 3:350–51, 354–55. For the House vote on the Senate's bill see ibid., 6:472–74; also Charles Ramsdell, ed., *Laws and Joint Resolutions of the Last Session of the Confederate Congress . . .* (Durham: Duke University Press, 1941), pp. 167–69; Richard Goff, *Confederate Supply* (Durham: Duke University Press, 1969), pp. 110–11; and Black, *Railroads of the Confederacy*, pp. 121–22.

47. Wadley to Seddon, 26 January 1863, in *Official Records*, Ser. 4, vol. 2, pp. 373–74.

48. U.S. War Department, *Journal of the Confederate Congress*, 3:409; see also Black, *Railroads of the Confederacy*, pp. 122–23; Official Correspondence referred to the Railroad Bureau after Wadley's appointment. See *Official Records*, Ser. 4, vol. 2, p. 885.

49. *Official Records*, Ser. 4, vol. 2, p. 579.

50. Wakelyn, ed., *Biographical Dictionary of the Confederacy*, p. 386. See also Black, *Railroads of the Confederacy*, pp. 110, 166–67.

51. Black, *Railroads of the Confederacy*, p. 172.

52. Sims to A. R. Lawton, 23 October 1863, in *Official Records*, Ser. 4, vol. 2, pp. 881–83.

53. Lawton to Seddon, 24 October 1863, ibid., p. 883; Seddon to Davis, 26 November 1863, ibid., pp. 1012–13.

54. For the orders that established the Iron Impressment Commission, see Special Orders No. 36, 12 February 1863, ibid., p. 393; I. M. St. John, "A plan for the immediate results toward restoring railroad track and machinery," April 1863, ibid., p. 508; Black, *Railroads of the Confederacy*, pp. 124, 200; *Official Records*, Ser. 4, vol. 2, pp. 393, 508.

55. Georgia Railroad Report in *Atlanta Southern Confederacy*, 17 May 1863; Atlantic & Gulf Railroad Annual Report in *Savannah Republican*, 12 March 1863; Western & Atlantic Annual Report in *Augusta Chronicle and Sentinel*, 8 November 1863; Central Railroad and Banking Company, *Reports*, p. 287.

56. Dutcher and Jones, *Memorial History of Augusta*, p. 495.

57. See, for example, Larkin Smith to John Rowland, 25 July 1862, War Department Collection of Confederate Records, chap. 5, Quartermaster Department, Letters and Telegrams Sent, vol. 16, p. 415.

58. *Augusta Chronicle and Sentinel*, 23 March 1863.

59. *Atlanta Southern Confederacy*, 29 November 1862, 11, 18 April 1863. For similar sentiments, see *Savannah Republican*, 17 March 1863.

60. Mary G. Cumming, *Georgia Railroad and Banking Company, 1833–1945* (Augusta: Walton Printing Co., 1945), p. 123; Central Railroad and Banking Company, *Reports*, pp. 248–71. Using machinery from Savannah, black labor built the Central's new Macon machine shop. See Robert C. Black III, "The Railroads of Georgia in the Confederate War Effort," *Journal of Southern History* 13 (November 1947): 524. The plans of the Railroad Steamship Company faced a formidable obstacle in obtaining needed materials from abroad: the Union blockade of Savannah. After Fort Pulaski fell in 1862, blockade running from Georgia's chief port came to an abrupt end.

61. Brown to Davis, 16 March 1863; Brown to Wadley (Sims), 16 March 1863; Brown to Davis, 25 May 1863, all in Governor's Letterbooks; Seddon to Cuyler, 19 August 1863, in U.S. War Department, *The War of Rebellion: A Compilation of the Official Records of the Union and Confederate Armies*, Ser. 1, 53 vols. (Washington, D.C.: U.S. Government Printing Office, 1880–1902), vol. 28, pt. 2, pp. 295–96.

62. Brown to Bragg, 23 November 1863; Brown to Joseph E. Johnston, 30 December 1863; Brown to Davis, 18 November 1863; Brown to Wadley (Sims), 17 June 1863, all in Governor's Letterbooks. See also Brown to the General Assembly, 2 December 1863, in Candler, ed., *Confederate Records*, 2:556–58.

63. *Augusta Chronicle and Sentinel*, 15 January 1864. The *Chronicle's* comments are virtually identical to Seddon's comments to Davis on 26 November 1863 (cited in note 53 above).

64. Johnston to Brown, 12 January 1864; Brown to Johnston, 16 January 1864; A. R. Lawton to Brown, 14 January 1864; Brown to Lawton, 15 January 1864, all in Candler, ed., *Confederate Records*, 3:451–55; Johnston to Henry C. Wayne, 13 January 1864, in *Official Records*, Ser. 1, vol. 32, pt. 2, p. 552; G. D. Phillips to Brown, 14 January 1864, Governor's Letterbooks; Brown to Davis, 27 January 1864, and Brown to Johnston, 10 February 1864, in Candler, ed., *Confederate Records*, 3:458, 464–67.

65. Sims to Lawton, 1 April 1864, in *Official Records*, Ser. 4, vol. 3, p. 228. Major S. B. French, commissary of subsistence in Richmond, voiced similar complaints to Commissary General Lucius Northrop in February 1864. French noted that Major W. H. Smith, commissary of subsistence for Georgia, South Carolina, and North Carolina, reported that "the Government is deprived of many facilities by the cupidity of the Railroad companies and the corruption of agents and employes [sic], who regard their personal interests as paramount to other considerations" (ibid., pp. 88–90).

66. Brown to Davis, 7 March 1864, Governor's Letterbooks.

67. Georgia Railroad Annual Report, reprinted in *Augusta Chronicle and Sentinel*, 11 May 1864.

68. Sims to Lawton, 22 February, 1 April 1864, in *Official Records*, Ser. 4, vol. 3, pp. 92–93, 228; A.A.G. Special Orders No. 60, 12 March 1864, ibid., p. 209; Quartermaster Circular, 11, 30 March 1864, War Department Collection of Confederate Records, chap. 5, Quartermaster Department, Letters and Telegrams Sent, February 1864–January 1865, vol. 19, pp. 92, 131; Seddon to Davis, 28 April 1864, in *Official Records*, Ser. 4, vol. 3, p. 339.

69. Hood to Bragg, 4 September 1864, in *Official Records*, Ser. 1, vol. 38, pt. 5, p. 1018. The Atlanta campaign is studied exhaustively in Thomas Lawrence Connelly's *Autumn of Glory: The Army of Tennessee, 1862–1865* (Baton Rouge: Louisiana State University Press, 1971), pp. 361–469.

70. Brown to General Assembly, 3 November 1864, in Candler, ed., *Confederate Records*, 2:761–63; Richard E. Prince, *Steam Locomotives and History: Georgia Railroad and West Point Route* (Green River, Wyo.: Richard Prince, 1962), p. 62; Dutcher and Jones, *Memorial History of Augusta*, pp. 496–97; *Augusta Chronicle and Sentinel*, 6 September 1864.

71. Black, *Railroads of the Confederacy*, p. 260.

72. For accounts of provisions and the lack of adequate transport to serve the armies, see S. B. French to L. Northrup, 8 February 1864, in *Official Records*, Ser. 4, vol. 3, p. 89; Lawton to Davis, 20 September 1864, War Department Collection of Confederate Records, chap. 5, Quartermaster Department, Letters and Telegrams Sent, vol. 20, p. 129; Frank E. Vandiver, ed., *The Civil War Diary of General Josiah Gorgas* (University, Ala.: University of Alabama Press, 1947), p. 157.

73. Sims to Lawton, 13 September 1864, in *Official Records*, Ser. 4, vol. 3, pp. 616–17; William E. Smith to Seddon, 7 January 1865, ibid., pp. 1006–7; Lawton to Seddon, 2 February 1865, ibid., pp. 1053–54; Sims to Lawton, 10 February 1865, ibid., pp. 1091–93; Gilmer to Breckinridge, 16 February 1865, ibid., pp. 1084–86.

74. U.S. Department of War, *Journal of the Confederate Congress*, 7:442, 583–87, 607, 4:571–74.

75. Charles W. Ramsdell, "The Confederate Government and the Railroads," *American Historical Review* 22 (1917): 794–810.

76. Cochran, *Railroad Leaders*, pp. 9, 144, 203.

77. See Maury Klein, "The Strategy of Southern Railroads," *American Historical Review* 73 (April 1968): 1054; Cochran, *Railroad Leaders*, p. 223. For an analysis of how stages of entrepreneurship relate to this development, see Arthur H. Cole, *Business Enterprise in Its Social Setting* (Cambridge: Harvard University Press, 1959), p. 124.

78. Cochran, *Railroad Leaders*, p. 223; Cole, *Business Enterprise in Its Social Setting*, p. 124.

79. Emory M. Thomas, *The Confederate Nation, 1861–1865* (New York: Harper Torchbooks, 1979), pp. 196, 211. In a broad sense, the failure to exercise tight control over all areas of the mobilization could lend credence to David Donald's notion that the Confederacy "died of democracy." But Davis's—and Richmond's—willingness to centralize and coordinate commissary supply, quartermaster production, ordnance manufacturing, and conscription seems to undermine Donald's assertions. See Donald, "Died of Democracy," in David Donald, ed., *Why the North Won the Civil War* (Baton Rouge: Louisiana State University Press, 1960). Moreover, the interference of states'-rights governors Joseph E. Brown of Georgia and Zebulon Vance of North Carolina also handicapped Davis in formulating policy. As Brown's biographer Joseph Parks points out, Brown's resistance to Confederate policies encouraged other Georgians to disobey what he termed arbitrary infringements of sovereign rights. Such resistance hit a chord among railroad managers. See Parks, *Joseph E. Brown of Georgia* (Baton Rouge: Louisiana State University Press, 1977), p. 322.

80. For an account of Haupt's service in conjunction with the Federal railroads and the reasons for his ouster in September 1863, see Francis A. Lord, *Lincoln's Railroad Man: Herman Haupt* (Rutherford, N.J.: Fairleigh Dickinson University Press, 1969), esp. chap. 13, "Haupt's Contributions to Military Railroading," pp. 258–80.

Chapter 5

1. William S. McFeely, *Grant: A Biography* (New York: Norton, 1981), pp. 180–82, 84–85.

2. Samuel P. Richards Diary, 10 July 1864, Atlanta Historical Society; Charles H. Olmstead to "wife," 31 July 1864, Charles H. Olmstead Papers, Southern Historical Collection, University of North Carolina, Chapel Hill.

3. Hood erroneously assumed that Confederate cavalry raids on Sherman's supply line induced Sherman to withdraw to the south to protect those lines. In reality, Sherman was moving counterclockwise to cut off Hood's railroad lifelines, the Atlanta & West Point and Macon & Western railroads. See Shelby Foote, *The Civil War: A Narrative*, 3 vols. (New York: Random House, 1974), 3:522–23.

4. Richards Diary, 1 September 1864; see also B. J. Semmes to "Eo," 7 September 1864, Benedict Joseph Semmes Papers, Southern Historical Collection, University of North Carolina, Chapel Hill.

5. Charles W. Hubner, "Some Recollections of Atlanta during 1864," *Atlanta Historical Bulletin* 1 (January 1928): 7. Hood did succeed in getting the bulk of the Atlanta Arsenal's stores to Augusta. See John M. Brooke to Stephen Mallory, 4 November 1864, in U.S. Navy Department, *Official Records of the Union and Confederate Navies in the War of the Rebellion*, Ser. 2, 3 vols. (Washington, D.C.: U.S. Government Printing Office, 1884–1922), 2:755–56. For Confederate government perceptions of the loss of Atlanta and its storehouses, see Frank E. Vandiver, ed., *The Civil War Diary of General Josiah Gorgas* (University, Ala.: University of Alabama Press, 1947), pp. 139–40. For civilian perceptions, see Charles H. Olmstead to "wife," 12, 17 September 1864, Olmstead Papers.

6. Richards Diary, 4 September 1864; George W. Nichols, *The Story of the Great March from the Diary of a Staff Officer* (New York: Harper & Brothers, 1865), p. 38.

7. U.S. War Department, *The War of Rebellion: A Compilation of the Official Records of the Union and Confederate Armies*, Ser. 1, 53 vols. (Washington, D.C.: U.S. Government Printing Office, 1880–1902), vol. 39, pt. 2, p. 356.

8. B. J. Semmes to "Eo," 11 September 1864, Semmes Papers; Sherman to Hood, 7 September 1864, in *Official Records*, Ser. 1, vol. 39, pt. 2, pp. 414–15. See also Hood to Sherman, 12 September 1864, and Sherman to Hood, 14 September 1864, ibid., pp. 419–22.

9. Henry Hitchcock, *Marching with Sherman* (New Haven: Yale University Press, 1927), p. 58.

10. Nichols, *Story of the Great March*, pp. 38–41; Poe, as quoted in Allen Phelps Julian, "Atlanta's Last Days in the Confederacy," *Atlanta Historical Bulletin* 11 (June 1966): 10–11. See also T. Conn Bryan, *Confederate Georgia* (Athens: University of Georgia Press, 1953), pp. 164–65; Elizabeth Bowlby, "The Role of Atlanta during the War between the States," *Atlanta Historical Bulletin* 5 (July 1940): 194–95. For Sherman's report, see *Official Records*, Ser. 1, vol. 39, pt. 3, pp. 740–41, and *Memoirs of William T. Sherman by Himself*, 2 vols. (1891; rpt. Bloomington: Indiana University Press for the Civil War Centennial Series, 1957), 2:179.

11. Rains to James Seddon, 23 July 1863, in U.S. War Department, *The War of Rebellion: A Compilation of the Official Records of the Union and Confederate Armies*, Ser. 4, 3 vols. (Washington, D.C.: U.S. Government Printing Office, 1902), 2:660–61. See also Florence Fleming Corley, *Confederate City: Augusta, Georgia, 1860–1865* (Columbia: University of South Carolina Press, 1960), pp. 84–85; *Augusta Chronicle and Sentinel*, 24 November 1864.

12. Sherman to Lincoln, 21 December 1864, in *Official Records*, Ser. 1, vol. 44, pp. 6–7, 89. Contemporaries wondered why Sherman bypassed Augusta on his way to the sea. After the war, Mayor Charles Estes of Augusta stated that the Union commander desired to protect Union men in the city. A more romantic—and erroneous—legend alleged that Sherman had fallen in love with an Augusta belle during a tour of duty in the city in 1844. The general explained his decision in a letter to Pleasant A. Stovall of the *Augusta Chronicle and Sentinel* in 1888. Sherman believed that Augusta was too heavily fortified and reasoned that the lightly defended Columbia, South Carolina, would fall more easily, thus rendering Augusta's facilities useless without a protracted and costly battle at Augusta. Sherman added, however: "If the people of Augusta think I slighted them in the winter of 1864 they are mistaken; or if they think I made a mistake in strategy let them say so and with the president's consent . . . I can send a detachment of 100,000 or so of Sherman's . . . 'Bummers' and their descendants, who will finish up the job without charging Uncle Sam a cent." See Corley, *Confederate City*, pp. 90–92.

13. Nichols, *Story of the Great March*, p. 96; Sherman to Ulysses S. Grant, 22 December 1864, in *Official Records*, Ser. 1, vol. 44, pp. 6–7; Sherman to Henry Halleck, 1 January 1865, ibid., p. 12.

14. Kenneth Coleman, ed., *A History of Georgia* (Athens: University of Georgia Press, 1977), p. 203; Nichols, *Story of the Great March*, pp. 108, 99; John McGlidden to William H. Gardiner, 29 January 1865, in Frank Otto Gatell, ed., "A Yankee Views the Agony of Savannah," *Georgia Historical Quarterly* 43 (December 1959): 429–30.

15. Wilson, *Under the Old Flag*, 2:266, as quoted in James Pickett Jones, *Yankee Blitzkrieg: Wilson's Raid through Alabama and Georgia* (Athens: University of Georgia Press, 1976), pp. 240–41. See also Jones, "Wilson's Raiders Reach Georgia: The Fall of Columbus, 1865," *Georgia Historical Quarterly* 59 (Fall 1975): 315–16.

16. Charles D. Mitchell, "Field Notes on the Selma Campaign," *Sketches of War History Read before the Ohio Commandery of the Loyal Legion of the United States* (1908), p. 192, as quoted in Jones, *Yankee Blitzkrieg*, pp. 142–43. See also Etta Blanchard Worseley, *Columbus on the Chattahoochee* (Columbus: Columbus Office Supply, 1951), pp. 296–98, and Diffee W. Standard, *Columbus, Georgia, in the Confederacy: The Social and Industrial Life of the Chattahoochee River Port* (New York: William Frederick Press, 1954), p. 61; *Official Records*, Ser. 1, vol. 49, pt. 2, pp. 424–25.

17. *Annual Report of the Comptroller General of the State of Georgia, Made to the Governor, 1866* (Macon: W. Burke & Co., 1866), pt. 1, p. 27, pt. 2, pp. 2–20, University of Georgia Library, Athens. See also Willard Range, *A Century of Georgia Agriculture, 1850–1950* (Athens: University of Georgia Press, 1954),

pp. 66–69; J. Horace Bass, "Civil War Finance in Georgia," *Georgia Historical Quarterly* 26 (Fall 1942): 224; and Alexander A. Lawrence, *A Present for Mr. Lincoln: The Story of Savannah from Secession to Sherman* (Macon: Ardvian Press, 1961), pp. 424–25.

18. For Sherman's report of the losses he inflicted during his March to the Sea, see Sherman to Halleck, 1 January 1865, in *Official Records*, Ser. 1, vol. 44, p. 13.

19. Eliza Frances Andrews, *The War-Time Journal of a Georgia Girl, 1864–1865* (New York: D. Appleton & Co., 1908), pp. 47, 198.

20. Eva B. Jones to Mary Jones, 14 July 1865, in Robert Manson Myers, ed., *The Children of Pride: A True Story of Georgia and the Civil War* (New Haven: Yale University Press, 1972), pp. 1280–81; Joseph H. Mahaffey, ed., "Carl Schurz's Letters from the South," *Georgia Historical Quarterly* 35 (1951): letter no. 4, 31 July 1865, pp. 243–44; George Anderson Mercer Diary, 11 June 1865, Southern Historical Collection, University of North Carolina, Chapel Hill.

21. John Stainback Wilson, *Atlanta as It Is: Being a Brief Sketch of Its Early Settlers* 1871; rpt. *Atlanta Historical Bulletin* 6 (1941): 15–16; Mercer Diary, 11 June 1865.

22. With the advent of peace, U.S. military authorities seized all railroads in the state and region. While Washington policy makers squabbled over how to deal with the captured property, the Quartermaster Department poured a whopping $1.3 million a month into Southern railroads. On 8 August 1865, the region's railroads were returned to their proper companies under the proviso that all boards of directors be reorganized and staffed by "loyalists"—those who had taken a loyalty oath to the government. For a complete analysis of Federal policy, see Carl Russell Fish, *The Restoration of Southern Railroads*, University of Wisconsin Studies in the Social Sciences and History, no. 2 (Madison: University of Wisconsin, 1919), pp. 11–13, 16–19, 27, and Peter S. McGuire, "The Railroads of Georgia, 1860–1880," *Georgia Historical Quarterly* 16 (March 1932): 187–88. See also Robert C. Black III, *Railroads of the Confederacy* (Chapel Hill: University of North Carolina Press, 1952), pp. 289–92, and R. E. Riegel, "Federal Operation of Southern Railroads during the Civil War," *Mississippi Valley Historical Review* 9 (September 1922): 126–37.

23. Sherman to Halleck, 1 January 1865, in *Official Records*, Ser. 1, vol. 44, p. 13; Salem Dutcher and Charles C. Jones, Jr., *Memorial History of Augusta, Georgia, from Its Settlement to the Close of the Eighteenth Century* (Syracuse, N.Y.: D. Mason, 1890), pp. 496–97; Richard E. Prince, *Steam Locomotives and History: The Georgia and West Point Route* (Green River, Wyo.: Richard Prince, 1962), p. 62.

24. Master Mechanic's Report, Western & Atlantic Railroad, 21 October 1865, Miscellaneous Bound and Unbound Records of Georgia Railroads before Regulation, 1859–1915, Georgia Department of Archives and History, Atlanta; *Augusta Chronicle and Sentinel*, 13 January 1865; Dutcher and Jones, *Memorial History of Augusta*, pp. 496–97; and Central Railroad and Banking Company, *Reports of the Presidents and Superintendents of the Central Railroad and Banking Company of Georgia, No. 20 to 32, Inclusive, and the Amended Charter*

of the Company (Savannah: G. N. Nichols, Printer, 1868), 1866, p. 337.

25. Alfred D. Chandler, Jr., *The Visible Hand: The Managerial Revolution in American Business* (Cambridge: Belknap Press of Harvard University Press, 1977), p. 95; Thomas C. Cochran, *Railroad Leaders, 1845–1890: The Business Mind in Action* (Cambridge: Harvard University Press, 1953), pp. 9, 11, 14; Dutcher and Jones, *Memorial History of Augusta*, p. 494.

26. *Reports of the Georgia Railroad and Banking Company* (Augusta, 1866), pp. 3–8; President's Report, 1867, pp. 4–5, Superintendent's Report, 30 April 1866, in Charles D. Saggus, "1865—Year of Despair, Year of Hope: Augusta Recovers from the War," *Richmond County History* 7 (Summer 1975): 42; Georgia, vol. 1b, pp. 111–12, R. G. Dun & Co. Collection, Baker Library, Harvard University Graduate School of Business Administration, Cambridge, Mass. Interestingly, the Georgia Railroad's board of directors remained virtually unchanged: the men who, with King, presided over the company in 1861 held similar positions after the war. See Henry V. Poor, *Manual of Railroads of the United States, 1870–71* (New York: H. V. and H. W. Poor, 1870), p. 48.

27. Henry V. Poor, *Manual of Railroads of the United States, 1869–70* (New York: L. G. Wemyss, 1869), p. 31; Poor, *Manual of Railroads, 1870–71*, p. 48.

28. Georgia, vol. 1b, p. 144, R. G. Dun & Co. Collection.

29. *Reports . . . Central of Georgia Railroad and Banking Co., 1865*, pp. 275–77; ibid., *1867*, pp. 312–13.

30. Black, *Railroads of the Confederacy*, p. 111.

31. Central Railroad and Banking Company, *Reports*, pp. 5, 303–4, 291–92, 332, 337; Dutcher and Jones, *Memorial History of Augusta*, pp. 505–6; C. Mildred Thompson, *Reconstruction in Georgia: Economic, Social, Political, 1865–1872*, Columbia University Studies in History, Economics and Public Law, vol. 64, no. 1 (1915; rpt. Savannah: Beehive Press, 1972), pp. 288–89.

32. Georgia, vol. 28, pp. 160–61, R. G. Dun & Co. Collection; Dutcher and Jones, *Memorial History of Augusta*, p. 506; Lease of the Southwestern to the Central of Georgia Railroad, 28 May 1871, *Annual Report of the Macon & Western Railroad Company to the Stockholders*, pp. 2–8, Georgia Department of Archives and History, Atlanta. This view runs counter to Klein's assessment of Wadley's policies as manager of the Central. Klein sees Wadley perpetuating policies that were ill-suited to the changes in the postbellum South. Yet Klein never takes into consideration Wadley's wartime experiences. His actions in extending the Central's operations were more than a continuation of "developmental" strategies. In essence, Wadley was bringing a new conception, a national orientation, to bear on the decision-making process. For evidence of this new conception, see Central Railroad, *Annual Reports*, 1865–73; and Maury Klein, "Southern Railroad Leaders, 1865–1893: Identities and Ideologies," *Business History Review* 42 (Autumn 1968): 288–310.

33. *Reports of the Superintendent and Treasurer of the Western & Atlantic Railroad . . . 1 October 1864* (Macon: Intelligencer Steam Press, 1864), pp. 3–4, Georgia Department of Archives and History, Atlanta.

34. Board Minutes, Board of Directors, Western & Atlantic Railroad, September 8, 18, 21–23, 27, 1865, Georgia Department of Archives and History. See also U.S. War Department, *The War of Rebellion: A Compilation of the Official Records of the Union and Confederate Armies*, Ser. 3, 5 vols. (Washington,

D.C.: U.S. Government Printing Office, 1902), 5:233–35.

35. James H. Johnston, *Western and Atlantic Railroad of the State of Georgia* (Atlanta: Stein Publishers, 1932), p. 58; Miscellaneous Bound and Unbound Records of Georgia Railroads before Regulation, 1859–1915; Jenkins to the General Assembly, 30 January 1866, ibid.

36. *Annual Reports of the Officers of the Western & Atlantic Railroad, 1867*; Jenkins to the General Assembly, 30 January 1866, both in Miscellaneous Bound and Unbound Records of the Georgia Railroads; Western & Atlantic Valuations; *Annual Report of the Western & Atlantic Railroad to . . . Charles J. Jenkins*, September 30, 1866 (Atlanta: Intelligencer Press, 1866), all in Georgia Department of Archives and History.

37. With the passage of the Military Reconstruction Act of 1867, the South was divided into five military districts. Major General John Pope took charge of Military District Number 3 and made Atlanta his headquarters. Under his direction, elections were held to select delegates to a state constitutional convention. Historian Charles E. Wynes notes that Georgia's constitutional convention was a "basically conservative body"—fewer than ten of the delegates could be considered "carpetbaggers." The guiding light of the convention was Northern émigré Rufus B. Bullock, a Republican who had served with the Confederate Quartermaster Department during the war. Bullock's role at the convention almost assured his nomination as the Georgia Republican party's gubernatorial candidate. Bullock defeated former Confederate war hero John Brown Gordon in a tight, heated election. With Bullock's election, the so-called radical phase of Georgia's reconstruction began. See Wynes, "The Politics of Reconstruction, Redemption and Bourbonism," in Coleman, ed., *History of Georgia*, pp. 211–13; Alan Conway, *The Reconstruction of Georgia* (Minneapolis: University of Minnesota Press, 1966), pp. 156–61; and Elizabeth Studley Nathans, *Losing the Peace: Georgia Republicans and Reconstruction, 1868–1872* (Baton Rouge: Louisiana State University Press, 1968). Bullock also owed a large political debt to former governor Joseph E. Brown. As a result, Brown openly endorsed Bullock's candidacy, and contemporaries and scholars have surmised that Brown deemed a Bullock administration the best vehicle for Georgia's political and economic recovery.

38. *Annual Reports of the Officers of the Western & Atlantic Railroad . . . to Rufus B. Bullock, 30 September 1869* (Atlanta: Samuel Bard, 1870), Georgia Department of Archives and History.

39. Georgia, vol. 1b, p. 142, R. G. Dun & Co. Collection.

40. The state legislature was almost evenly divided between conservative Democrats and Republicans, and crossovers on certain measures often occurred. See Nathans, *Losing the Peace*, p. 105, and Coleman, ed., *History of Georgia*, p. 213; Conway, *Reconstruction of Georgia*, pp. 192–93; *Report of the Joint Committee to Investigate the Condition of the Western & Atlantic Railroad . . . February 25, 1869* (Atlanta: Samuel Bard, 1869), pp. 82–84, Georgia State Library; Thompson, *Reconstruction in Georgia*, p. 225; Russell Duncan, "Rufus Brown Bullock, Reconstruction, and the 'New South,' 1834–1907: An Exploration into Race, Class, Party and the Corruption of the American Creed" (Ph.D. dissertation, University of Georgia, 1988).

41. Western & Atlantic Lease, 26 October 1870, Western & Atlantic Rail-

road Minutes, 1870–90, Atlanta Historical Society; Mark W. Summers, *Railroads, Reconstruction and the Gospel of Prosperity: Aid under the Radical Republicans, 1865–1877* (Princeton: Princeton University Press, 1984), p. 264.

42. Executive Department, Lessees of the Western & Atlantic Railroad, 24 December 1870, Western & Atlantic Railroad Minutes, 1870–90; Thompson, *Reconstruction in Georgia*, pp. 228–30; Nathans, *Losing the Peace*, pp. 205–12.

43. President's Report, Western & Atlantic Railroad, 1 January 1872, Western & Atlantic Railroad Minutes.

44. See, for example, Brown to Judah P. Benjamin, 2 October 1861, in Allen D. Candler, ed., *The Confederate Records of the State of Georgia*, 6 vols. (Atlanta: Charles P. Byrd, 1909–12), 3:132–33; also Black, *Railroads of the Confederacy*, pp. 194–95, 172.

45. President's Report, Western & Atlantic Railroad, 1 January 1872, Georgia Department of Archives and History; Georgia, vol. 13, pp. 224, 363, R. G. Dun & Co. Collection.

46. Nathans, *Losing the Peace*, pp. 118–20; Numan V. Bartley, *The Creation of Modern Georgia* (Athens: University of Georgia Press, 1983), p. 56. As Bartley points out, the Bullock administration was not nearly as extravagant as Democratic critics charged. Bullock's debt amounted to $3.5 million, whereas the debt accrued during presidential Reconstruction—the administrations of Governors James Johnson and Charles Jenkins—amounted to $3.7 million (ibid., p. 71).

47. See *Report of the Committee of the Legislature to Investigate the Bonds of the State of Georgia, 1872*, pp. 69–70, 106, 117, Georgia Department of Archives and History; Conway, *Reconstruction of Georgia*, pp. 205–7; Summers, *Railroads, Reconstruction and the Gospel of Prosperity*, p. 77; Carter Goodrich, *Government Promotion of American Canals and Railroads, 1800–1890* (New York: Columbia University Press, 1960), pp. 209–10; Eric Foner, *Reconstruction: America's Unfinished Revolution, 1863–1877* (New York: Harper & Row, 1988), pp. 379–92; and Bartley, *Creation of Modern Georgia*, pp. 68–72, 79. Local initiative and urban rivalry spurred the revival of interest in the Atlanta Air Line and the Georgia Western projects. The air line traced its roots to the 1850s, when Atlanta capitalists decided that through routes to the upper South would substantially aid the city's economy. Boosters again considered plans for the air line during the war, but not until 1868 were conditions favorable to begin construction. Persistent appeals for action were tempered by the realization that boosterism could not be instantly converted into cash. City subscriptions and aid from the Richmond & Danville Railroad Company finally turned the air line dream into reality, and construction began in 1869. The road reached the North Carolina Piedmont by 1871. See James Michael Russell, "Atlanta, Gate City of the South, 1847 to 1885" (Ph.D. dissertation, Princeton University, 1972), pp. 198–201; *Atlanta Constitution*, 21 November 1868; *Atlanta Daily New Era*, 7 January 1868; Georgia, vol. 14, p. 33, vol. 13, p. 282, R. G. Dun & Co. Collection.

The editorial staff of the *Atlanta Constitution* also resurrected the Georgia Western project in 1869. This road, like the Atlanta Air Line, had antebellum roots and was designed to link Atlanta with the coal fields of south Alabama.

Despite vigorous editorials in favor of the project, it languished until the 1880s, when General John Brown Gordon sold his rights in the company to the powerful Louisville & Nashville. See John F. Stover, *The Railroads of the South, 1865–1900: A Study in Finance and Control* (Chapel Hill: University of North Carolina Press, 1955), p. 240; *Atlanta Constitution*, 23, 25 May 1871, 11 January 1872, 20 July 1873.

48. Maury Klein, "The Strategy of Southern Railroads," *American Historical Review* 73 (April 1968): 1054.

49. Changes in trade were largely the result of more competitive railroads and the rise of Atlanta. See Russell, "Atlanta, Gate City of the South," p. 173; Randolph Dennis Werner, "Hegemony and Conflict: The Political Economy of a Southern Region, Augusta, Georgia, 1865–1895" (Ph.D. dissertation, University of Virginia, 1977), pp. 34–36, 95–96; Maury Klein, "Southern Railroad Leaders, 1865–1893: Identities and Ideologies," *Business History Review* 42 (Autumn 1968): 304; *Augusta Chronicle and Sentinel*, 13–16 April, 24 May 1881. The Georgia Railroad's board of directors remained intact even after the lease.

50. This view runs slightly counter to Klein's assessment of Wadley's managerial policies. Klein argues that Wadley perpetuated "localistic" policies designed to enrich Savannah that were ill-suited to conditions in the postbellum South. Yet Klein never takes into consideration Wadley's wartime stint as railroad chief. Wadley's extension of the Central's operations was more than a continuation of local developmental policies. In essence, Wadley was managing his road with a new, national orientation. Such a conception made state and national concerns as important as local ones in Central Railroad decision making. For evidence of this new orientation, see Central Railroad Company, *Reports*, 1865–73, and Klein, "Strategy of Southern Railroads," p. 1059.

51. President's Report [Brown] to the General Assembly, 1 August 1872. See also President's Report for 1 January 1872, Georgia Department of Archives and History.

52. The drive for expansion and consolidation produced cutthroat competition. The shaky finances of some roads were damaged beyond repair by the Panic of 1873 and the depression that followed. As John F. Stover has pointed out, the depression opened the door to a Northern invasion, and by the 1880s Southern-dominated lines were coming under the control of Northern financial interests. See Stover, *Railroads of the South*, pp. 202–10.

Chapter 6

1. *Louisville Courier-Journal*, as reprinted in *Atlanta Constitution*, 11 September 1875; Grigsby H. Wotton, Jr., "New City of the South: Atlanta, 1843–1873" (Ph.D. dissertation, Johns Hopkins University, 1973), p. 15; Franklin M. Garrett, *Atlanta and Environs: A Chronicle of Its People and Events*, 2 vols. (Athens: University of Georgia Press, 1954), 1:828.

2. James Michael Russell, "Atlanta, Gate City of the South, 1847 to 1885"

(Ph.D. dissertation, Princeton University, 1972), p. 127.

3. Sidney Andrews, *The South since the War* (1866; rpt. New York: Arno Press, 1969), p. 339.

4. *Barnwell's Atlanta City Directory* (Atlanta: Intelligencer Book & Job Office, 1867), pp. 32–35; Garrett, *Atlanta and Environs*, 1:675; Allen Phelps Julian, "Atlanta's Last Days in the Confederacy," *Atlanta Historical Bulletin* 11 (June 1966): 13; Russell, "Atlanta, Gate City of the South," pp. 163–64.

5. *Barnwell's Atlanta City Directory*, p. 35; Russell, "Atlanta, Gate City of the South," p. 167. By the end of 1866, Atlanta's population stood at 20,228; by 1869, it had reached 29,169. See *Hanleiter's Atlanta City Directory for 1870* (Atlanta: William R. Hanleiter, 1870), p. 24.

6. Andrews, *The South since the War*, pp. 340, 375; John H. Kennaway, *On Sherman's Track, or the South after the War* (London: Seeley, Jackson and Halliday, 1867), pp. 115–16; C. W. Tebeau, " 'Visitors' Views of Georgia Politics and Life, 1865–1880,' " *Georgia Historical Quarterly* 20 (March 1942): 4.

7. *Albany* (Ga.) *News*, as reprinted in *Atlanta Daily New Era*, 21 April 1870; *Chicago Railroad Gazette* as reprinted in ibid., 5 October 1870; *Daily New Era*, 23 December 1866. See also Fulton County Grand Jury Memorial, 1866, as reprinted in Garrett, *Atlanta and Environs*, 1:708; *Atlanta Daily Intelligencer*, 14 May 1866. See also *Barnwell's Atlanta City Directory*, pp. 33–35.

8. *Milledgeville Federal Union*, 12 February 1867; *Southern Field and Fireside*, as reprinted in *Atlanta Daily New Era*, 30 October 1866.

9. *Atlanta Daily New Era*, 3 January 1867; *Atlanta Daily Intelligencer*, 8 February 1870.

10. Georgia, vol. 13, p. 32, R. G. Dun & Co. Collection, Baker Library, Harvard University Graduate School of Business Administration, Cambridge, Mass.

11. Ibid., p. 162; Garrett, *Atlanta and Environs*, 1:350; Wotton, "New City of the South," p. 175.

12. Georgia, vol. 13, pp. 245, 277; vol. 14, pp. 255, 371, R. G. Dun & Co. Collection.

13. U.S. Census Office, *Ninth Census of the United States: Part III, Wealth and Industry* (Washington, D.C.: U.S. Government Printing Office, 1872), p. 506; Fulton County Tax Digest, reprinted in *Atlanta Constitution*, 5 August 1871; *Annual Report of the Comptroller General of the State of Georgia* (Atlanta: Samuel Bard, 1870), pp. 42–47.

14. *Atlanta Daily New Era*, 30 January 1868; *Atlanta Constitution*, 17 November 1868, 13 July, 7 February 1871. The *Atlanta Daily New Era* covered the plans to attract immigrants in its 25 April, 16, 29 May 1868, and 25 September 1870 issues. A company was finally formed in 1873: the Georgia Real Estate and Immigration Company. The company was based in Atlanta, but its directors represented Atlanta, Augusta, and Savannah. Those individuals planned to sell land through lottery agencies. The company planned to hold lotteries once the "requisite amount" of overseas tickets were sold and the proceeds invested in the lottery fund. The Georgia Real Estate and Immigration Company folded in June 1874, when it failed to sell enough tickets to hold a land lottery. See Georgia, vol. 13, p. 381, R. G. Dun & Co. Collection;

City Council Minutes, selected years, 1869–73, as cited in Wotton, "New City of the South," pp. 178–79; Russell, "Atlanta, Gate City of the South," p. 156; Garrett, *Atlanta and Environs*, 1:866–67; *Atlanta Daily New Era*, 17 January 1867; *Atlanta Constitution*, 17 September 1868, 9 January 1873.

15. Georgia, vol. 23, pp. 110, 24, 125, 61, 3, 14, and 102, R. G. Dun & Co. Collection; *Atlanta Daily New Era*, 5 May 1867; C. Mildred Thompson, *Reconstruction in Georgia: Economic, Social, Political, 1865–1872*, Columbia University Studies in History, Economics and Public Law, vol. 64, no. 1 (1915; rpt. Savannah: Beehive Press, 1972), p. 89.

16. Thompson, *Reconstruction in Georgia*, p. 89.

17. Georgia, vol. 23, pp. 156, 110, R. G. Dun & Co. Collection; Etta Blanchard Worseley, *Columbus on the Chattahoochee* (Columbus: Columbus Office Supply Co., 1951), pp. 319–20.

18. Georgia, vol. 23, p. 156, vol. 24, p. 272, R. G. Dun & Co. Collection; *Atlanta Constitution*, 7 December 1870, 7 February 1880; *Columbus Sun*, reprinted in *Mobile* (Ala.) *Daily Register*, 16 January 1880; *St. Louis Republican*, reprinted in *Mobile Daily Register*, 13 February 1880; Worseley, *Columbus on the Chattahoochee*, pp. 377–78.

19. Georgia, vol. 23, pp. 41, 109, R. G. Dun & Co. Collection; Worseley, *Columbus on the Chattahoochee*, p. 376; Thompson, *Reconstruction in Georgia*, p. 285.

20. Georgia, vol. 23, p. 79, vol. 24, p. 311, R. G. Dun & Co. Collection; Worseley, *Columbus on the Chattahoochee*, p. 378.

21. *New Orleans Picayune*, reprinted in *Atlanta Constitution*, 5 September 1871; *Atlanta Daily New Era*, 5 May 1867.

22. Georgia, vol. 23, pp. 160, 63, R. G. Dun & Co. Collection.

23. Ibid., pp. 102–3, 90.

24. Ibid., pp. 75, 234, 3, 32.

25. Ibid., pp. 101, 56. In the 1880s, Elias moved to Cleveland, Ohio. See *Atlanta Constitution*, 15 March 1885.

26. Worseley, *Columbus on the Chattahoochee*, pp. 319–21.

27. *Columbus Daily Sun*, 18 April 1866.

28. Ibid., 22 May 1866; see also 17 and 24 May 1866.

29. U.S. Census Office, *Ninth Census, Wealth and Industry*, p. 506; Edward King, *The Great South* (1879; rpt. Baton Rouge: Louisiana State University Press, 1972), pp. 373–74; *Atlanta Constitution*, 7 December 1871. The *Constitution* devoted extensive coverage to Columbus's postwar resurrection in its 19 December 1886 issue.

30. B. C. Truman in *New York Times*, 3 December 1865.

31. For changes in perceptions, see *Augusta Chronicle and Sentinel*, 14 April, 26 May 1864; Richard H. L. German, "The Economic Development of Augusta in the Gilded Age, 1860–1900," *Richmond County History* 3 (Winter 1971): 10. Georgia Railroad president John P. King had encouraged the board of directors to allow the bank's charter to lapse in 1864 owing to the Confederacy's desperate financial situation. The bank thus suspended its active operations but remained, as German points out, a "*de facto* institution" in the community. See also James F. Doster, "The Georgia Railroad and

Banking Company in the Reconstruction Era," *Georgia Historical Quarterly* 48 (March 1964): 1.

32. Martin V. Calvin, *Augusta City Directory, 1865,* as cited in Florence Fleming Corley, *Confederate City: Augusta, Georgia, 1860–1865* (Columbia: University of South Carolina Press, 1960), p. 98; *Augusta Chronicle and Sentinel,* 4, 12 May 1865.

33. Georgia, vol. 1b, pp. 126, 255, 60, R. G. Dun & Co. Collection; Corley, *Confederate City,* pp. 48–49.

34. Georgia, vol. 1b, pp. 126, 255, 60, R. G. Dun & Co. Collection; Salem Dutcher and Charles C. Jones, Jr., *Memorial History of Augusta, Georgia, from Its Settlement in 1735 to the Close of the Eighteenth Century* (Syracuse, N.Y.: D. Mason, 1890), pp. 418–19; Richard W. Griffen, "The Augusta (Georgia) Manufacturing Company in Peace, War and Reconstruction, 1847–1877," *Business History Review* 32 (Spring 1958): 70; William Ludwick Whatley, "A History of the Textile Development of Augusta, Georgia, 1865 to 1883" (M.S. thesis, University of South Carolina, 1964), p. 7; *Atlanta Daily New Era,* 30 January 1870.

35. Georgia, vol. 1b, pp. 139, 85, R. G. Dun & Co. Collection.

36. Ibid., pp. 57, 11, 97, vol. 13, p. 313.

37. Thompson, *Reconstruction in Georgia,* pp. 278–79.

38. Randolph Dennis Werner, "Hegemony and Conflict: The Political Economy of a Southern Region, Augusta, Georgia, 1865–1895" (Ph.D. dissertation, University of Virginia, 1977), pp. 34–36; Russell, "Atlanta, Gate City of the South," p. 173. The Georgia Railroad's annual reports for the period also demonstrate the decline in the cotton trade. See Georgia Railroad, *Annual Reports,* 1865–73, Georgia State Library, Atlanta; also Harold Woodman, *King Cotton and His Retainers: Financing and Marketing in the South, 1800–1920* (Lexington: University Press of Kentucky, 1968), pp. 269–75, 279–88; see also Harry Hammond, Beech Island, South Carolina, to William Courtenay, 27 November 1883, in William A. Courtenay Papers, South Caroliniana Library, as cited in Werner, "Hegemony and Conflict," p. 35. Hammond's correspondence highlights the unpredictable nature of the postbellum cotton trade.

39. Whatley, "History of the Textile Development," pp. 10–11. One of the leading advocates of canal expansion was General George Washington Rains, builder and superintendent of the Confederacy's Augusta Powder Works and Arsenal. Rains was probably more aware than most of how inadequate the canal was to meet the city's manufacturing needs. See Edward J. Cashin, *The Story of Augusta* (Augusta: Richmond County Board of Education, 1980), p. 149.

40. Dutcher and Jones, *Memorial History of Augusta,* p. 413; Whatley, "History of the Textile Development," pp. 11–12.

41. Dutcher and Jones, *Memorial History of Augusta,* pp. 414–15; Cashin, *Story of Augusta,* pp. 150–51; Whatley, "History of the Textile Development," pp. 12–13.

42. Whatley, "History of the Textile Development," p. 55; Cashin, *Story of Augusta,* p. 149.

43. German, "The Economic Development of Augusta," p. 9; Whatley,

"Textile Development of Augusta," pp. 18–30; *Atlanta Constitution*, 26 December 1886; Griffen, "The Augusta (Georgia) Manufacturing Company," pp. 71–72.

44. See *Augusta Chronicle and Sentinel*, 4, 25 May 1864, 12 May 1865. The 1870 census credited Augusta with 97 manufacturing establishments that were capitalized at $1,345,155. The annual value of products was $2,614,405. See U.S. Census Office, *Ninth Census, Wealth and Industry*, p. 507.

45. Many Georgians were disgusted with Savannah's behavior after Sherman's occupation of the city. Citizens meetings were held in January 1865, and resolutions were adopted calling for the governor to call a state convention to consider Georgia's withdrawal from the Confederacy and its reentry into the Union. Other resolutions, deeming secession a "hasty and unwise act," and expressions of thanks to Sherman for his fairness understandably rankled many Georgians who had lived in the path of the March to the Sea. See *Savannah Republican*, 3 January 1865, and George W. Nichols, *The Story of the Great March from the Diary of a Staff Officer* (New York: Harper & Brothers, 1865), pp. 99, 108.

46. John McGlidden to William H. Gardiner, 29 January 1865, in Frank Otto Gatell, ed., "A Yankee Views the Agony of Savannah," *Georgia Historical Quarterly* 43 (December 1959): 429.

47. *Savannah Republican*, 26 January 1865; T. M. Haddock, comp., *Haddock's Savannah, Ga., Directory and General Advertiser* (Savannah: J. H. Estill, 1871), p. 18; Charles C. Jones, Jr., *History of Savannah, Georgia, from Its Settlement to the Close of the Eighteenth Century* (Syracuse, N.Y.: D. Mason, 1890), pp. 356–57, 388; Nichols, *Story of the Great March*, p. 108.

48. *Savannah Republican*, 24, 25 March, 12 June, 20 October 1865. Trade with the Federals could assume impressive dimensions. Sarah Lachlison, the daughter-in-law of one of Savannah's most prominent civic and mercantile leaders, recalled that Union troops had ample money but few provisions. Her family possessed flour and sorghum but little else. Because the Lachlisons needed ready cash, they opened a bakery in their basement. The soldiers, "ready to pay exorbitant prices for eatables other than Army rations," eagerly bought up the cakes that were sold through an "iron barred window[,] fearing to allow any closer contact with the dreaded enemy." The Lachlisons netted a hefty $1,500 through trading with the "dreaded enemy." See Sarah Lachlison Papers, Georgia Historical Society, Savannah.

49. Andrews, *The South since the War*, pp. 365–66.

50. Mayor's Report, 1 October 1871, clipping in Edward C. Anderson Papers, Georgia Historical Society; also Mayor's Reports, 1866–70, ibid.; George Anderson Mercer Diary, 25 April 1869, Southern Historical Collection, University of North Carolina, Chapel Hill; and F. D. Lee and J. L. Agnew, *Historical Record of the City of Savannah* (Savannah: J. H. Estill, 1869), pp. 135–37, 150–51.

51. *Atlanta Constitution*, 28 February, 11 April, 4 June 1871; Haddock, *Haddock's Savannah Directory*, pp. 18–19, 23; U.S. Census Office, *The Statistics of the Population of the United States from the Original Returns of the Ninth Census* (Washington, D.C.: U.S. Government Printing Office, 1872), p. 121.

52. King, *The Great South*, p. 366.

53. U.S. Census Office, *Ninth Census, Wealth and Industry*, p. 506; *Savannah Republican*, 12 June 1865; *New York Sun*, as reprinted in *Atlanta Constitution*, 28 February 1871; Haddock, comp., *Haddock's Savannah Directory*, p. 18, illustrates local perceptions of Savannah's rivals reaping gains from wartime service.

54. Don H. Dodd and Wynelle Dodd, *Historical Statistics of the South, 1790–1970* (University, Ala.: University of Alabama Press, 1975), pp. 18–20.

55. James Michael Russell, *Atlanta, 1847–1890: City Building in the Old and New South* (Baton Rouge: Louisiana State University Press, 1988), pp. 260–65.

56. Don Harrison Doyle, "Urbanization and Southern Culture: Economic Elites in Four New South Cities (Atlanta, Nashville, Charleston, Mobile) c. 1865–1910," in Orville Vernon Burton and Robert C. McMath, Jr., eds., *Toward a New South? Studies in Post–Civil War Southern Communities* (Westport, Conn.: Greenwood Press, 1982), pp. 15–16, 18, 24–28.

57. Werner, "Hegemony and Conflict," pp. 19–21.

58. C. Vann Woodward, *Origins of the New South, 1877–1913* (Baton Rouge: Louisiana State University Press, 1951), p. 20.

59. Dodd and Dodd, *Historical Statistics of the South*, pp. 18–20.

60. Ibid.; David R. Goldfield, *Cotton Fields and Skyscrapers: Southern City and Region, 1607–1980* (Baton Rouge: Louisiana State University Press, 1982), pp. 85–86; Howard N. Rabinowitz, "Southern Urban Development, 1860–1900," in David R. Goldfield and Blaine A. Brownell, eds., *The City in Southern History: The Growth of Urban Civilization in the South* (Port Washington, N.Y.: Kennikat Press, 1977), pp. 102–4; Mark W. Summers, *Railroads, Reconstruction, and the Gospel of Prosperity: Aid under the Radical Republicans* (Princeton: Princeton University Press, 1984), esp. chap. 16, " 'Men are Giting Desperate . . .': The Panic, Collapse and Survival of the Gospel of Prosperity, 1873–1880," pp. 268–98.

Selected Bibliography

Primary Sources

Manuscript Collections

Athens, Georgia
  University of Georgia Library
    Annual Report of the Comptroller General of the State of Georgia, Made to the Governor, 1857–70.
    Quartermaster Department, Letters and Telegrams Sent, 1861–65. Microfilm copy.
    War Department Collection of Confederate Records.
      Record Group 109. Records of Ordnance Establishments at Dalton, Savannah, Augusta, and Atlanta, Georgia, and Nashville, Tennessee. Microfilm copy.
Atlanta, Georgia
  Atlanta Historical Society
    Lemuel P. Grant Papers.
    William McNaught Papers.
    Samuel P. Richards Papers.
    Western & Atlantic Railroad Minutes, 1870–90.
  Georgia Department of Archives and History
    Adjutant General's Reports, 1861–64.
    Board Minutes, Board of Directors, Western & Atlantic Railroad, September 1865.
    Governor's Letterbooks, 1831–61, 1861–65.
    Incoming Correspondence to the Governor, Georgia, 1861–65.
    Macon & Brunswick Railroad, *Annual Reports,* 1859–70.
    Macon & Western Railroad, *Annual Reports,* 1857–71.
    Miscellaneous Bound and Unbound Records of Georgia Records before Regulation, 1859–1915.
    Report of the Committee of the Legislature to Investigate the Bonds of the State of Georgia, 1872.
    Western & Atlantic Railroad, *Reports of the Superintendent and Treasurer,* 1857–71.
    Western & Atlantic Railroad Valuations and Cash Journals, 1856–66.
  Georgia State Library
    Atlantic & Gulf Railroad Company, *Reports of the President of the Atlantic & Gulf Railroad,* 1859–61.
    Georgia Railroad and Banking Company. *Reports of the Directors &c of the Georgia Railroad and Banking Company,* 1859–73.
    Report to the Joint Committee to Investigate the Condition of the Western & Atlantic Railroad . . . February 25, 1869, 1869.

Report of the Railroad Convention, Chattanooga, Tennessee, 4–5 June 1861.
Cambridge, Massachusetts
  Baker Library, Harvard University Graduate School of Business Administration
  R. G. Dun & Co. Collection.
Chapel Hill, North Carolina
  Southern Historical Collection
    Arnold-Screven Papers.
    Lucy Hull Baldwin Papers.
    Bulloch Family Papers.
    Farish Carter Papers.
    Jeremy F. Gilmer Papers.
    Alexander R. Lawton Papers.
    George Anderson Mercer Papers.
    Charles H. Olmstead Papers.
    George Washington Rains Papers.
    Benedict Joseph Semmes Papers.
Chicago, Illinois
  Center for Research Libraries
    War Department Collection of Confederate Records, Chapter V, Quartermaster Department, Letters and Telegrams Sent, rolls 8, 10, and 13.
    Records of the States of the United States, 1782–1872.
      Georgia. Treasurers' Reports.
Savannah, Georgia
  Georgia Historical Society
    Edward C. Anderson Papers.
    Augusta & Savannah Railroad Company, *Annual Reports*, 1853–61.
    Joseph E. Brown Papers.
    Chatham County, State of Georgia, Minutes of Council, City of Savannah, 1855–69.
    Constitution and By-Laws of the Savannah Chamber of Commerce.
    Constitution and By-Laws of the Savannah Chamber of Commerce, Adopted 4th April 1870.
    Sarah Lachlison Papers.
    Municipal Reports, City of Savannah, Reports of the Mayor's Office, 1856–72.
    Muscogee Railroad Company, *Annual Reports*, 1853, 1867.
    Records of the U.S. Collector of Customs, Savannah, Georgia, 1799–1910.
    Savannah Cotton Exchange Papers.
    Henry Frederick Willink, Jr., Papers.

Newspapers and City Directories

Atlanta Constitution, 1868, 1871–74
Atlanta Daily Intelligencer, 1861–64
Atlanta Daily New Era, 1866–71

Atlanta Southern Confederacy, 1861–65
Augusta Chronicle and Sentinel, 1848–64
Columbus Daily Sun, 1860–66
Columbus Tri-Weekly Enquirer, 1857–59
Milledgeville Southern Recorder, 1849–55, 1858–64
Savannah Republican, 1861–72

Alex Abrams & Co., comp. *Directory of the City of Savannah for 1870.* Savannah: J. H. Estill, 1870.
Barnwell's Atlanta City Directory. Atlanta: Intelligencer & Job Office, 1867.
Directory for the City of Augusta & Business Advertiser for 1859. Augusta: R. A. Watkins, 1859.
Haddock, T. M., comp. *Haddock's Savannah, Ga., Directory and General Advertiser.* Savannah: J. H. Estill, 1871.
Hanleiter's Atlanta City Directory for 1870. Atlanta: William R. Hanleiter, 1870.
Hanleiter's Atlanta City Directory for 1871. Atlanta: William R. Hanleiter, 1871.
Hanleiter's Atlanta City Directory for 1872. Atlanta: Plantation Publishing, 1871.
Purse's Directory of the City of Savannah Together with a Mercantile & Business Directory. Savannah: Purse & Son, 1866.
Savannah City Directory for 1867. Savannah: N. T. Darrell & Co., 1867.
Williams' Atlanta Directory, City Guide and Business Mirror. Vol. 1, 1859–60. Atlanta: M. Lynch, 1859.

Official Documents

Candler, Allen D., ed. *The Confederate Records of the State of Georgia.* 6 vols. Atlanta: Charles P. Byrd, 1909–12.
Matthews, James M., ed. *Private Laws of the Confederate States of America, Passed at the First Session of the First Congress, 1862.* Richmond: R. M. Smith, 1862.
————. *The Statutes at Large of the Provisional Government of the Confederate States of America, from the Institution of the Government, February 8, 1861, to its Termination, February 18, 1862.* Richmond: R. M. Smith, 1864.
Superintendent of the United States Census. *Statistical View of the United States . . . Being a Compendium of the Seventh Census.* Washington, D.C.: Beverly Tucker, 1854.
U. S. Census Office. *Manufactures of the United States in 1860: Compiled from the Original Returns of the Eighth Census.* Washington, D.C.: U.S. Government Printing Office, 1865.
————. *Ninth Census of the United States: Part III, Wealth and Industry.* Washington, D.C.: U.S. Government Printing Office, 1872.
————. *Population of the United States in 1860, Compiled from the Original Returns of the Eighth Census.* Washington, D.C.: U.S. Government Printing Office, 1864.
————. *The Statistics of the Population of the United States from the Original Returns of the Ninth Census.* Washington, D.C.: U.S. Government Printing Office, 1872.
U.S. Navy Department. *Official Records of the Union and Confederate Navies in*

the War of Rebellion. Ser. 1, 27 vols., Ser. 2, 3 vols. Washington, D.C.: U.S. Government Printing Office, 1884–1922.

U.S. War Department. *The War of Rebellion: A Compilation of the Official Records of the Union and Confederate Armies*. Ser. 1, 53 vols., Ser. 4, 3 vols. Washington, D.C.: U.S. Government Printing Office, 1880–1902.

U.S. War Department. *Journal of the Congress of the Confederate States of America, 1861–1865*. 7 vols. Washington, D.C.: U.S. Government Printing Office, 1904–5.

Other Printed Primary Sources

Andrews, Eliza Frances. *The War-Time Journal of a Georgia Girl, 1864–1865*. New York: D. Appleton and Co., 1908.

Andrews, Sidney. *The South since the War*. 1866. Reprint. New York: Arno Press, 1969.

Central Railroad and Banking Company. *Reports of the Presidents and Superintendents of the Central Railroad and Banking Company of Georgia, No. 20 to 32 Inclusive, and the Amended Charter of the Company*. Savannah: G. N. Nichols, Printer, 1868.

DeBow, J. D. B. *The Industrial Resources, Statistics, &c of the United States and More Particularly of the Southern and Western States*. 3 vols. 1854. Reprint. New York: Augustus Kelly, 1966.

Fremantle, Arthur J. L., *Three Months in the Southern States, April–June 1863*. Edinburgh : William Blackwood and Sons, 1863.

Hundley, D. R. *Social Relations in Our Southern States*. 1860. Reprint. Ann Arbor: University Microfilms, 1973.

Jones, J. B. *A Rebel War Clerk's Diary*. 2 vols. New York: J. B. Lippincott, 1866.

Kennaway, John H. *On Sherman's Track, or the South after the War*. London: Seeley, Jackson and Holliday, 1867.

King, Edward. *The Great South*. 1879. Reprint. Baton Rouge: Louisiana State University Press, 1972.

Lesley, J. P. *The Iron Manufacturer's Guide to the Furnaces, Forges and Rolling Mills of the United States*. New York: John Wiley, 1859.

Mallet, John W. "Work of the Ordnance Bureau of the War Department of the Confederate States, 1861–1865." *Southern Historical Society Papers*, vol. 37. Richmond: Southern Historical Society, 1909.

Merrill, James M., ed. " 'Personne' Goes to Georgia: Five Civil War Letters." *Georgia Historical Quarterly* 43 (June 1959): 202–11.

Myers, Robert Manson, ed. *The Children of Pride: A True Story of Georgia and the Civil War*. New Haven: Yale University Press, 1972.

Olmsted, Frederick Law. *A Journey in the Seaboard Slave States*. New York: Dix and Edwards, 1856.

Rains, George Washington. *History of the Confederate Powder Works*. Augusta: Chronicle & Constitutionalist, 1881.

Reid, Whitelaw. *After the War: A Tour of the Southern States*. 1866. Reprint. New York: Harper & Row, 1965.

Russell, William Howard. *My Diary North and South*. 1863. Reprint. New York: Knopf, 1988.

Shryock, Richard H., ed. *Letters of Richard D. Arnold, M.D., 1808–1876. Papers of the Trinity College Historical Society*. vols. 18–19. Durham: Trinity College, 1929.

Somers, Robert. *The Southern States since the War, 1870–1*. 1871. Reprint. University, Ala.: University of Alabama Press, 1965.

Trowbridge, J. T. *The South: A Tour of Its Battlefields and Ruined Cities*. 1866. Reprint. New York: Arno Press, 1969.

Vandiver, Frank E., ed. *The Civil War Diary of General Josiah Gorgas*. University, Ala.: University of Alabama Press, 1947

Younger, Edward, ed. *Inside the Confederate Government: The Diary of Robert Garlick Kean, Head of the Bureau of War*. New York: Oxford University Press, 1957.

Secondary Works

Books

Aitken, Hugh G. J., ed. *Explorations in Enterprise*. Cambridge: Harvard University Press, 1965.

Albaugh, William A. III, Hugh Benet, Jr., and Edward N. Simmons, *Confederate Handguns: Concerning the Guns, the Men Who Made Them, and the Times of Their Use*. Philadelphia: Riling and Lentz, 1963.

Albaugh, William A. III, and Edward N. Simmons. *Confederate Arms*. New York: Bonanza Books, 1967.

Andreano, Ralph, ed. *The Economic Impact of the American Civil War*. Cambridge: Schenkman, 1962.

Atherton, Lewis E. *The Southern Country Store, 1800–1860*. Baton Rouge: Louisiana State University Press, 1949.

Bateman, Fred, and Thomas Weiss. *A Deplorable Scarcity: The Failure of Industrialization in the Slave Economy*. Chapel Hill: University of North Carolina Press, 1981.

Bell, Earl L., and Kenneth C. Crabbe. *The Augusta Chronicle: Indomitable Voice of Dixie, 1785–1960*. Athens: University of Georgia Press, 1960.

Black, Robert C. III. *Railroads of the Confederacy*. Chapel Hill: University of North Carolina Press, 1952.

Brownell, Blaine A., and David R. Goldfield., eds. *The City in Southern History: The Growth of Urban Civilization in the South*. Port Washington, N.Y.: Kennikat Press, 1977.

Bryan, T. Conn. *Confederate Georgia*. Athens: University of Georgia Press, 1953.

Cashin, Edward J. *The Story of Augusta*. Augusta: Richmond County Board of Education, 1980.

Chandler, Alfred D., Jr. *The Visible Hand: The Managerial Revolution in American Business*. Cambridge: Belknap Press of Harvard University Press, 1977.

Cochran, Thomas C. *Railroad Leaders, 1845–1890: The Business Mind in Action*. Cambridge: Harvard University Press, 1953.

Cole, Arthur C. *The Whig Party in the South*. Washington, D.C.: American Historical Association, 1913.

Cole, Arthur H. *Business Enterprise in Its Social Setting*. Cambridge: Harvard University Press, 1959.

Coleman, Kenneth, ed. *A History of Georgia*. Athens: University of Georgia Press, 1977.

Conway, Alan. *The Reconstruction of Georgia*. Minneapolis: University of Minnesota Press, 1966.

Corley, Florence Fleming. *Confederate City: Augusta, Georgia, 1860–1865*. Columbia: University of South Carolina Press, 1960.

Coulter, E. Merton. *The Confederate States of America, 1861–1865*. Vol. 7 of *A History of the South*, ed. Wendell Holmes Stephenson and E. Merton Coulter. Baton Rouge: Louisiana State University Press, 1950.

———. *Georgia: A Short History*. Chapel Hill: University of North Carolina Press, 1947.

Cumming, Mary G. *Georgia Railroad and Banking Company, 1833–1945*. Augusta: Walton Printing Co., 1945.

Dew, Charles B. *Ironmaker to the Confederacy: Joseph R. Anderson and the Tredegar Iron Works*. New Haven: Yale University Press, 1966.

Dutcher, Salem, and Charles C. Jones, Jr. *Memorial History of Augusta, Georgia, from Its Settlement in 1735 to the Close of the Eighteenth Century*. Syracuse, N.Y.: D. Mason, 1890.

Eaton, Clement. *The Growth of Southern Civilization, 1790–1860*. New York: Harper and Brothers, 1961.

Fish, Carl Russell. *The Restoration of Southern Railroads*. University of Wisconsin Studies in the Social Sciences and History, no. 2. Madison: University of Wisconsin Press, 1919.

Fuller, Claud E., and Richard D. Steuart. *Firearms of the Confederacy*. Huntington, W. Va.: Standard Publications, 1944.

Garrett, Franklin M. *Atlanta and Environs: A Chronicle of Its People and Events*. 2 vols. Athens: University of Georgia Press, 1954.

Goff, Richard D. *Confederate Supply*. Durham: Duke University Press, 1969.

Goldfield, David R. *Cotton Fields and Skyscrapers: Southern City and Region, 1607–1980*. Baton Rouge: Louisiana State University Press, 1982.

———. *Urban Growth in an Age of Sectionalism, Virginia, 1847–1861*. Baton Rouge: Louisiana State University Press, 1977.

Hahn, Steven. *The Roots of Southern Populism: Yeoman Farmers and the Transformation of the Georgia Upcountry, 1850–1890*. New York: Oxford University Press, 1983.

Hattaway, Herman, and Archer Jones. *How the North Won: A Military History of the Civil War*. Urbana: University of Illinois Press, 1983.

Heath, Milton Sydney. *Constructive Liberalism: The Role of the State in Economic Development in Georgia to 1860*. Cambridge: Harvard University Press, 1954.

Hesseltine, William B. *Confederate Leaders in the New South*. Baton Rouge: Louisiana State University Press, 1950.

Johnson, Michael P. *Toward a Patriarchal Republic: The Secession of Georgia*. Baton Rouge: Louisiana State University Press, 1977.

Johnston, James H. *Western and Atlantic Railroad of the State of Georgia*. Atlanta: Stein Printing, 1932.

Jones, Charles C., Jr. *History of Savannah, Georgia, from Its Settlement to the*

Close of the Eighteenth Century. Syracuse, N.Y.: D. Mason, 1890.

Jones, James Pickett. *Yankee Blitzkrieg: Wilson's Raid through Alabama and Georgia.* Athens: University of Georgia Press, 1976.

Lawrence, Alexander A. *A Present for Mr. Lincoln: The Story of Savannah from Secession to Sherman.* Macon: Ardvian Press, 1961.

Lee, F. D., and J. L. Agnew. *Historical Record of the City of Savannah.* Savannah: J. H. Estill, 1869.

Luraghi, Raimondo. *The Rise and Fall of the Plantation South.* New York: Franklin Watts, 1978.

Martin, John H., comp. *Columbus, Georgia, from Its Selection as a "Trading Town" in 1827 to Its Partial Destruction by Wilson's Raid in 1865.* Columbus: Thomas Gilbert, 1874.

Massey, Mary Elizabeth. *Ersatz in the Confederacy.* Columbia: University of South Carolina Press, 1952.

Nathans, Elizabeth Studley. *Losing the Peace: Georgia Republicans and Reconstruction, 1868–1872.* Baton Rouge: Louisiana State University Press, 1968.

Niemi, Albert W., Jr. *State and Regional Patterns in American Manufacturing, 1860–1900.* Westport, Conn: Greenwood Press, 1974.

Phillips, Ulrich B. *A History of Transportation in the Eastern Cotton Belt to 1860.* New York: Columbia University Press, 1908.

Pioneer Citizens' Society of Atlanta. *Pioneer Citizens' History of Atlanta, 1833–1902.* Atlanta: Byrd Printing Co., 1902.

Poor, Henry V. *Manual of Railroads of the United States, 1869–70.* New York: L. G. Wemyss, 1869.

———. *Manual of the Railroads of the United States, 1870–71.* 3d ser. New York: H. V. and H. W. Poor, 1870.

Prince, Richard E. *Steam Locomotives and History: Georgia Railroad and West Point Route.* Green River, Wyo.: Richard Prince, 1962.

Ramsdell, Charles W. *Behind the Lines in the Southern Confederacy.* Baton Rouge: Louisiana State University Press, 1944.

Research Center in Entrepreneurial History, Harvard University. *Change and the Entrepreneur.* Cambridge: Harvard University Press, 1949.

Russel, Robert Royal. *Economic Aspects of Southern Sectionalism, 1840–1861.* 1924. Reprint. New York: Arno Press, 1973.

Schwab, John Christopher. *The Confederate States of America, 1861–1865: A Financial and Industrial History of the South during the Civil War.* 1901. Reprint. New York: Burt Franklin, 1968.

Shryock, Richard H. *Georgia and the Union in 1850.* Durham: Duke University Press, 1926.

Standard, Diffee W. *Columbus, Georgia, in the Confederacy: The Social and Industrial Life of the Chattahoochee River Port.* New York: William Frederick Press, 1954.

Stover, John F. *The Railroads of the South, 1865–1900: A Study in Finance and Control.* Chapel Hill: University of North Carolina Press, 1955.

Summers, Mark W. *Railroads, Reconstruction and the Gospel of Prosperity: Aid under the Radical Republicans, 1865–1877.* Princeton: Princeton University Press, 1984.

Taylor, George Rogers, and Irene D. Neu. *The American Railroad Network,*

1861–1890. Cambridge: Harvard University Press, 1956.

Telfair, Nancy. *A History of Columbus, Georgia, 1828–1928*. Columbus: Historical Publishing Co., 1929.

Thomas, Emory M. *The Confederacy as a Revolutionary Experience*. Englewood Cliffs, N.J.: Prentice-Hall, 1971.

———. *The Confederate Nation, 1861–1865*. New York: Harper Torchbooks, 1979.

Thompson, C. Mildred. *Reconstruction in Georgia: Economic, Social, Political, 1865–1872*. Columbia University Studies in History, Economics and Public Law, vol. 64, no. 1. 1915. Reprint. Savannah: Beehive Press, 1972.

Vandiver, Frank E. *Ploughshares into Swords: Josiah Gorgas and Confederate Ordnance*. Austin: University of Texas Press, 1952.

———. *Rebel Brass: The Confederate Command System*. 1956. Reprint. Westport, Conn: Greenwood Press, 1969.

———. *Their Tattered Flags: The Epic of the Confederacy*. New York: Harpers Magazine Press Book, 1970.

Wakelyn, Jon L., ed. *Biographical Dictionary of the Confederacy*. Westport, Conn.: Greenwood Press, 1977.

Wilson, John Stainback. *Atlanta as It Is: Being a Brief Sketch of Its Early Settlers*. 1871. Reprint. *Atlanta Historical Bulletin* 6 (1941): 9–161.

Worseley, Etta Blanchard. *Columbus on the Chattahoochee*. Columbus: Columbus Office Supply Co., 1951.

Articles

Bass, J. Horace. "Civil War Finance in Georgia." *Georgia Historical Quarterly* 26 (Fall 1942): 213–24.

Bateman, Fred, James Foust, and Thomas Weiss. "The Participation of Planters in Manufacturing in the Antebellum South." *Agricultural History* 48 (April 1974): 277–94.

Black, Robert C. III. "The Railroads of Georgia in the Confederate War Effort." *Journal of Southern History* 13 (November 1947): 511–34.

Bowlby, Elizabeth. "The Role of Atlanta during the War between the States." *Atlanta Historical Bulletin* 5 (July 1940): 177–97.

Brownell, Blaine A. "Urbanization in the South: A Unique Experience?" *Mississippi Quarterly* 26 (Spring 1973): 105–20.

Cappon, Lester J. "Trend of the Southern Iron Industry under the Plantation System." *Journal of Economic and Business History* 2 (1930): 353–81.

Collins, Herbert. "The Southern Industrial Gospel before 1860." *Journal of Southern History* 12 (August 1946): 386–402.

Cotterill, R. S. "Southern Railroads and Western Trade, 1840–1850." *Mississippi Valley Historical Review* 3 (March 1917): 427–41.

Coulter, E. Merton. "The Movement for Agricultural Reorganization in the Cotton South during the Civil War." *Agricultural History* 1 (January 1927): 3–17.

Davidson, Philip G. "Industrialism in the Antebellum South." *South Atlantic Quarterly* 27 (October 1928): 405–25.

DuBose, Beverley M. III. "The Manufacture of Confederate Ordnance in Georgia." *Atlanta Historical Bulletin* 12 (December 1967): 8–22.

Gatell, Frank Otto, ed. "A Yankee Views the Agony of Savannah." *Georgia Historical Quarterly* 43 (December 1959): 428–31.

German, Richard H. L. "Augusta Entrepreneurs, Artisans and Politicians." *Richmond County History* 5 (Summer 1973): 15–22.

———. "The Economic Development of Augusta in the Gilded Age, 1860–1900." *Richmond County History* 3 (Winter 1971): 5–20.

Gibbons, Robert. "Life at the Crossroads of the Confederacy: Atlanta, 1861–1865." *Atlanta Historical Bulletin* 23 (Summer 1979): 11–73.

Goldfarb, Stephen J. "A Note on Limits to the Growth of the Cotton Textile Industry in the Old South." *Journal of Southern History* 48 (November 1982): 545–58.

Griffen, Richard W. "The Augusta (Georgia) Manufacturing Company in Peace, War, and Reconstruction, 1847–1877." *Business History Review* 32 (Spring 1958): 60–73.

———. "The Origins of the Industrial Revolution in Georgia: Cotton Textiles, 1810–1865." *Georgia Historical Quarterly* 42 (1958): 355–75.

Hay, Thomas R. "Gazaway Bugg Lamar, Confederate Banker and Businessman." *Georgia Historical Quarterly* 37 (June 1953): 89–128.

Heath, Milton S. "Public Railroad Construction and the Development of Private Enterprise in the South before 1861." *Journal of Economic History* 10, Supplement (1950): 40–53.

Hesseltine, William B., and Larry Gara. "Georgia's Confederate Leaders after Appomattox." *Georgia Historical Quarterly* 35 (March 1951): 1–15.

Hubner, Charles W. "Some Recollections of Atlanta during 1864." *Atlanta Historical Bulletin* 1 (January 1928): 5–8.

Johnson, J. G. "Notes on Manufacturing in Antebellum Georgia." *Georgia Historical Quarterly* 16 (March 1932): 214–32.

Jones, James P. "Wilson's Raiders Reach Georgia: The Fall of Columbus, 1865." *Georgia Historical Quarterly* 59 (Fall 1975): 313–29.

Julian, Allen Phelps. "Atlanta's Last Days in the Confederacy." *Atlanta Historical Bulletin* 11 (June 1966): 9–18.

Klein, Maury. "Southern Railroad Leaders, 1865–1893: Identities and Ideologies." *Business History Review* 42 (Autumn 1968): 288–310.

———. "The Strategy of Southern Railroads." *American Historical Review* 73 (April 1968): 1052–68.

Luraghi, Raimondo. "The Civil War and the Modernization of American Society: Social Structure and Industrial Revolution in the Old South before and during the War." *Civil War History* 18 (September 1972): 230–50.

McGuire, Peter S. "The Railroads of Georgia, 1860–1880." *Georgia Historical Quarterly* 16 (March 1932): 179–214.

Mitchell, Stephens. "Atlanta: The Industrial Heart of the Confederacy." *Atlanta Historical Bulletin* 1 (May 1930): 20–28.

Olmstead, Charles H. "Fort Pulaski." *Georgia Historical Quarterly* 1 (June 1917): 98–105.

Ramsdell, Charles W. "The Confederate Government and the Railroads." *American Historical Review* 22 (1917): 794–810.

———. "The Control of Manufacturing by the Confederate Government." *Mississippi Valley Historical Review* 8 (December 1921): 231–49.

Saggus, Charles D. "1865—Year of Despair, Year of Hope: Augusta Recovers from the War." *Richmond County History* 7 (Summer 1975): 21–42.

Shryock, Richard H. "The Early Industrial Revolution in the Empire State." *Georgia Historical Quarterly* 11 (June 1927): 109–29.

Tebeau, C. W. "Visitors' Views of Georgia Politics and Life, 1865–1880." *Georgia Historical Quarterly* 20 (March 1942): 1–15.

Wallenstein, Peter. "Rich Man's War, Rich Man's Fight: Civil War and the Transformation of Public Finance in Georgia." *Journal of Southern History* 50 (February 1984): 15–42.

Ward, James A. "A New Look at Antebellum Southern Railroad Development." *Journal of Southern History* 39 (August 1973): 409–20.

Ward, Judson C., Jr. "The New Departure Democrats of Georgia: An Interpretation." *Georgia Historical Quarterly* 41 (September 1957): 227–36.

Wood, W. K. "The Georgia Railroad and Banking Company." *Georgia Historical Quarterly* 57 (Winter 1973): 543–61.

———. "A Note on Pro-Urbanism and Urbanization in the Antebellum South: Augusta, Georgia, 1820–1860." *Richmond County History* 6 (Winter 1974): 23–31.

Dissertations and Theses

Cooley, McWhorter S. "Manufacturing in Georgia during the Civil War Period." M.S. thesis, University of Georgia, 1929.

DeBats, Donald Arthur. "Elites and Masses: Political Structure, Communication and Behavior in Antebellum Georgia." Ph.D. dissertation, University of Wisconsin, 1973.

Griffen, James David. "Savannah, Georgia, during the Civil War." Ph.D. dissertation, University of Georgia, 1963.

Haunton, Richard H. "Savannah in the 1850's." Ph.D. dissertation, Emory University, 1968.

Russell, James Michael. "Atlanta, Gate City of the South, 1847 to 1885." Ph.D. dissertation, Princeton University, 1972.

Singer, Ralph Benjamin, Jr. "Confederate Atlanta." Ph.D. dissertation, University of Georgia, 1973.

Werner, Randolph Dennis. "Hegemony and Conflict: The Political Economy of a Southern Region, Augusta, Georgia, 1865–1895." Ph.D. dissertation, University of Virginia, 1977.

Whatley, William Ludwick. "A History of the Textile Development of Augusta, Georgia, 1865 to 1883." M.S. thesis, University of South Carolina, 1964.

Wotton, Grigsby H., Jr. "New City of the South: Atlanta, 1843–1873." Ph.D. dissertation, Johns Hopkins University, 1973.

Index